RICHLAND FRIENDS' MEETING HOUSE
(Quakertown)

OLD
RICHLAND FAMILIES

INCLUDING

DESCENDANTS OF EDWARD ROBERTS, THOMAS ROBERTS, THOMAS
LANCASTER, PETER LESTER, CASPER JOHNSON, HUGH
FOULKE, JACOB STRAWN, RICHARD MOORE,

WILLIAM JAMISON, ROBERT PENROSE, JOSEPH BALL, MORRIS
MORRIS, THE GREENS, SHAWS, EDWARDSES, HEACOCKS,
THOMSONS, HALLOWELLS AND SPENCERS.

HISTORICAL AND GENEALOGICAL DATA BEING DERIVED LARGELY
FROM THE RECORDS OF FRIENDS AND OTHER
ORIGINAL SOURCES.

BY

ELLWOOD ROBERTS,

Author of "Lyrics of Quakerism," Etc., and Librarian of the Montgomery
County Historical Society.

Southern Historical Press

Book Publishers

**Greenville
South Carolina**

Please direct all correspondence and orders to:

www.southernhistoricalpress.com
or
SOUTHERN HISTORICAL PRESS, Inc.
PO BOX 1267
Greenville, SC   29601
southernhistoricalpress@gmail.com

Originally published: Norristown, PA.   1895
ISBN #978-1-63914-023-7
All rights Reserved.
Printed in the United States of America

"I used to think blood a delusion and quite at odds with democratic doctrine ; but the older I grow the more I am led to believe that an honorable lineage is the best of heritages.

"To one who is not a pessimist or a cynic, traditions as to his father's father's wisdom or his great-grandmother's engaging charms, act as spurs or incentives to noble effort—even though the lustre of his house has been dimmed by adversity and its usefulness foreshortened by death."—ROBERT GRANT.

CONTENTS.

ILLUSTRATIONS.

PREFACE.

It has long been a cherished design of the author to collect into permanent shape traditions and records of his own family, that the recollections familiar to him for years might thus be transmitted to posterity which has a right to them, and because otherwise they might be irretrievably lost. In the course of his labors, however, he has taken a wider range and included many other families connected by the ties of relationship or intermarriage, with his own.

On reaching middle age, matters of this kind are viewed in a very different light from that of youthful days. What was once put off lightly until a more convenient season, one is admonished to do at once, lest haply he may be unable to do it at all.

At such a time, it is readily seen that the great majority of those who started out with us on the journey of life, have fallen by the wayside, or are so widely scattered, if still alive, that they are no longer within call. There is real danger of our being left quite alone, unless new friendships have been made or new alliances formed to take the place of old associations.

In early life we look constantly forward. Fancy paints the grand triumphs that are yet to be won. It is quite natural, after the meridian of life has been passed, to look backward to the days of youth, or even beyond them to generations preceding our own.

How swiftly pass the generations! Persons who live to an advanced age, see two or three of them come and go, almost before they are aware of the fact. Full of their own projects, they fail to realize the value of the companionship of the friends of youth until it is too late. Dazzled by visions of fame or fortune, such treasures vanish almost before the possibility of loss dawns upon the mind. "Too late!" How often are we constrained to utter the dreadful words as we turn away with tear-dimmed eyes from the open graves of near kindred or of dear friends!

The sundering of such ties, time after time, serves notice upon us, as it were, that whatever is to be done must be done at once. Life is uncertain, and no one may tell what a day shall bring forth. The " divinity that stirs within us " impels us onward. If we pause, we know not that the work shall ever be accomplished.

The hours spent in untangling the complicated web of past generations have been pleasant as well as profitable. We are the product of the generations gone before us. We are what our ancestors have made us, to a greater extent than most people imagine. Our posterity, in the same way, will be largely the creatures of influences derived from ourselves.

The study of genealogy is of great value. Its effects should be beneficial, because thus can be discerned the importance of maintaining the honor of a family extending back through long lines of progenitors whose virtues, perhaps, only remain in remembrance, while their faults have been forgotten. It is well to be familiar with one's own family history, and, having gained such knowledge, it may be regarded as eminently proper to put it on record for the benefit of future generations, ere the opportunity be lost forever.

In the preparation of this volume, the author has kept in mind the danger of excessive laudation of living or dead, and endeavored to avoid equally the other extreme of injustice to any of whom he has written. Just praise to either is right and proper, and there is no valid reason for withholding it.

It need hardly be said that the collection, arrangement and publication of the great mass of names, facts, dates and other information contained in the pages of this volume, obtained, as they have been, mostly from original sources, has been a work of incredible labor, to say nothing of the expense involved in their accumulation and preparation.

Those who are familiar with such undertakings will at once recognize the truth of this statement. That labor could not have been performed without the aid of others whom a kindly Providence, the bond of a common ancestry and their own generous natures have impelled to assist the author in his self-appointed task.

The friendships which have been renewed and the acquaintances which have been formed in this way are of themselves compensation for the energy and care bestowed upon the work, not to be undervalued or ignored. It has been truly said, "One touch of nature makes the whole world kin." The ascertaining of the precise degree of relationship among those who are descended from the same stock, strengthens the ties of kindred, however remote they may be, and brings us nearer to each other.

Acknowledgment has been made in the subsequent pages of favors rendered to the author, but it may be well to put on record on this page the names of those whose interest and aid have been most effective, including the following: Clarence V. Roberts and Ida Jamison, Philadelphia; Annie L. Croasdale, Byberry; Benjamin F. Penrose, Ogontz; Mary Emma Green, Jane G. Kinsey, Eleanor Foulke, Eli W. Strawn, Charles F. Strawn, Henry Johnson, A. J. Croman, Uriah S. Stauffer, Seward M. Rosenberger, J. Levi Heacock, Stephen Foulke, Quakertown; Warren S. Ely, Doylestown, and many others. It is not intended that they shall be held responsible for errors which have crept in, as must necessarily happen in a work of this character. Let them be attributed to the author, to whom they properly belong.

Ellwood Roberts.

Norristown, Pa., Sixth-month 1, 1898.

DENGLER RESIDENCE, QUAKERTOWN
(On the site of the house of Morris Morris, the first erected at Richland)

I

THE GREAT SWAMP.

Located less than forty miles from Philadelphia, the vicinity known successively as Great Swamp, Richland and Quakertown, is one of the most interesting in Eastern Pennsylvania. Settled almost two centuries ago by English and Welsh Friends or Quakers and by Germans who, like them, sought a refuge from the assaults of religious intolerance at home, the community has, to a very remarkable extent, retained the characteristics which have marked it from the beginning. The phlegmatic Teuton and the imperturbable Quaker have lived side by side, generation after generation, for nearly two hundred years, without a difference to disturb the mutual kindness and forbearance which have marked their intercourse.

The site of the first house erected in the settlement by Morris Morris is occupied by a quaint structure, the successor, a century ago, of the original log house. It stands at an angle with the wide avenue extending to the station from the older portion of the town and known as Main street. The name Morris has disappeared from the vicinity as have those of others of the old settlers, although the large majority are still represented in the citizenship of the borough.

Among the first settlers were Edward Roberts, Thomas Roberts, Peter Lester, Abraham Griffith, Thomas Nixon, Thomas Lancaster, John Edwards, John Ball and others. The largest landowner of earlier times, Griffith Jones, a Welshman, never reached America. His holdings, including several thousand acres, were rapidly absorbed by others.

The settlement included a large tract of country, embracing several townships adjoining Richland, as it was termed when it was organized and laid out in 1734, extending even into the adjoining counties, Montgomery and Lehigh. While the settlement now Quakertown was the central point, members of the meeting were located in Springfield, Rockhill, Milford, Saucon and elsewhere. Here their descendants lived for generations, founding substantial homes, many of which exist at the present day, in nearly their original condition.

The designation "Great Swamp" disappeared about a century ago; the term Richland is applied to the Monthly Meeting and to the township; the name Quakertown is likely to cling for all time to come to the pleasant town, still tinctured with the flavor of Friendly hospitality, although the bulk of the population is largely of German origin, and has been for many years. The Germans are the descendants, in most cases, of sires who came to America prior to the Revolutionary War, and they may be considered as thoroughly Americanized as any of its residents, although they still cling to the old country speech, especially in conversation with each other. They are more than ordinarily attached to the customs of their forefathers. There is, perhaps, not a more conservative race in the world than the Pennsylvania Germans.

The settlement was peopled by those who left home on account of their religious convictions, and there was thus a common bond of sympathy. It was Penn's foresight in providing a place of refuge for his people, and his liberality in throwing it open to all comers, regardless of creed or nationality, that gave to the population of the state he founded its cosmopolitan character and brought together such apparently incongruous and discordant elements to form a community which has retained its peculiarities for nearly two centuries.

The English and Welsh Friends who settled the vicinity were desirous of enjoying that freedom of thought and independence not to be found at home. They were a simple, thrifty people, addicted to agricultural pursuits, leading quiet lives; the different families intermarrying with each other for generations; surviving to a good old age; seldom mingling in the strife and bustle of the gay world outside; presenting such an example of industry, honesty and morality as is rarely to be found in this world of ours.

Their German neighbors were also steady-going people who cultivated the homely virtues, seldom concerning themselves with the usually unsatisfactory pursuit of worldly honor or political ambition. While few of them became Friends, they respected their plain-speaking neighbors—often sending their children to the Friends' school, they attending the midweek meeting with their teachers, thus tacitly admitting the propriety of customs which they could not always comprehend. Side by side the two have dwelt in peace and friendship. They have mingled together at funerals and weddings, at school and elsewhere, but each has kept its characteristics, practically unchanged by the associations of years.

German immigration was influential next to that of the Friends in the early history of Pennsylvania. They have left a lasting impression on every community to which they came, and especially upon the one of which I am writing. Many of them came from the Palatinate, whence they were forced by religious persecution. They belonged mostly to what became known as the German Reformed denomination. Following the valley of the Perkiomen from what is now Montgomery county, they reached Milford in Bucks, and by 1730, when the first permanent Friends' meeting-house was built at Richland, they had become very numerous.

So far as the name "Swamp" is concerned, it would appear to-day to be very decidedly a misnomer, but it may be readily imagined that it was different before the timber was cut down and the land drained and cultivated. When the vicinity was settled, the water lay in some places upon the surface at certain seasons of the year.

From the date of location of some of the original surveys, much of what is now comprised within the limits of Milford and Springfield must have been originally called Richland. This view is borne out by the fact that much of the land surveyed as part of Richland Manor, was located in the adjacent townships. Tradition tells of the early settlers finding the place covered with a luxurious growth of grass. It was mostly heavily timbered, but the forest was interspersed with small prairies, with a rich soil, hence the place was called Richland.

That the richness of the soil was known to the proprietor and to the numerous individuals who were at that time laying warrants on the best land may be inferred. Griffith Jones obtained his release from Penn October 11, 1681, for 6000 acres surveyed to him in 1701. It appears to have been the first land surveyed in the vicinity—2616 acres, a part of which was patented to him in 1703.

Penn designed reserving a manor in the place for his own use, but it was surveyed at different times as warrants for manor land were taken out. Anterior to the surveys, other warrants were laid, and the most desirable land was taken up.

A part of the manor was located several miles from where it was originally intended.

The township when first visited by the white man was heavily timbered, covered with grass, even among the timber, and interspersed with spots of cleared ground similar to a prairie, called Indian fields, some of which were cleared by the Indians, ready for cultivation. The proportion of prairie was, however, small. Nearly all was wet and swampy, and in the spring of the year covered with water, until cultivation had effected a change.

Wolves, bears, deer and panthers were abundant and continued so for years. Rattlesnakes were very troublesome to the early settlers for many years. Mowers were compelled to wrap their legs with hay or other protecting substances to ward off their bites.

The circumstances which gave rise to the name "Swamp" were rapidly modified under the benign ministry of the axe and the plow. The industry of the early settlers soon changed the appearance of things. The rude habitations at first erected gave way to substantial dwellings, and the crops and cattle were housed in ample barns. Everywhere was smiling abundance in keeping with the name by which the locality became known, although still the Great Swamp to the outside world. If its people were not wealthy, they lived comfortably, and if they lacked the superfluities which are so highly prized by the denizens of towns, they enjoyed all the comforts that were necessary to the

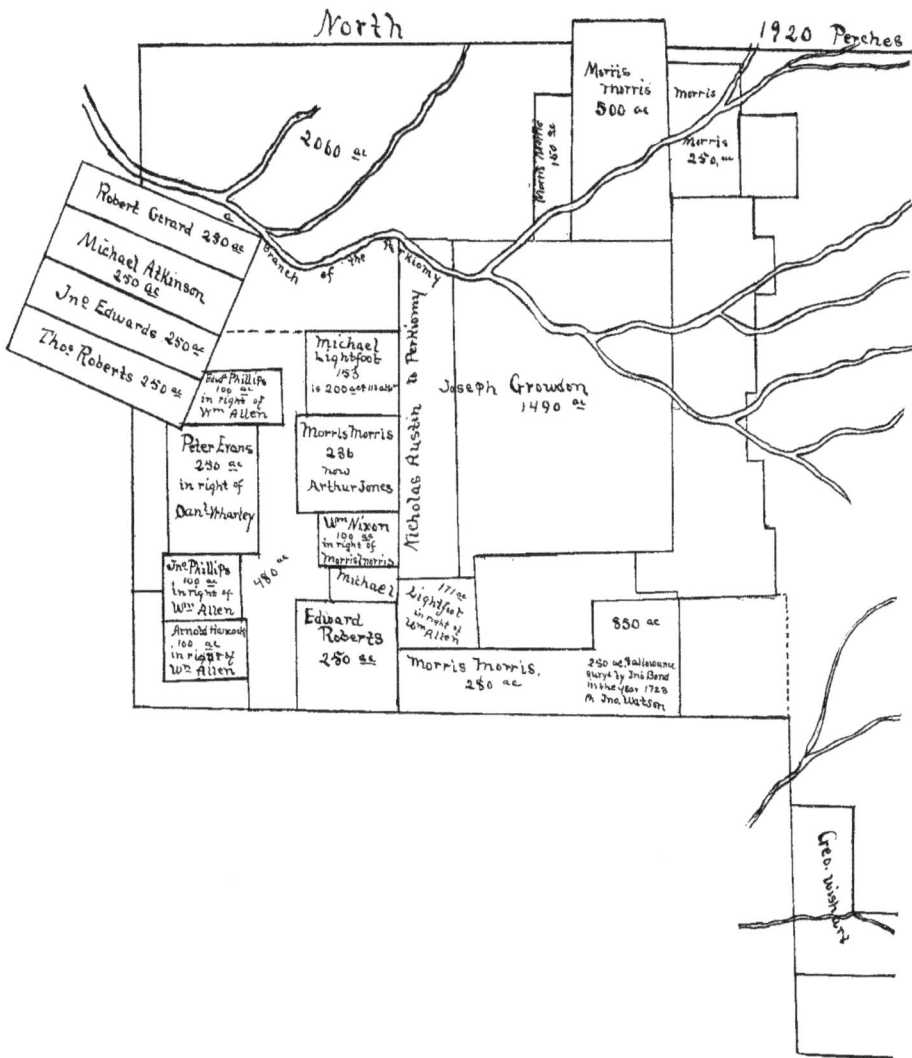

North   1920 Perches

Morris Morris 500 ac

Morris

Morris Morris 160 ac

Morris 250 ac

2060 ac

Branch of the

Robert Gerard 250 ac

Michael Atkinson 250 ac

Jnº Edwards 250 ac

Thoſ Roberts 250 ac

Edwᵈ Phillips 100 ac in right of Wᵐ Allen

Michael Lightfoot 150 is 200 acᵗ incals.

Nicholas Austin to Perkiomy

Joseph Growdon 1490 ac

Peter Evans 250 ac in right of Danᵗ Wharley

Morris Morris 286 now Arthur Jones

Wᵐ Nixon 100 ac in right of Morris Morris

Jnº Phillips 100 ac in right of Wᵐ Allen

Arnold Hancock 100 ac in right of Wᵐ Allen

480 ac

Michael

17 ac Lightfoot in right of Wᵐ Allen

Edward Roberts 250 ac

850 ac

Morris Morris 250 ac

250 ac Kallowance survᵈ by Jnᵒ Bond in the year 1728 & Jnᵒ Watson

Geo. Wishart

THE MANOR OF RICHLANDS
(Showing various property owners in 1784)

proper enjoyment of life, and examples of survival to a great age were very frequent.

The story of the six or seven generations that have passed is recorded with tolerable fullness in the Meeting record books, two of which (the earliest) have been lost for nearly a dozen years, but were found recently.

At Great Swamp was organized a branch of the first Society for maintaining friendly relations with the aboriginal inhabitants. It was called "Ye Friendly Association for Regaining and Preserving Peace with ye Indians." All through the bloody and devastating wars with the infuriated red men, lasting for years, there was no clash between them and the followers of Penn at Richland. Under a giant oak on the grounds deeded by Morris Morris to the Society for the erection of a meetinghouse and school, ten acres in all, which stood until within four or five years, when it was blown down by a storm, the Indians of the olden time were accustomed to sit and string their beads or fashion their rude implements.

Samuel Foulke was Treasurer and guiding spirit of this organization as of others of his day. It was kept up until the Peace of 1759, and accomplished good work for humanity.

Indians were located in different places. The wigwams were generally along the banks of the creeks, more particularly along Swamp creek, a branch of the Perkiomen, and the Tohickon. The Indians considered the vicinity one of the best of their hunting grounds. On Swamp creek, as late as 1770, there continued a remnant of the once powerful tribe which in its better days numbered nearly a hundred wigwams. They were kind and social. There was a beaten path having a north and south course that passed through the "Swamp."

The neighborhood of Quakertown is a sort of basin, four miles or more in diameter. This basin is drained by tributaries of the Tohickon, running to the Delaware, and by Swamp creek, which empties into the Perkiomen, a tributary of the Schuylkill. The little rivulet known as Licking run, which empties into the Tohickon, was named from a salt lick on its bank. The site of the town was a springy wooded meadow when emigration first reached the place into which the cattle were turned to pasture, while the first dwellings were erected upon the elevated ground around the basin.

The Great Swamp was settled largely by English and Welsh Quakers, the overflow as it were from Gwynedd, Abington and Byberry which were comparatively close to Philadelphia and whose land was mostly absorbed by the time the eighteenth century had fairly opened. As years passed, these were reinforced by others who had heard of the advantages of the vicinity. The name Quakertown was naturally enough applied to a settlement largely made up of Friends, by the people surrounding them who belonged to other denominations. Thus the designation of the village, which has become a flourishing borough in our own day, was permanently fixed as years rolled on.

William Penn, as already stated, in October, 1681, granted six thousand acres to Griffith Jones, to be located, like many other tracts thus conveyed in London, as convenience or opportunity might permit. Jones made some attempt to take up land in Gwynedd, but, finding that impracticable, after the lapse of a few years he decided to have his entire grant surveyed to him in the Great Swamp, which was done accordingly in 1701. A part of it was patented in 1703. Jones owned nearly half of what is now Richland township.

Griffith Jones left it to others to settle the neighborhood, they purchasing his land at a nominal figure; cutting down a portion of the timber and thus enlarging the area fit for cultivation; erecting rude dwellings to be replaced later by habitations more capacious and comfortable, and, in general, reaping the advantages of entering upon and possessing the land.

Abraham Griffith, of Byberry, settled in the southern part of the present township, known then by the name of "The Bog." A rude shelter was erected by the side of a rock and the rock's leaning portion formed a part of the dwelling.

In this rude habitation was born the first white child in that portion of Bucks county, Abraham Griffith, Jr. The father was married in 1708 to Hannah, daughter of Peter Lester, or Leicester, at Byberry, and it is supposed he went to Quakertown soon afterwards, locating on a part of the Griffith Jones tract. In 1712 he became the purchaser of a tract belonging to

Jones. About the same time, Peter Lester bought 600 acres of Griffith Jones, and some time after settled there also.

Edward Roberts went from Byberry to Great Swamp in the spring of 1716. He located on the property owned later by Evan Roberts, one of his descendants, now Stephen Foulke's. Himself and wife went on horseback from Byberry and took all their movables with them. They had one daughter at that time, Martha, who grew to womanhood and married John Roberts, the son of Thomas, another early settler. Soon after his arrival, he found his wife had become infected with small-pox, probably from their Indian neighbors, and he was under the necessity of returning along the Indian path to Gwynedd, or North Wales, the nearest settlement, where proper care could be taken of her. Here she was nursed back to health and in five or six weeks she and her husband returned to the "Swamp." She was the daughter of Everard and Elizabeth Bolton, of Abington.

Edward Roberts first erected a temporary shelter, composed mostly of bark, reared up against some of the large white oak trees that were then so abundant in that vicinity, until a more comfortable cabin could be built. In this last they lived until the year 1728, when he erected the south end of the house afterwards occupied by Evan Roberts, but taken down later by Stephen Foulke, the present owner, the stone for which was quarried on the farm formerly Abel Roberts', where Aaron Penrose resided later. It was built without lime, using clay for mortar, but stood very firm for nearly a century and a half.

Peter Lester, as his name indicates, came from Leicestershire, England. He and his son-in-law were the pioneers of the extensive immigration which occurred between 1708 and 1720. He had settled in Gwynedd, twenty miles distant. Peter Lester and his family located a short distance below where is now Quakertown, but later removed to the upper portion of the settlement, where five or six generations of the family dwelt.

The first settlers had no facilities for building houses. They came in detached parties and probably at first depended almost entirely upon the Indians of the vicinity, who, fortunately, were kindly disposed towards these peaceable followers of Penn. The first dwellings, as we have seen, were of bark, and they were erected beside great rocks or under the shadow of trees.

Other settlers, in addition to those mentioned, were James McVaugh, who was granted a hundred acres with a mill site; Morris Morris, to whom was transferred a tract containing a thousand acres; John Moore, Michael Atkinson, Michael Lightcap, Thomas Nixon, William Nixon, Thomas Lancaster; Hugh Foulke, who purchased over three hundred acres; John Edwards, of Abington, whose wife was Martha Foulke, both being acknowledged ministers of the Society of Friends; William Jamison, William Morris, John Ball, Samuel Thomas and many others whose names appear further on in the transcripts from the original records of Friends, which form a considerable portion of this volume.

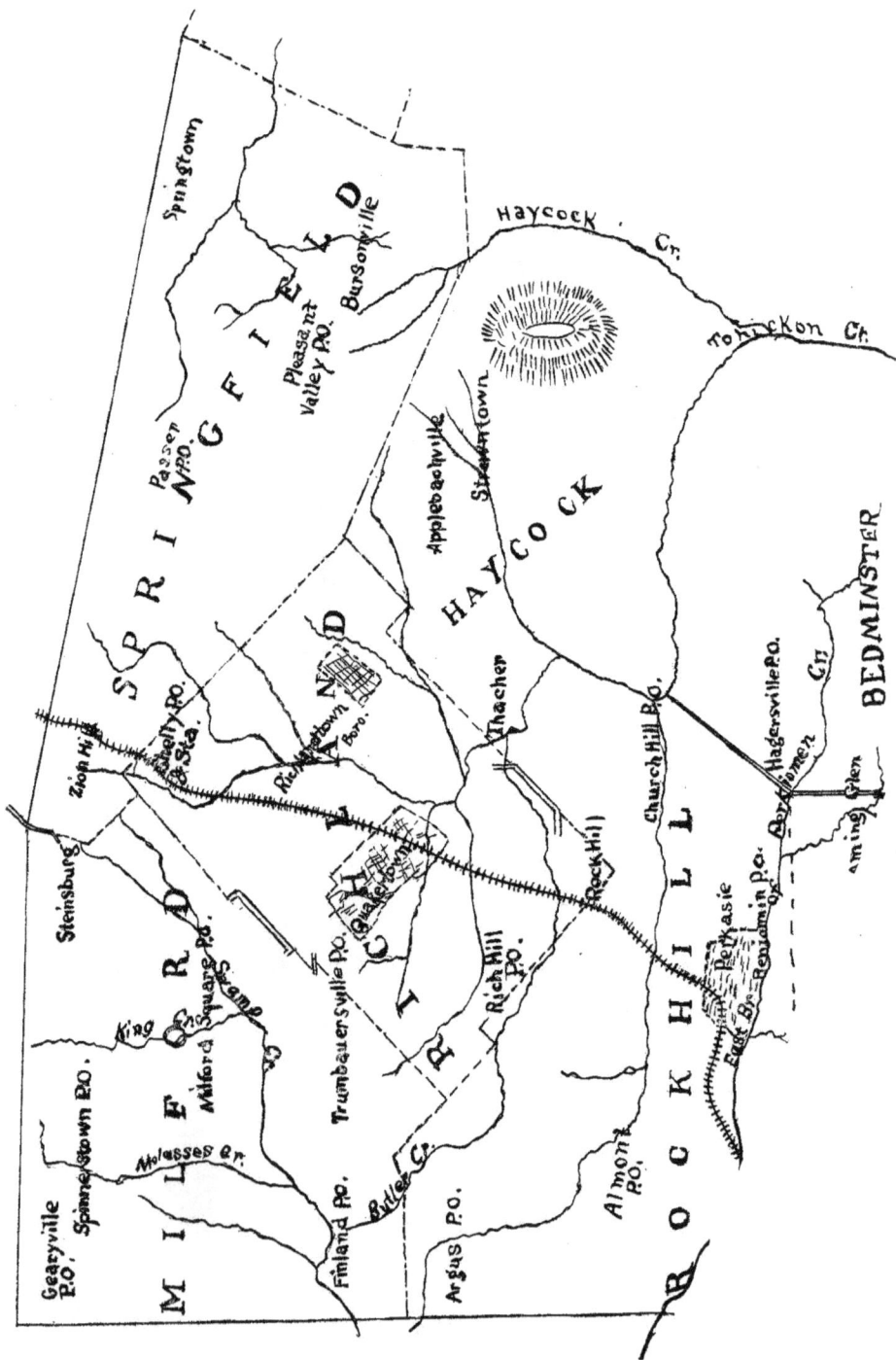

MAP OF RICHLAND AND SURROUNDING TOWNSHIPS IN BUCKS COUNTY

(The Eastern and Western boundary lines of the Township extend nearly North and South)

Springtown

Haycock Cr.

Burgonville

Tohickon Cr.

Pleasant Valley P.O.

S P R I N G F I E L D

Passer N.P.O.

Appleeaohville

Strawntown

H A Y C O C K

BEDMINSTER

Zion Hill

Shelly P.O. & Sta.

Richlandtown Boro.

Thacher

Church Hill P.O.

Hagersville P.O.

aming Glen

Steinsburg

King

R I C H L A N D

Rock Hill

women Cr.

M I L F O R D

Enos Square P.O.

Skamb Cr.

Quakertown

Rock Hill P.O.

Bethasie

Hagersville P.O.

Benjamin P.O.

Geasyville P.O.

Spinnerstown P.O.

Milford Square P.O.

Trumbauersville P.O.

R O C K H I L L

East Br.

Molasses Cr.

Finland P.O.

Butler Cr.

Argus P.O.

Almont P.O.

II.

RICHLAND TOWNSHIP.

The township was not organized until 1734. By this time there had been a large influx of the German element, which, as we have seen, predominated later in that entire section of Bucks county, cont'nuing to do so until the present time. In 1729, the inhabitants of Richland petitioned for a road laid out "from near a creek called Sacking, or Sucking (Saucon), to the place where the Quaker meeting-house is building, and from thence to the end of Abraham Griffith's lane." In 1730, thirty-two of the residents petitioned for a road from the "new meeting-house to the county line near William Thomas's, in order to go to Philadelphia by the Montgomery road." Prior to that time, the route to Philadelphia was by the Old York road, which, it was alleged, was "marshy, the ground not fitting for carts or loaded horses."

The names annexed to this petition will give the reader an idea of the resident property owners in the settlement at that time. They were Hugh Foulke, John Lester, John Adamson, Arnold Heacock, John Phillips, George Phillips, William Morris, Edward Roberts, Arthur Jones, William Nixon, John Ball, John Edwards, Thomas Roberts, Joshua Richards, William Jamison, Edmund Phillips, Johannes Bleiler, Michael Everhart, Joseph Everhart, Abraham Hill, Johannes Landis, Jacob Klein, John Jacob Klemmer, Jacob Musselman, Jacob Sutar, Peter Cutz, Jacob Drissel, Henry Walp, Samuel Yoder, George Hix (Hicks), John Jacob Zeits, Heinrich Ditterly. The names clearly of German origin indicate how extensive had become the admixture of that element in the population in so short a time, comparatively speaking.

The petition for a township by the name of "Richland" was filed in September, 1734, the signers being Peter Lester, Duke Jackson, Lawrence Growden, John Ball, George Hyatt, John Phillips, Edward Roberts, John Lester and Thomas Heed. On the draft of the survey the real estate owners marked are Joseph Gilbert, James Logan, Joseph Pike, Lawrence Growden, Griffith Jones, Michael Lightfoot, Samuel Pierson and Henry Taylor, but this part of the work seems not to have been fully performed, as there are known to have been many other landowners within its bounds at that time. Griffith Jones' land occupied one-fifth of the entire township.

Richland township is over five miles in length, from north to south, and about four and a-half miles in breadth. Its area is nearly 14,000 acres, the adjacent townships being Springfield, Haycock, Rockhill and Milford. In the northwest corner is a tract of a few acres covered with rocks, which emit a ringing sound when struck like the Ringing Rocks near Pottstown, in Montgomery county. The progress of the township is shown by the population at different censuses: 1790, 860 inhabitants, 147 dwellings; 1810, 1317; 1820, 1385; 1830, 1719, and 344 taxables; 1840, 1781; 1850, 1729; 1860, 2058 white and 16 colored; 1870, 2104 white and 7 colored, there being 93 of foreign birth; 1880, 1994, additions having been made meantime to the borough of Quakertown; 1890, 2088.

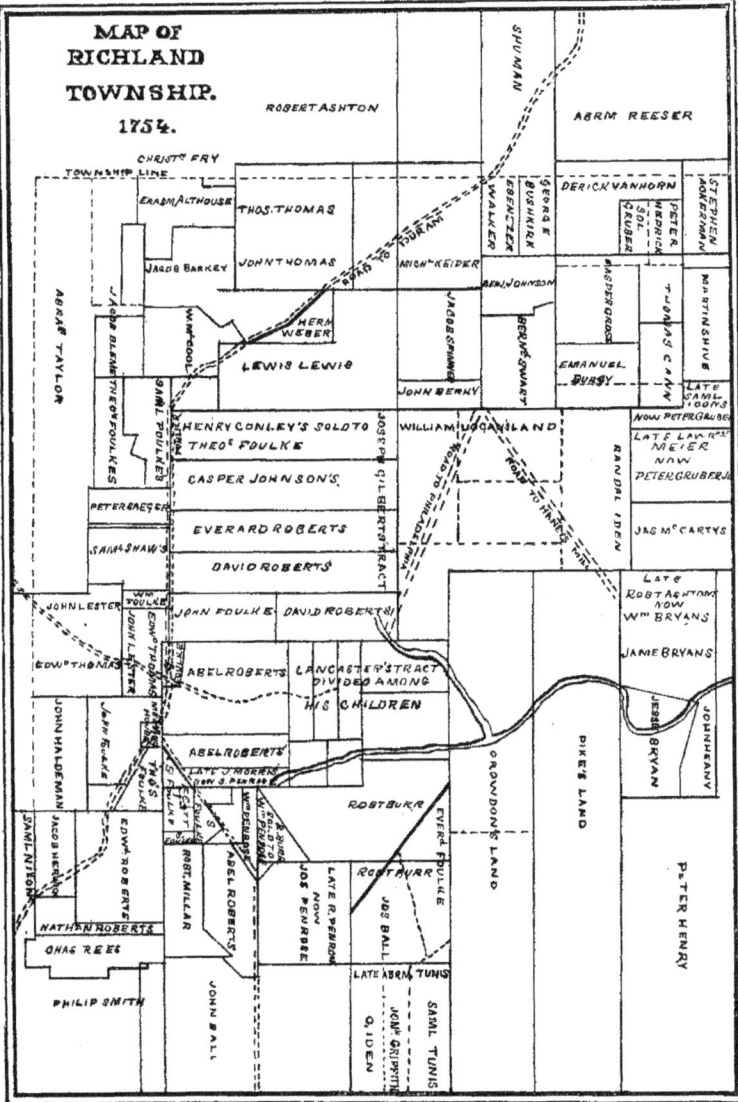

MAP OF RICHLAND TOWNSHIP. 1754.

III.

THE FRIENDS' MEETING.

The first Friends' meetings were held at the houses of members. Many of the little colony had come from Abington, Byberry or Gwynedd, where they belonged, and to which they journeyed on horseback to attend Monthly Meetings, the Quarterly and Yearly Meetings being held in Philadelphia. Among them was Peter Lester, at whose house, conveniently located for many who attended, meetings for worship had become permanently fixed for several years before authority was obtained from the parent meeting at Gwynedd to hold Richland Preparative Meeting in 1721. In 1723 a small house was built where William Shaw now lives.

This location is on the road to Philadelphia, about a mile below the present site. The object in changing it to the present site was probably two-fold—to get on the higher ground and to place the meeting-house more in the centre of the settlement, as it was then constituted, although in the course of time the village came to be built on one side of the house which is now at the western extremity of Quakertown.

The Friends of Richland, while they were in full sympathy, as elsewhere, with the patriot cause during the Revolutionary War, refrained as a rule from any active support thereof, their principles precluding them from bearing arms. In 1781, eleven members, more or less prominent in the meeting, were disowned on the ground that they had taken the oath of allegiance to the new government, it being contrary to the usage of Friends to take an oath at all. They were Samuel Foulke, James Chapman, Thomas Edwards, Enoch Roberts, Everard Foulke, Thomas Thomas, John Thomas, John Foulke, Thomas Foulke, John

Lester and William Edwards. About the same time Elizabeth Potts was disowned for holding slaves contrary to the testimony of the Society.

At the Monthly Meeting of Friends held at Richland Fourth-month 15, 1773, the following report was presented:

"The Friends appointed by last meeting to draw up an account of the first settlement of our meeting, to be transmitted to the next Quarterly Meeting, have performed the service as follows:

"The first settlement of Friends in this place was about the year 1710, by our ancient Friend Peter Lester, of Leicestershire, England, who, with his wife and children and other families, became members of Gwynedd Monthly Meeting, and a meeting for worship was, with the concurrence of that Monthly Meeting, held at the said Peter Lester's house for several years; Friends living in an amicable intercourse with the Indian natives, who at that time were numerous in these parts, and often helpful to these new settlers, in furnishing them with necessary provisions, which is gratefully remembered by some yet living among us.

"About the year 1723, a small meeting-house was built and a Preparative Meeting then held, by the assent of said Monthly Meeting, and Friends continuing to increase in number, by the youth growing up and the accession of several families of Friends from other places, it became necessary, in the year 1730, to build a new meeting-house, which was done on a commodious lot of ground near the centre of the settlement, and our said Meeting, through the blessing of Divine Providence, both spiritually and temporally bestowed, still continued increasing in strength and numbers until the year 1742, when Friends thought it expedient to make application to the Quarterly Meeting, held at Philadelphia on the first of Ninth-month, 1742, to have a Monthly Meeting erected amongst themselves, which was granted them, to be held the third Fifth-day in each month, and called Richland Monthly Meeting, which from that time has continued, and Friends here have since made considerable additions to their meeting-house, to accommodate the meeting.

"The above account being approved by the meeting, was signed by order and on behalf thereof by

"Samuel Foulke, Clerk."

The following is the minute made at the opening of Richland Monthly Meeting in 1742:

"Inasmuch as it hath pleased God, the author of all our mercies, to increase the number of Friends belonging to our

OLD FRIENDS' MEETING HOUSE AT RICHLAND
(Torn down in 1862. From an oil painting by Joseph John)

meeting at Richland, and the adjacent places thereunto belonging; many of the elders growing in years, and the youth coming up; and also living far remote from Gwynedd Monthly Meeting whereunto we belonged; and the difficulty we sometimes had to attend the same: under these considerations, a concern came upon Friends here to make application to the Monthly Meeting to have a Monthly Meeting established among ourselves, desiring their consideration and concurrence to propose our request to the Quarterly Meeting at Philadelphia; which, after deliberate consideration of the Monthly and Quarterly Meetings, our said request was allowed of and granted.

"At a Quarterly Meeting held at Philadelphia the first of the Ninth-month, 1742, the motion from Gwynedd Monthly Meeting for the Friends at the Swamp being a Monthly Meeting to themselves, to be held the third Fifth-day of the month, monthly, is granted. "Samuel Preston, Clerk."
[Richland Monthly Meeting.]

The meeting at Stroudsburg, in Monroe county, close relations between the members of which and those of Richland have always been maintained, was indulged by Richland Monthly Meeting in 1809, and, two years later, a Preparative Meeting was established there and so continues to the present day.

It should be mentioned that Abington Quarterly Meeting was instituted in 1786.

The Commissioners of Property, by letters patent, dated in 1728, granted to Morris Morris, as already stated, one thousand acres of land on part of which the borough of Quakertown is now located. The meeting-house erected in 1730 was on the present site, on land leased of Morris. It was intended that this house should be of stone, but the matter being laid before Gwynedd Monthly Meeting, it was advised that the structure be of wood, being more in accordance with the means of Richland Friends. This advice was followed, though it seems to have been a mistake, necessitating frequent alterations and additions. An extension was made in 1749, thirty-eight subscribers joining in raising the money required for the work.

In 1759, Morris Morris deeded to the meeting ten acres of land, and a year or two later a further enlargement of the building was completed. It was 20 by 26 feet, at the north end of the structure. The meeting-house was located in a fine grove of oaks, and there is a traditionary recollection that the Indians, always friendly to the settlers of Quakertown, were wont to make the shade of these their resting-places. Some of the older people who passed away thirty or forty years ago, could remember them sitting under a tree at the south end of the house.

There is also a well-authenticated tradition that the young men of the vicinity, many of them members of the Society of Friends, were accustomed to make a drill ground of that portion of the enclosure which was covered by the shade of these spreading oaks.

Lizzie Yost, who read a paper on the history of Quakertown before the Bucks County Historical Society a few years ago, says in reference to the health and longevity of the settlers:

"Davis, in his history of Bucks county, speaks of the longevity and health of the citizens of this vicinity. To corroborate that statement it was found that within a distance of 200 yards on Main street there were nine persons whose ages averaged 86 years 1 month; also seven others who averaged 74 years and 4 months; and eight others who averaged 62 years and 3 months. All of these but six owned the houses wherein they lived, and all but one were capable of attending to their household and outdoor duties regularly.

"The records of the meeting show that at one time there were four families who had forty children, ten each—every one of whom grew up to full manhood and womanhood, and made good and useful citizens, wherever their lot was cast.

"At the wedding of two of the heads of two of these families in 1799, seventeen of their children—nine of one and eight of the other—attended the wedding."

In reference to the customs of the olden time, she says, most of her information having been derived from John J. Moore and Jane Kinsey:

"The temperance element was not very strong in the earlier days. It is in evidence that, at the funeral of one of the wealthiest and most respected citizens, there was a kettle of buttered rum set between the gate and the house for all to partake of freely.

"The changing of the people from the old ways seems to have been slow work, for the report of the committee of the Monthly Meeting that had charge of this matter for several years, was in 1804: 'That our testimony against the use of spirituous liquors has not gained much strength since last year.' So far as known, it was not until the year 1834 when Richard Moore built the first large dwelling in the upper section of the county without the use of any spirituous or malt liquor among the workmen. Things have changed since then, but still there are six places licensed to sell strong drink within the borough."

By way of continuation of the history given in the committee's report, a few pages back, it may be here added that Richland Monthly Meeting granted permission to Saucon Friends to hold meetings for worship in 1742, and to Springfield Friends in 1745. A year or two later Abraham Griffith, Samuel Thomas and Lewis Lewis were a committee to assist Springfield Friends in selecting a site for a meeting-house.

The first marriage after the Monthly Meeting was formed was solemnized Ninth-month 24, 1743, the parties being Samuel Foulke and Ann Greasly.

As to the attitude of Richland Friends in regard to slavery, it may be mentioned that an act of Assembly passed March 1, 1780, required that all slaves in the state should be registered on or before November 1, 1782. The number registered at the Prothonotary's office in Newtown, then the county-seat of Bucks, was 520, but there were none from Richland, showing that their German neighbors were as clear of slaveholding as were Friends.

The old meeting-house was further improved in 1795, when a roof of cedar shingles was put on which remained in good condition when the building was torn down to make room for the structure in which the Friends of Richland now assemble for worship and to transact the business of the Preparative and Monthly Meetings.

IV.

QUAKERTOWN.

The precise date when the name Quakertown began to be applied to the settlement is not known, but it was probably about the time of the Revolutionary War. In 1770 Walter McCoole kept the only hotel in the place, at the cross roads. It was kept by a man named Zavitz during the war period.

The first store in the place was opened by William Green, in an old house built by Moses Shaw. It stood where is now the residence of Jane Kinsey. He occupied it until he built the large brick house at Broad and Main streets, in 1805.

William Green was the first Postmaster of Quakertown, the post-office being established in his store in 1803. He held the office many years.

Continuing the reminiscences from the paper of Lizzie Yost:

"The next hotel was the old Red Lion, built by Enoch Roberts and kept by him for many years. He died at the age of ninety-six years, being hale and hearty to the time of his death.

"The Abraham Barndt house and the old tannery were built by John Lester, the latter for his son Shipley in 1792. Shipley afterwards built the house now owned by Eliza Lott, and his brother Thomas the one owned by Joshua Bullock.

"The tradition is that when John Fries, the leader of the local rebellion of 1799 against the payment of tax on window glass, was convicted of treason, it was ordered that he should be executed at the cross roads in Quakertown—the intersection of Broad and Main streets. The gallows was prepared, but he was afterwards reprieved by President Adams.

"In 1799 the government sent a body of a thousand soldiers to suppress the rebellion. They camped for some time at the

WILLIAM GREEN
(First Postmaster of Quakertown)

spring in the meadow in front of the house now owned by H. W. Weiss. Relics of their stay are still extant.

"Morris Morris built part of the house lately owned by Joshua Foulke and now owned by William Dengler, and the old springhouse of which has recently been removed. Morris sold a portion of the land to his son-in-law, Abel Roberts, including the buildings. He conveyed the same to his son-in-law, Samuel Nixon.

"Either Abel or Samuel built the present house and Samuel lived there till his death. Two of his daughters built the older part of the large building now occupied by Mary Steinhauer, and his widow married William Edwards, who lived in the old house that stood on the corner of Sixth and Broad streets, which was probably built by him."

The pretext for Fries' Rebellion, it should be stated, was not a tax on window glass, but a direct tax apportioned among the states, the proceeds being used in preparation for the threatened war with France. The President had been given power to borrow $5,000,000, and $2,000,000 additional was to be raised by this tax, which was upon houses and slaves. Owners of slaves were required to pay fifty cents each for all between the ages of twelve and fifty years. On every house worth $200 to $500, twenty cents per $100 was assessed, while on those valued at $500 to $1000, thirty cents per $100 was the rate. As Pennsylvania was practically a free state, the tax fell on property. The connection which windows had with the matter was the fact that assessors determined the value of houses by counting the windows and measuring their size.

Seth Chapman was the collector of the direct tax in the Third district of Pennsylvania, consisting of Bucks and Montgomery counties. The opposition to the law arose from ignorance and failure to comprehend its provisions, arising among the German element, whose first knowledge of the law was the advent of the assessor. They decided to resist the imposition on general principles. Fries, who was a native of Hatfield, Montgomery county, but a resident of Milford township, rallied several of his neighbors and drove off the assessors when they appeared, the latter taking refuge in Quakertown.

Governor Mifflin issued a proclamation, and Secretary of War McHenry ordered out the cavalry of Philadelphia, Chester, Montgomery, Bucks and Lancaster. General MacPherson was in command of them. The troops encamped at Springhouse, and moved to Quakertown. Fries was arrested while at his occupation of vendue crier and, with thirty others, taken to Philadelphia for trial. He and two others were found guilty of treason. The verdict was based on the forming of associations to resist the tax; interference with the assessors, and the fact that Fries and others had gone to Bethlehem and intimidated the authorities there until rioters who had been arrested were liberated. The most remarkable circumstance about this remarkable resistance to national authority was the fact that those who were most violent in opposition to the "house tax," owned no property.

The Bethlehem turnpike was begun in 1813. Its construction gave an impetus to improvement in that section of Bucks county in which Quakertown is located.

It has many industrial establishments, including cigar factories, eight churches and the Friends' meeting-house; shops, stores and schools. For the last-named, public and private, it has a well-deserved reputation. Friends opened a school, in a building adjacent to the meeting-house, soon after the Monthly Meeting was established.

Richard Moore and Thomas Lester opened a boarding school at Quakertown in 1818, which was successful, but was maintained only for a short time. In 1858 Rev. A. R. Horne opened a normal school, which was continued for five years, and was attended during that time by over four hundred students. This was changed into a soldiers' orphan school. When the writer was principal of the Quakertown public school in 1865-6, it was in operation as such, but was abandoned in 1867, the pupils being removed to other schools.

The first teachers' institute ever held in Bucks county was at Quakertown, on December 12, 1860, and it was through the instrumentality of Mr. Horne that it was arranged and carried through to a successful conclusion.

For many of the facts contained in the following summary

THE EDWARDS FEED STORE
(Built in 1772)

of educational progress in Quakertown, the author of this volume is indebted to S. M. Rosenberger, the capable principal of the borough schools at the present time.

The Friends' school, established soon after the settlement of Richland, was probably kept in early times at the house of the teacher. A frame building was erected on the grounds near the meeting-house a short time prior to the Revolutionary War.

It was a frame structure, and located not far from the present building at the west end of the town, erected in 1857. Among the teachers at the Friends' school in the course of the present century may be mentioned Dr. Walton, Dr. Arthur Cernea, Hannah Mather, Joseph Large, Thomas Hobson (1832), Benjamin Naylor (the originator of a system of singing geography, which was very popular in its day), Benjamin L. Thomas, William Morris Jackson (who taught several years and closed his engagement in the spring of 1865), Catharine Underwood, of Philadelphia, who taught two or three years; Charles M. Foulke (now a resident of Washington), Susan Hayhurst (now living in Philadelphia), Levi Heacock, Anna Blakey and others; John Ball was a teacher for a dozen years. William M. Jackson afterwards became principal of the Friends' School, New York. The school has been closed nearly twenty years.

Levi Heacock and James Brunner conducted a school during the summer of 1866, their specialty being preparing pupils for teachers' examinations. The winter following it was continued by Levi Heacock, James Brunner going West, where he ultimately became Superintendent of the public schools of Omaha, Nebraska. Levi Heacock and Rev. George M. Lazarus conducted a school in the early seventies in the lower room of St. John's Lutheran Church. The last-named was superintendent of the borough schools at the time of his death, being thrown from his carriage by a runaway horse while in attendance at a funeral on January 31, 1874. Quakertown was thus for many years a sort of educational centre for Upper Bucks and several adjoining counties, young people of German parentage who were anxious to acquire a knowledge of English forming a large proportion of the pupils. Many of them have attained more or less prominence in various walks of life. Reunions of those who attended Dr. Horne's school (previously mentioned) are held every five years.

The first public school in the immediate vicinity was located at the western limit of the town. It was a stone structure, still standing and now a dwelling. The first teacher was Thomas Smith, of Wrightstown. Soon after Quakertown became a borough, June 4, 1855, the Directors fixed the term at ten months, so that the borough has always stood at the head of the list as to length of term. Miss Sarah Aaron was then teacher. For the summer session, 1856, Miss Lizzie Callender was teacher, with thirty-five pupils. Dr. William Chambers, of Doylestown, took charge the next winter. He died during the term and was succeeded by Miss Anna Hartshorn.

Her salary was $25 a month. At that time one or more directors visited the school weekly. The next teacher was Miss Rachel Bowman. The new building on Tenth street was erected, and still stands, forming the front part of the present building. Two schools were established. Successive teachers were: Albina Reeder, elected in 1860; William G. Foulke, 1860; Oliver Fell, 1865; Sallie Reeder, 1865; Ellwood Roberts, 1865-6; Mr. Fackenthall, 1866; Mr. Snyder, 1866; Andrew Cope, 1867; Lizzie Edmunds, 1868; Mr. Rambo, 1869. Primary teachers were: Bella Meredith, Lizzie Edmunds (elected in 1865), Lizzie Butler, Mr. Hoot (1867), Mary Hibberd (1870), Miss Snyder (1872), Annie Smith, 1873. History and grammar were in use when the writer was principal of the school, and a class of young women and men, several of whom afterward taught successfully, attended.

The salary of principal in 1865 and 1866, was $50 per month, a figure much higher than that paid in surrounding districts. An addition was erected in 1876. The district was one of the first to introduce free text-books and stationery, and in general the School Board has been among the most progressive in the state.

The High school was opened in 1873, the idea being an outgrowth of the local institutes held under the County Superintendency of Hugh B. Eastburn. Prof. Campbell took charge. He introduced an annual dinner.

The teachers at present are: Seward M. Rosenberger, Mahlon S. Nicholas, W. H. Mininger, W. H. Wimmer, Elizabeth Brough, Carrie Ozias, Helen Evans, Ella Ommeren, Kate Fluck, Annie Mumbauer, Lilla Oberly, Elmira Ochs.

Quakertown was made a borough in 1854. At that time there were forty-five property-owners within its limits. The increase in population which took place was due largely, as a matter of course, to the construction of the North Pennsylvania railroad commenced in 1853, and finished to the Lehigh in 1857, trains running through from Philadelphia to Bethlehem in July of the latter year. It had been opened as far as Gwynedd two years earlier.

The population of Quakertown in 1870 was 863; in 1880, 1769, and in 1890, 2169.

Charles Strawn, the postmaster of Quakertown, has a taste for old relics. He exhibits a map of Pennsylvania, dating back to 1792, which he inherited from his grandfather, Benjamin Foulke. The place is marked on it "The Swamp." The counties of the state then in existence were few, the greater portion of Pennsylvania being a wilderness.

Quakertown's homes are substantial, comfortable; its people generous in their hospitality to strangers. Farmers of the surrounding country remove to the place when they retire from active work on the old homestead and are succeeded by a son or grandson, as in the larger country towns generally. An empty house is rarely seen.

There is a wealth of unwritten history in the shape of traditions. The place has long been known for the longevity of its people, centenarians and nonagenarians being more common than elsewhere. Their simple habits and freedom from exhausting excitements that beset the denizens of cities, prolong life and keep memory and other faculties in their normal condition even in old age.

A trolley line through the town to Trumbauersville, three miles distant, in one direction, and to Richlandtown, four miles, in another, is in course of construction and will be completed by midsummer. It will stimulate improvement as a matter of course.

The Richland Library Company was chartered in 1795, the directors being Abraham Stout, Everard Foulke, Israel Lancaster, Samuel Sellers, Joseph Lester and Israel Foulke, Secretary. The following were the original members: James Chapman, Shipley Lester, Benjamin Foulke, Cadwallader Foulke, Israel Foulke, Jesse Foulke, Nathan Roberts (2 shares), Jacob Baker, Levi Roberts, John Griffith, John Engle, Evan Foulke, David Roberts, Hugh Foulke, Edward Foulke, Samuel Iden, Theophilus Foulke, Samuel Sellers, Everard Foulke, Abraham Stout, Israel Lancaster, Benjamin Green, John Lester, Jr. The original catalogue, printed in Philadelphia by Richard Folwell, No. 33 Carter's alley, shows that the library contained 131 works, many of them consisting of two or more volumes each.

The borough limits were extended in 1874 so as to include Richland Centre, a thriving village which had grown up around the railroad station, the road from that point to the older village being almost impassable in winter. The progress of improvement at the station had been hastened by John Strawn and Joel B. Roberts, property owners, who laid out streets and building lots. A post office was established in 1867. The road between the two was macadamized and the two villages have become one town.

Quakertown has two English newspapers, the Free Press and Times, the latter published at the station. The editor and proprietor of the Free Press, the leading paper, is Uriah S. Stauffer. It was founded by his father, John G. Stauffer, August 13, 1881. The family are of Swiss origin. The first ancestor in this country, Hans Stauffer, came to America in the spring of 1710, and settled in the vicinity of Valley Forge. The family are numerous in counties adjoining Bucks. The other newspaper is of more recent origin.

While the Germans formed so important an element in Quakertown, the first church organization aside from Friends was not formed until 1860. This was St. John's Evangelical Lutheran. St. John's Reformed congregation was organized in 1861 by Rev. P. S. Fisher. Methodists formed a congregation in 1872, and soon afterward erected their building. In due time other denominations secured a foothold. St. John's Reformed

JOSEPH R. LANCASTER'S HOUSE
(On the North side of Broad Street, Quakertown. Torn down in 1891)

congregation has completed a handsome place of worship within three or four years, its cost being considerably above $10,000.

There have been banking facilities at Quakertown since 1871, first by a state bank, and later by the Quakertown National Bank, organized in 1877.

William Green's tenure as Postmaster has been mentioned. He held the office twenty-six years. In 1829 John F. Walker was appointed; in 1832, John J. Horn; 1833, John Schantz; 1834, Benjamin Shroyer. Up to the establishment of the office in 1803 there had been none nearer than Allentown or Bethlehem. One was established at Sellers' Tavern (Sellersville) in 1820, and one at Richlandtown in 1832. There are now over a dozen within a radius of three or four miles of Quakertown, as may be seen by consulting the map opposite page 21. The mails, prior to the construction of the North Pennsylvania railroad, were carried by stage daily to and from Allentown, Bethlehem and Philadelphia, and weekly in the same way to and from Doylestown. In February, 1836, there was a delay of sixteen hours on the latter route, owing to the severe snow storm, said to have been four feet on a level.

Joseph R. Lancaster succeeded Shroyer as Postmaster, remaining until 1838; Jacob Slifer succeeded to him, and in 1840, Benjamin Griffith. Joseph Lancaster was reappointed in 1844. From 1844 to 1846 the office was kept in the old log house in which J. R. Lancaster lived, which is shown on the opposite page. It stood about forty yards west of the cross roads, on the north side of Broad street. It was torn down in 1891. The rate charged on a letter contained on an ordinary half-sheet at that time varied with the distance. If it were directed to Bethlehem the postage was 6 cents, to Philadelphia 10, Washington 25, Pittsburg 18¾, Newtown 25, Springhouse 12, Line Lexington 6, Buckingham 10, and so on through the list, according to the distance or the nature of the route. James L. Gold became Postmaster in 1846, Richard R. Green (son of William) in 1849, Levi Ochs in 1853, Peter Smith a year later, J. H. Kaull in 1855. Stamps came into use about this time. A story is told of a sender of a letter who asked that a stamp be placed on it, saying he would pay for it when he called again. He failed to do so, after repeated requests, and suit was brought for the value of the stamp, five cents. It cost the defendant over two dollars. Manasses Ochs became Postmaster in 1857, dying in office August 19, 1860. His widow, Mary J. Ochs, succeeded him, serving for many years. The present Postmaster is Charles Strawn, as already noted.

A weekly mail from Quakertown to Durham was established in 1819.

The old Bethlehem road, long an important highway from Philadelphia, was opened part of the way many years earlier, but not to Bethlehem until 1745. The new Bethlehem road was laid out later on an old Indian trail. The former was a well-known stage route for the greater part of a century. Down the Bethlehem road, later the Bethlehem turnpike, the farmers of Richland and other townships in that vicinity were accustomed to transport their produce to the Philadelphia market in heavy wagons, stopping on the way to feed or to remain over night at Line Lexington, Springhouse or Flourtown. They patronized the old taverns on Second street, Philadelphia, which were very popular in their day, known as the Black Horse, Red Lion, etc., from the figures on the huge swinging signs at the entrances to their yards. The construction of the railroad modified all this, the bulk of the produce from the vicinity, sometimes known as the "garden spot of Bucks county," being sent to market in that way. The distance from market was the greatest objection in earlier days among farmers to the locality. There are worse defects than this, however. There was compensation in the remoteness from city life and the changing fashions which belong to it, enabling them and their families to retain that simplicity of manners and freedom from affectation which marked them formerly, in common with other communities similarly situated, and which still characterize them to a certain extent at least.

HEADING OF FIRST QUAKERT[...]

(The STAR SPANGLED BANNER was published by David B. Overholt and Rynear T. Donatt, in the interest of the Know-
There have been various other newspaper ventures since, of which the FREE PRESS and T[...]

V.

RECORDS OF RICHLAND MEETING.

The records of Richland Monthly Meeting begin with its establishment in 1742, already mentioned. Those relating to births and deaths, removals and marriages, possess special interest, because of their value from a genealogical standpoint. They follow in order of time as nearly as possible, the births being grouped in families, wherever it can be done.

It may be said, by way of explanation, that a date occurring immediately after a name, without any intervening character, is the date of birth. The abbreviation d. before a date signifies that it is the month, day and year of death, in all dates the custom of Friends of calling the months by their numbers being adhered to, unless in exceptional instances. Under the head " Births and Deaths" are included some marriages, the latter mostly for the purpose of identification.

BIRTHS AND DEATHS.

JOHN AND DOROTHY LESTER.

Catharine 9, 23, 1733.
Priscilla 1, 18, 1736; m. Wm. Foulke.
John 1, 31, 1738.
William 3, 18, 1740.
Catharine, wife of John, d. in the winter of 1732.
Mary, dau. of John and Catharine, b. 1716; d. 5, 30, 1761.
Isaac died 1, 30, 1762.
John died 1, 27, 1771, in his 82d year.

EDWARD AND MARY (BOLTON) ROBERTS
Married at Abington 10, 29, 1714.
⎧ Edward d. 11, 25, 1768, in his 82d
⎪   year.
⎨ Mary d. 7, 22, 1784, aged 96 years, 6
⎩   months, 9 days.
Martha 8, 16, 1715; died 1, 26, 1768.
Abel 8, 23, 1717; d. 1, 5, 1808
John 11, 22, 1719.
David 1, 10, 1722; d. 8, 14, 1805.
·Everard 3, 9. 1725.
Nathan 6, 13, 1727; d 12. 10, 1806.
Mary 4, 26, 1730; d. 10, 2, 1787; m. John Foulke.
Jane 11, 3, 1732; d. 7, 25, 1822; m. Thomas Foulke.

WILLIAM AND MARTHA EDWARDS, OF MILFORD.

{ William d. 8, 13, 1764, in his 52d year.
{ Martha d. 4. 17, 1781, in her 65th year.
Mary 7, 14, 1739; d. 12, 17, 1755.
Thomas 1, 6, 1742; d. 5, 13, 1745.
Ann 12, 26, 1743-4.
William, Jr., 5, 13, 1746.
Thomas 2, 28, 1749.
Martha 6, 7, 1751.
Hugh 2, 13, 1754; d. 8, 30, 1760.
Mary 6, 15, 1756; d. 1, 19, 1770.
Hannah 7, 10, 1758.
Hugh 3, 16, 1761; d. 10, 4, 1764.

MORRIS AND SUSANNA MORRIS.

David d. 5, 28, 1752.
Susanna, wife of Morris Morris, died 4, 28, 1755.
Morris Morris d. 6, 2, 1764, in 87th year.
Samuel, of Whitemarsh, d. 11, 31, 1770.

JOHN AND MARGARET ROBERTS, OF MILFORD.

Hannah 4, 19, 1754.
Uriah 10, 28, 1755; d. 8, 14, 1762.
Enoch 2, 28, 1757.
David 11, 27, 1758.
Samuel 1, 13, 1761; d. 8, 8, 1762.
Uriah 11, 13, 1762.
Margaret 8, 11, 1768.
Martha 10, 25, 1764; d. 8, 13, 1831; m. Benjamin Foulke.
Abel 9, 27, 1770.
John d. 8, 8, 1776.

ABEL AND GAINOR (MORRIS) ROBERTS.

{ Gainor d. 1, 16, 1779.
{ Abel d. 1, 5, 1808.
Susanna 12, 13, 1748; d. 2, 26, 1818; m. 5, 11, 1769, Samuel Nixon.
Sidney 7, 5, 1756.
Sarah 6, —, 1758.

HUGH AND ANN HILLES.

Anne 1, 11, 1749.
Mary 10, 2, 1750.
William 10, 11, 1752.
David 9, 11, 1755.
Hugh d. 9, 12, 1756.

HUGH AND ANN FOULKE.

{ Hugh d. 5, 21, 1760, in his 75th year.
{ Ann d. 9, 10, 1763, in her 70th year.
He was a son of Edward, formerly of Wales, Great Britain; he was born 7, 6, 1685; she 11, 6, 1693.
Mary 9, 24, 1714.
Martha 5, 2, 1716.
Samuel 12, 4, 1718; m. Ann Greasley.
Eleanor 1, 19, 1720; m. Isaac Lester.
John 12, 21, 1722; d. 5, 25, 1787; m. Mary Roberts.
Thomas 1, 14, 1724; d. 3, 31, 1786; m. Jane Roberts.
Theophilus 12, 21, 1726; d. 11, 4, 1785: m. Margaret Thomas.
William 12, 10, 1728; d. 4, 11, 1796; m. Priscilla Lester.
Edward 10, 10, 1729; d. 1, 8, 1747.
Ann 1, 1, 1732; m. William Thomas.
Jane 1, 3, 1734; m. John Greasley.
Mary Boon d. 2, 20, 1756.
Jane Greasley, daughter of Hugh and Ann Foulke, d. 8, —, 1771.
James Boon d. 7, 1, 1785, of Exeter, in his 75th year.
John Boon d. 8, 5, 1785, of Exeter.
Ann Thomas d. 12, 14, 1786.
Samuel Foulke d. 1, 21, 1797, in his 78th year.

JOHN AND ANN GRIFFITH.

Hannah 5, 14, 1734.
Sarah 7, 16, 1735.

——— Parvin d. 10, 16, 1736.

LEWIS AND ANN LEWIS.

{ Lewis, Sr., d. 2, 16, 1778, in 72d year.
{ Ann d. 11, 8, 1785.
Elizabeth 11, 5, 1729.
Hannah 1730.
Ellis 3, 1, 1732; d. 12, 7, 173-.
Ellis (2d) 5, 20, 1734.
Lewis, Jr., 5, 30, 1736; d. 5, 9, 1738.
Ann, Jr., 8, 11, 1738.
Margaret 12, 11, 1741.
Lewis 9, 13, 1744; d. 1, 15, 1778.
Joseph 9, 3, 1746; d. 5, —, 1753.
Jane 11, 29, 1748.
Mary 12, 20, 1750; d. 5, —, 1759.
Martha 3, 21, 1754.

SAMUEL AND MARY CLARK.

William 2, 6, 1739.
Sarah 1, 23, 1741.
Elizabeth 9, 11, 1743.
Michael 1, 2, 1744.
Mary 9, 24, 1746.
Abigail 4, 21, 1747.
Walter 6, 3, 1749; d. 11, 22, 1785.
Samuel, Jr., 12, 7, 1751.
Morris Fell d. 11, 24, 1785 (son of Sarah Fell).
Walter Hadock d. 1, 22, 1789, near kinsman of Samuel Clark.

JOHN AND ANN ADAMSON.

Thomas 12, 23, 1717.
Betty 6, 9, 1719.
Hester 10, 9, 1721.
John 2, 15, 1726.
Ann 9, 25, 1728.
Susanna 9, 1, 1730.

JOHN AND SARAH BOND.

Benjamin 3, 11, 1726.
John, Jr., 5, 7, 1727; d. 10, 4, 1731.
Joshua 9, 12, 1729.
Abraham 5, 21, 1731.
Rebeckah 3, 31, 1733.
John ye 2d 2, 14, 1735.
Hannah 9, 6, 1736.
Edward 9, 4, 1738.
Mary 7, 6, 1741.

GEORGE AND SARAH HICKS.

Martha 2, 25, 1728.
Mary 10, 6, 1729.
William 7, 20, 1732; d. 2, 19, 1800.
Hannah 11, 18, 1734.
George 6, 31, 1736.
John 2, 26, 1740.

SAMUEL AND BETTY PEIRSON.

George 8, 27, 1729.
Hannah 4, 20, 1731; d. 4, 22, 1732.
Samuel, Jr., 7, 27, 1733.
Tom 2, 15, 1736.
Ann 9, 12, 1738; d. 12, 19, 1739.
Isabel 10, 19, 1740.
Betty, Jr., 12, 23, 1743.

THOMAS AND ALICE ROBERTS.

John 6-mo., 1716; d. 2, 2, 1797.
Ann 6, —, 1718.
Thomas 2, 1720; d.* 6, 5, 1767.

*This is the date that Thomas, Sr., died.
Thomas, Jr., died 5, 30, 1786.

Richard 12, 1722.
Alice 2, 1724; d. 8, 6, 1767; m. Edward Thomas.
Rachel 2, 1727.
Abraham 1, 14, 1730.

William d. 8, 13, 1731.

Rachel Jones d. 8, 1767.
Ann Hacock d. 3, 1807.

BENJAMIN AND SARAH GILBERT.

Rachel 11, 14, 1732.
Abigail 9, 3, 1734.
Sarah 2, 24, 1737; d. 8, 23, 1738.
Joseph 12, 10, 1738.
Benjamin, Jr., 1, 31, 1741.
John 5, 23, 1743.
Sarah 4, 26, 1745.
Joshua 3, 3, 1748.
Caleb 9, 19, 1754.

EDWARD AND ALICE THOMAS.

{ Edward d. 4, 4, 1782, aged 59 years, 2 mos., 13 days.
{ Alice Thomas d. 8, 6, 1807.
Margaret 9, 2, 1751.
Miriam 9, 2, 1753.
Mary 10, 2, 1755; d. 12, 19, 1731.
Martha 1, 22, 1758.
Samuel 7, 15, 1760; d. 5, 17, 1847.
Andrew 1, 20, 1764; d. 5, 15, 1765.
Samuel Thomas d. 5, 7, 1755, in his 65th year.
Margaret Thomas (wife of Samuel) d. 10, 24, 1750, in her 57th year.
Mary Thomas, daughter of Samuel and Margaret Thomas, d. 2, 27, 1756, in her 27th year.
Thomas Thomas, son of Samuel and Margaret Thomas, d. 10, 12, 1780, in his 62d year.

JOHN AND MARY EDWARDS.

{ John, Sr., d. 3, 29, 1756.
{ Mary d. 5, 10, 1770.
Margaret 8, 13, 1753.
William 6, 5, 1755; d. 8, 1, 1760.
Mary 8, 13, 1756.
John 8, 3, 1759.

{ William Newman 5, 3, 1759.
{ Margaret (his wife) 3, 23, 1759.

JOHN AND MARY FOULKE.

{ John d. 5, 25, 1787, in his 66th year.
Mary d. 10, 2, 1787; in her 57th year,
  much lamented.

Edward 7, 16, 1758.*
Anne 10, 27, 1760.
Jane 8, 2, 1763; d. 3, 18, 1780.
Aquilla 3, 2, 1766.
Margaret 10, 17, 1768.
Evan 5, 6, 1771.
Lydia 10, 2, 1775.
*The record has this Martha, but it is known to be Edward.

SAMUEL AND ANN FOULKE.

Eleanor 11, 5, 1744; d. 7, 6, 1833.
Thomas 4, 11, 1746; d. 10, 7, 1784.
Israel 9, 13, 1749; d. 9, 19, 1754.
Judah 4, 20, 1752; d. 6, 16, 1752.
Amelia 7, 3, 1753; d. 8, 7, 1811.
Hannah 9, 15, 1756.
Israel 2, 4, 1760; d. 9, 27, 1824.
Judah 1, 18, 1763.
Cadwallader 7, 14, 1765.
John 12, 6, 1767; d. 4, 5, 1840.
Ann d. 5-mo., 1797.

THOMAS AND JANE (ROBERTS) FOULKE.

Everard 9, 8, 1755; d. 9, 5, 1827.
Edward 12, 17, 1756; d. 1, 17, 1757.
Samuel 1, 3, 1761; d. 5-mo., 1763.
Abigail 10, 4, 1763.
Susanna 11, 5, 1766.
Samuel 11, 19, 1769; d. 12, 25, 1787.
Jane 11, 3, 1732; d. 7, 25, 1822.

DAVID AND PHEBE ROBERTS.

Amos 4, 1, 1755.
Mary 4, 19, 1758; d. 8, 22, 1760.
Elizabeth 7, 4, 1760.
Nathan 6, 29, 1762; d. 5, 28, 1763.
Jane 12, 19, 1764.
Abigail 2, 14, 1767.
Nathan 9, 24, 1769.
David 9, 21, 1772.
Evan 4, 20, 1775; d. 3, 26, 1849.

EVERARD AND ANN ROBERTS.

Susan 2, 7, 1771; d. 4, 11, 1854.

THOMAS AND MARY ADAMSON.

Rachel 9, 4, 1739.
Ann 9, 12, 1742; d. 8, 8, 1784; m. Abraham Ball.
Joseph 1, 17, 1745.
Mary 12, 7, 1747.

Hannah 5, 15, 1749.
Esther 4, 2, 1751.
John 11, 1, 1753.
Deborah 12, 8, 1755.
James 1, 4, 1757.
Martha 11, 2, 1760.
Sarah 1, 14, 1763.

WILLIAM AND PRISCILLA FOULKE.

Asher 2, 15, 1758.
Issachar 1, 31, 1760.
Jesse 4, 28, 1762.
John 10, 18, 1764; d. 12, 28, 1765.
Mary 10, 24, 1766.
Phebe 10, —, 1769; d. 11, 13, 1773.
Sarah (wife of Jesse Foulke) d. 9, 21, 1791.
Priscilla Foulke d. 3, 17, 1795, aged 59.
William Foulke d. 4, 11, 1796, in his 68th year.

Elizabeth Sichaverel d. 3, 6, 1773.

Sarah Ashton, daughter of Samuel and Margaret Thomas, d. 1, 25, 1786.
Mary, daughter of Sarah Ashton, d. 2, 15, 1786.

JOSEPH AND CATHARINE GREEN.

{ Joseph d. 5, 26, 1757, in his 40th year.
Catharine d. 7, 12, 1770.

Margaret 11, 28, 1744.
Joseph, Jr., 12, 23, 1745.
Samuel 10, 21, 1748.
Jane
Benjamin } 2, 27, 1750.
Jane d. 2, 2, 1767.
Benjamin d. 5, 22, 1828.
Ezekiel 5, 14, 1752.
James 3, 22, 1754.
Thomas 7, 27, 1756.

JOHN AND KEZIA DENNIS.

Joseph 12, 14, 1741.
Ezekiel 12, 17, 1742.
Catharine 11, 1, 1744.
John, Jr., 1, 26, 1746.
Sarah 12, 21, 1749.
Kezia 2, 22, 1753.
Tamar 8, 10, 1755.

THEOPHILUS AND MARGARET FOULKE.

{ Theophilus d. 11, 4, 1785, in 60th year.
Margaret born 4, 3, 1734, old style.

Hugh 8, 29, 1758.
Jane 8, 22, 1759.

WILLIAM AND ANN HOGE.

(m. 2, 9, 1723.)
James 12, 6, 1724-5.
William, Jr., 1, 4, 1726.
Solomon 3, 21, 1729.
George 2, 6, 1733.
Joseph 12, 1, 1735-6.
Zebulon 4, 15, 1738.
Ann 12, 26, 1740-1.
Ann, wife of William, d. 2, 21, 1759.

ISAAC AND ELINOR LESTER.

Margaret 11, 13, 1749.
Samuel 9, 6, 1750.
Joseph 2, 26, 1752.
John 1, 19, 1754.
Elijah 11, 20, 1755.
Mary 7, 16, 1757.
Catharine 6, 10, 1759.
Isaac 1, 6, 1761.

Owen Owens (of Saucon) d. 8, 21, 1742.
Mary d. 3, 14, 1760, in her 96th year.

Patrick Ogleby d. 7, 23, 1760.

ROBERT AND MARY PENROSE.

Jonathan 1, 1, 1735-6.
Joseph 6, 10, 1737.
John 11, 19, 1739-40; d. 2, 12, 1813;
    m. Ann Roberts.
William 2, 15, 1742; d. 1, 26, 1808; m.
    Mary Roberts.
Robert, Jr., 3, 6, 1744.
Samuel 6, 21, 1748; m. Sarah Roberts.
Benjamin 10, 30, 1749-50.
Mary 6, 5, 1753, new style.
Jesse 5, 2, 1755.

ISAAC AND ANN GRIFFITH.

Abraham 4, 2, 1746.
Rachel 9, 23, 1747.
Hannah 7, 6, 1749.
Mary 7, 28, 1752.
Ann 2, 1, 1754.
Sarah 11, 15, 1756.
Joseph 10, 22, 1758.
Martha 8, 23, 1760.
Isaac, Jr., 6, 7, 1764.
John 5, 29, 1766.
James 1, 16, 1769.
Abraham d. 10, 3, 1760, in his 82d year.

WILLIAM AND ANN THOMAS.

Absalom 7, 11, 1761.
Jane 12, 8, 1762.

JOHN AND ANN GREASLEY.

Rachel 10, 30, 1757.

WILLIAM AND MARY NIXON.

{ William d. 12, 16, 1747-8, in 68th year.
{ Mary (his wife) d. 4, 21, 1758, in her
    78th year. William came from Eng-
    land.
Mary 7, 27, 1713.
Samuel 11, 30, 1715; d. 1, 29, 1747-8.

THOMAS AND ELIZABETH BLACKLEDGE.

William 1, 16, 17—; d. 12, 8, 1761.
Elizabeth 6, 11, 1758.
Rachel 4, 13, 1760.

THOMAS, JR., AND LETITIA ROBERTS.

{ Thomas d. 5, 30, 1786, aged about 65 ys.
{ Letitia d. 10, 12, 1802.
Abigail 7, 28, 1751.
Martha 3, 9, 1753.
Alice 4, 3, 1755.
Israel 1, 14, 1757.
Elizabeth 8, 7, 1759; d. 7, 25, 1793.
Isaac 1, 25, 1762.

JOSEPH AND SARAH BALL.

{ Joseph d. 10, 31, 1792, aged 74 years.
{ Sarah d. 3, 21, 1796, aged 72 years.
John 4, 18, 1750.
Jesse 5, 26, 1756.
Margaret 9, 28, 1758.
Elizabeth 1, 13, 1763.
Catharine Ball d. 3, 28, 1764, in her 73d
    yr. (wife of John). John Ball d. 9, 22,
    1767, aged upwards of 80 years.

WILLIAM AND MARGARET HICKS.

Mary 12, 21, 1751.
Abigail 4, 21, 1756; d. 5, 29, 1820.
Margaret d. 12, 29, 1758.
    Hannah, second wife:
Jesse 9, 21, 1761.
Margaret 11, 30, 1762.
Samuel 9, 6, 1764.
George 6, 12, 1770; d. 8, 12, 1847.
William 12, 6, 1771.
Hannah 5, 11, 1774.
John 7, 31, 1776; d. 8, 14, 1830.
Hannah d. 11, 24, 1781, in her 43d year.

BENJAMIN AND RACHEL LANCASTER.

Jesse 1, 1, 1751.
Ann 6, 28, 1753.
Benjamin 2, 28, 1756; d. 7-mo. 1760.

Joseph 11, 7, 1758.
Benjamin 10, 10, 1761.
Nathan 12, 8, 1763.
Thomas Lancaster d. 9-mo. 1750 (O. S.),
    of Warwick, England; came to this
    country with Ann Chapman. In his
    48th year.

WILLIAM AND ANN BURR.

Martha 6, 6, 1764; d. 3, 31, 1765.
Reuben 3, 14, 1766.
Jane 5, 1, 1768.
Timothy 4, 19, 1770; d. 8, 17, 1801.
Samuel 3, 2, 1772; d. 8, 26, 1798.
Martha 1, 25, 1775.
David 5, 10, 1777.
William 2, 13, 1779.
Joseph 12, 31, 1780.
Henry 11, 27, 1782.
Ann d. 10, 10, 1795, in her 53d year.
Timothy d. at Penn's Neck, Salem co.,
    New Jersey.
Samuel d. at Philadelphia.

JOSEPH AND HANNAH DENNIS.

Ezekiel 6, 12, 1753.
Jesse 1, 30, 1755.
Sarah 4, 11, 1757.
Anne 10, 11, 1758.
Lewis 4, 22, 1761.
Joseph 7, 18, 1763.
Hannah 5, 22, 1765.

JOHN AND HANNAH CHAPMAN.

John Chapman 1, 30, 1742; d. 2, 2, 1771.
Jane (daughter of John and Hannah) 10,
    20, 1770; d. 12, 20, 1770.
Hannah (wife of John) 2, 3, 1742; d.
    10, 30, 1778.

JONATHAN AND ANN GRIFFITH.

Rachel 10, 18, 1752.
Jonathan, Jr., 9, 21, 1754; d. 3, 18, 1809.
John 5, 1, 1761.
Jonathan, Sr., d. 8, 1, 1767.

JOHN AND ANN PENROSE.

Martha 10, 13, 1765; d. 3, 20, 1849.
Enoch 8, 1, 1767; d. 8, 22, 1842.
Nathan 4, 1, 1769.
Rachel 2, 7, 1771.
Jane 11, 3, 1773; d. 5, 24, 1848.
Thomas 5, 2, 1775.
John 2, 7, 1777.
Ann 6, 22, 1779.
Evan 4, 2, 1782; d. 2, 11, 1864.

Mary 5, 9, 1785; d. 12, 16, 1849.
Rachel Shaw d. 3, 9, 1797 (late Penrose).

SAMUEL AND SUSANNA NIXON.

Margaret 2, 25, 1770.
Sarah 8, 26, 1771.
William 4, 29, 1775; m. Martha Roberts.
Hannah 1, 27, 1777.
Mary 1, 25, 1779; m. Isaac Parry.
Tacey 5, 15, 1781.
Abel 4, 13, 1783.
Samuel 12, 27, 1785.
Beulah, 1, 1, 1790.
Abigail, 3, 19, 1792.

JACOB AND STAUNCHY STRAWN.

William 11, 17, 1749.
Daniel 3, 27, 1752; d. 9, 10, 1819.
Mary 2, 21, 1754.
Hannah 4, 8, 1756.
Josiah 10, 28, 1758.
Job 10, 12, 1760.
Jerusha 12, 14, 1762.
Abel 3, 12, 1765.
Enoch 9, 1, 1768.
Mary (wife of Thomas) d. 3, 27, 1770.

JOHN AND ELIZABETH LANCASTER.

{ John d. 2, 26, 1791, aged about 59
    years.
  Elizabeth d. 12, 11, 1796, aged about
    67 years.
Abigail 8, 26, 1754.
Israel 7, 25, 1756; d. 8, 7, 1760.
Jonah 3, 28, 1758.
Anne 6, 27, 1759.
Israel 5, 22, 1761.

WILLIAM AND HANNAH CLARK.

Thomas 12, 13, 1766.
Gabriel 3, 13, 1769.
Thomas (2d) 4, 25, 1770.
William 8, 17, 1771.
Eleazer 1, 18, 1773.
Martha 11, 11, 1776--7.

WILLIAM AND MARY PENROSE.

Abigail 9, 11, 1771.
Margaret 5, 5, 1775; d. 10, 31, 1826.
Sarah 11, 21, 1778; d. 1860.
William d. 1, 26, 1808, aged nearly 66
    years.
Mary d. 11, 30, 1843.

LEWIS, JR., AND MARY LEWIS.

Sarah 7, 27, 1770; d. 5, 11, 1771.
James 3, 30, 1772; d. 1, 11, 1776.
Lewis 1, 10, 1774.
Joseph 10, 9, 1775.
Jane 11, 7, 1777; d. 11-mo., ——

EDWARD AND MARY ROBERTS.

{ Edward 11, 7, 1743.
{ Mary 12, 4, 1752.
Martha 7, 24, 1780.
James 11, 27, 1783.
Peninah 4, 7, 1788.

BENJAMIN AND JANE (ROBERTS) GREEN.

William 11, 10, 1776; d. 9, 24, 1851.
Hannah 9, 29, 1778; d. 4, 12, 1826.
Evan 11, 10, 1780.
Benjamin 12, 10, 1782.
Jane 2, 8, 1785; d. 3, 3, 1835.
James 3, 4, 1787; d. 7, 27, 1832.
Lydia 12, 20, 1789; d. 10, 26, 1850.
Joseph 2, 14, 1791.
Martha 2, 14, 1793; m. Samuel Carey.
Abigail 3, 18, 1797; d. 8, 21, 1854.
Jane, widow of Benjamin, d. 5, 18, 1841,
    aged 88 years.

JOHN AND JANE LESTER.

{ John 1, 31, 1738.
{ Jane 10, 26, 1739; d. 11, 26, 1805.
Sarah 4, 5, 1763.
Shipley 11, 23, 1764; d. 3, 24, 1832.
Hannah 2, 2, 1767.
Thomas 3, 1, 1769; d. 3, 22, 1828.
Jane 9, 8, 1771.
John 8, 11, 1774.
Isaac 2, 20, 1777; d. 3, 18, 1780.
Peter 9, 10, 1779; d. 8, 22, 1785.

JOSEPH AND ELEANOR PENROSE.

Israel 12, 31, 1768.
Jane 1, 7, 1771.
Benjamin 1, 3, 1773; died 9-mo., 1777.
Joseph 1, 27, 1777.

JAMES AND MARTHA GREEN.

Ann 1, 10, 1780.
Elizabeth 11, 1, 1781.
Thomas 9, 7, 1783.
Margaret 10, 5, 1785.
James d. 8, 10, 1786, in his 33d year,
    much lamented.

SAMUEL AND MARY SHAW.

{ Samuel d. 2, 21, 1781, in his 72d year.
{ Mary, d. 12, 23, 1794, aged 81 years,
{   2 weeks.
Hannah 7, 29, 1738.
Mary 5, 30, 1740; d. 11, 14, 1779.
John 10, 16, 1742; d. 9, 24, 1826.
Joseph 6, 25, 1744.
William 2, 23, 1750; d. 6, 17, 1818.
Samuel 8, 25, 1756.
Moses, 8, 20 1758; d. 9, 6, 1826.

JOHN AND PHEBE SHAW.

Israel 9, 3, 1765; d. 9, 30, 1833.
Hannah 12, 12. 1766.
William Nixon 11, 12, 1769.
Joseph 2, 6, 1772; d. 2 16, 1823.
Gulielma 9, 25, 1774.
Phebe 1, 4, 1778; d. 5, 1, 1830.
Mary 1, 17, 1780.
Miriam 1, 11, 1782; d. 11, 14, 1814; m.
    David Foulke.
John 7, 27, 1783; d. 3, 17, 1839.

WILLIAM AND SARAH SHAW.

Mary 12, 1, 1778; d. 1, 21, 1817.
Jonathan 9, 26, 1781; d. 1, —, 1859.
Samuel 2, 26, 1784; d. 2, 6, 1863; m.
    Sidney Foulke.
Moses 7, 24. 1786.
Abigail 7, 3, 1789; d. 8, 29, 1858.
Hannah 3, 7, 1793; d. 5, 28, 1859; m.
    James Foulke.
Sarah d. 7, 22, 1820.

ISRAEL AND ANN ROBERTS.

Lydia 4, 14, 1783; d. 1, 5, 1866.
Jane 3, 10, 1785.
Thomas 7, 16, 1787.
Letitia 8, 21, 1789.
Lewis 12, 21, 1791.

ISRAEL AND ELIZABETH FOULKE.

William 8, 18, 1783; d. 9, 2, 1784.
Thomas 12, 31, 1784; d. 6, 4, 1832.
David 12, 21, 1786.
Cadwallader 5, 22, 1789; d. 8, 22, 1794.
Jane 3, 26, 1791; d. 6, 24, 1794.
Hugh 9, 8, 1793; d. 4, 3, 1853.
Phebe 12, 27, 1795.
Amos 8, 10, 1798.
Deborah 8, 13, 1800; d. 12, 29, 1806.
Elizabeth d. 12, 17, 1831.

EDWARD AND ELIZABETH FOULKE.

{ Edward 7, 16, 1758.
{ Elizabeth 8, 7, 1759; d. 7, 25, 1793;
  daughter of Thomas, Jr., and Letitia
  Roberts.
Jane 8, 20, 1782.
Rowland 12, 29, 1783.
Agnes 8, 27, 1785.
Mary 9, 29, 1787.
John 10, 28, 1789.
Edward 5, 26, 1792; d. 2, 16, 1859.

THOMAS AND ELIZABETH MCCARTY.

Phebe 8, 2, 1766; d. 3, 30, 1850.
Samuel 11, 8, 1767.
Silas 11, 30, 1768.
Sarah }
Mary } 12, 19, 1769.
Joel 12, 16, 1771.
John 5, 6, 1773.
James 6, 11, 1774.
Jane 9, 18, 1775.
Elizabeth 9, 17, 1776.
Thomas 3, 8, 1778.
Job 8, 10, 1779.
Hannah 2, 19, 1781.
Benjamin 7, 20, 1783.

STEPHEN AND PHEBE KIRK.

Isaac 1, 11, 1762.
Sarah 2, 3, 1764.
Jonas 10, 20, 1766.
Hannah 1, 18, 1769.
Benjamin 6, 26, 1771.
Elizabeth 10, 19. 1773.
Rachel 6, 2, 1776.

Sarah Brock d. 10, 6, 1802.

SAMUEL AND SUSANNA SHAW.

John 11, 24, 1780.
Thomas 10, 16, 1782.
Letitia 12, 14, 1784.
Susanna d. 6, 17, 1788, aged 35 years 2
  months.

RANDAL AND ELEANOR IDEN.

{ Randal 1. 4, 1736; d. 5, 16, 1812.
{   Son of Randal and Margaret.
{ Eleanor, d. 7, 6, 1833, in 89th year.
John ―― d. 4, 4, 1779.
Margaret 9, 1, 1774.
Samuel 2, 2, 1779; m. Eliz. Chapman.
Jesse 10, 23, 1782.
Jane 10, 24, 1785.
Sarah, 10, 26, 1789.

Susanna 12, 8, 1791.
Albion 8, 29, 1793; d, 10, 6, 1806.
Beulah Iden d. 1, 2, 1817.

JUDAH AND SARAH FOULKE.

Samuel 8, 12, 1787.
Eleanor 2, 25, 1789.
Mary 3, 8, 1791.
Ann 12, 9, 1792.
Thomas 5, 7, 1795.
Elizabeth 5, 19, 1797.
Jane 6, 19, 1799.
Amelia 6, 20, 1801.
Cadwalader 5, 25, 1803.
Jesse 9, 18, 1805.
Mercy 5, 6, 1808.
Grace 1, 29, 1810.
Silas 3, 18, 1812.

SAMUEL AND SARAH PENROSE.

Abel 8, 7, 1778; d. 12, 7, 1824.
Gainor 3, 14, 1780.
William 3, 14, 1782.
Edward 10, 7, 1784.
Mary 5, 11, 1787.
Benjamin 9. 16, 1791.
Susanna 8, 21, 1793.
Samuel 8, 10, 1796
Margaret 9, 20, 1798.
Morris 6, 15, 1801.
Kezia d. 11, 11, 1803 (wife of Abel).
Abel m. (2d) Abigail Foulke.

JAMES AND REBECCA CHAPMAN.

Jacob Abbot 2, 19, 1773.
Elizabeth 9, 8, 1776; m. Samuel Iden.
Abigail 12, 31, 1779.

JOHN AND LETITIA FOULKE.

{ John 12, 6, 1767 (son of Samuel and
{   Ann).
{ Letitia 9, 10, 1767; d. 10, 18, 1854;
{   dau. of Thomas and Letitia Roberts.
James 8, 2, 1790; d. 4, 8, 1866.
Sidney 12, 30, 1791; d. 12-mo., 1862;
  m. Samuel Shaw.
Abigail 1, 5, 1794; m. Thomas Wright.
Elizabeth 10, 13, 1795.
Ann 11, 23, 1797.
Hannah 7, 4, 1799; m. Bartholomew
  Mather.
Kezia 4, 4, 1804.
Mary 12, 5, 1806; m. Jos. Paul.

AMOS AND MARGARET ROBERTS.

Mordecai 8, 29, 1776.
Mary 3, 17, 1778.
Alice 4, 28, 1780.
Hugh 2, 16, 1782.
Andrew 1, 31, 1784.
George 1, 9, 1786 ; d. 11, 17, 1789.
Phœbe 3, 7, 1788.
Margaret 2, 20, 1790.

JAMES AND MARGARET WALTON.

Ann 9, 15, 1764.
James 7, 22, 1776.
Joseph 10, 27, 1780.
Ellis 7, 23, 1783.

Daniel 4, 16, 1754 (son of Isaac) ; d. 1809.

GEORGE AND MARY CUSTARD.

Joseph 5, 1, 1751 ; d. 1, 12, 1837.

JOSEPH AND AMELIA CUSTARD.

Amelia 7, 3, 1753 ; d. 8, 7, 1811 ;
    daughter of Samuel Foulke.
Ann 8, 14, 1787.
George 11, 30, 1789 ; d. 10, 1, 1854,
    suddenly.
Mary 11, 19, 1792.

MOSES AND MARY SHAW.

Deborah 12, 15, 1782 ; d. 1, 10, 1860.
Sarah 11, 30, 1784.
Mary 1, 25, 1787 ; d. 12, 29, 1808.
William 10, 9, 1790.
Mary d. 4, 30, 1833 ; widow of Moses.

ASHER AND ALICE FOULKE.

Phebe 10, 27, 1781.
Anthony 6, 19, 1784.
William 5, 15, 1786 ; d. 9, 20, 1787.
Anne 6, 6, 1788.
Elizabeth 8, 23, 1790 ; d. 10, 4, 1791.

EVERARD AND ANN FOULKE.

Abigail 5, 18, 1779.
Eleanor 7, 18, 1781 ; d. 4, 28, 1815.
Caleb 8, 29, 1783 ; d. 2, 22, 1852.
Samuel 3 28, 1786.
Thomas 4, 13, 1789.
Susanna 9, 18, 1791.
Anna 5, 3, 1794 ; d. 9, 16, 1820.
Margaret 12, 24, 1796 ; m. Peter Lester.
Everard 7, 21, 1800.
Ann d. 3, 13, 1827.

ISRAEL AND SUSANNA PENROSE.

Elizabeth 12, 25, 1791.
Edith 6, 25, 1794.
Enos 10, 15, 1796.
Jane 1, 31, 1801.
Benjamin 7, 9, 1803.
Edith 10, 7, 1806.
Joseph 9, 6, 1808.

SAMUEL AND RACHEL GREEN.

Catharine 3, 11, 1770.
Mary 8, 28, 1771.
Jane 2, 5, 1773.
Green 8, 17, 1774.
Rachel 6, 18, 1776.
Thomas 1, 22, 1778.
Alice 8, 7, 1781.
Samuel 8, 3, 1783.

WILLIAM AND REBECCA ROBERTS.

Joseph 8, 7, 1786.
Sarah 12, 18, 1787.
Maria 7, 23, 1789.
Martha 4, 2, 1791.
John   } 12, 25, 1796.
Rebecca }
Nathan 2, 26, 1800 ; d. 10 21, 1805.

ISSACHAR AND JANE FOULKE.

Priscilla 8, 11, 1793.
Bathsheba 11, 15, 1794.
Mary 8, 3, 1797.
Sarah 10, 3, 1799.
Rebecca 5, 30, 1801.
Jane 12, 1, 1802.
Aaron 10, 26, 1804.
Mercy 9, 25, 1806 ; d. 11, 5, 1806.
Barton 5, 22, 1808.

JOHN AND ANN BALL.

Joel 9, 29, 1779.
Joseph 4, 29, 1782.
Margaret 6, 30, 1784.
Jesse 9, 20, 1786.
Sarah 3, 4, 1788.
James 2, 5, 1790.
Susanna 6, 5, 1792.
Iden 9, 25, 1794.

JONATHAN AND SARAH GRIFFITH.

James 3, 12, 1788.
Joseph 8, 29, 1790.
Mary 4, 23, 1797 ; d. 9, 15, 1799.

JESSE AND SARAH FOULKE.

Ellen 9, 29, 1798.
Hannah 7, 16, 1800.
Rachel 9, 16, 1802.
William 5, 6, 1805.
Sarah d. 9, 21, 1791.

THOMAS AND ANNE RAWLINGS.

Joseph 12, 3, 17— ; d. 12, 22, 1796.
Margaret 1, 25, 1786.
Thomas 12, 23, 1787.
Ann 10, 17, 1789.
Jane 3, 3, 1792.

JESSE AND MARY HICKS.

Ann 9, 23, 1787.
Mahlon 6, 9, 1790.
Hannah 5, 6, 1793.
Rebecca, 8, 9, 1795.
Jesse 3, 9, 1798.
Thomas 1, 31, 1801.

BENJAMIN AND MARTHA FOULKE.

Hannah 12, 25, 1789; d. 2, 11, 1859
  m. George Custard.
Jane 1, 25, 1793; d. 2d-mo., 1859; m.
  Wm. L. Strawn.
Charles 10, 14, 1795.
Rachel 1, 16, 1800; d. 1803.
Rachel (2d) 3, 14, 1803.
Martha 10, 25, 1764; d. 8, 13, 1831;
  wife of Benjamin.

DANIEL AND ELIZA D. STROUD.
(Stroudsburg.)

Charles 4, 9, 1793.
MacDowell 10, 12, 1795.
William 8, 19, 1797.
Jacob D. 3, 28, 1799.
James Hollinshead 11, 12, 1800.
Susan 3, 31, 1804.
Simpson 7, 31, 1806.
Elizabeth 1, 5, 1808.
Eliza D. d. 10, 29, 1809.

ISRAEL AND HANNAH LANCASTER.

Harriet 1, 20, 1799.
John 4, 5, 1801.
William 10, 28, 1802.
Morris 3, 10, 1806.

NATHAN AND MARGARET ROBERTS.

{ Nathan 9, 24, 1769.
{ Margaret 3, 24, 1765.
Ashton 3, 8, 1792.

Theophilus 3, 13, 1794.
Guy 8, 2, 1796.

WM. H. AND MARTHA BALL.

{ Wm. H. 11, 9, 1790; d. 2, 19, 1863.
{ Martha.
Margaret 12, 28, 1815 (m. to Charles
  Reeder).
Elmina 9, 24, 1817; d. 5, 19, 1842; m.
  William Blaker.
Joel 8, 24, 1819.
Mary 8, 7, 1821; m. 1st, —— Edwards,
  2d, Penrose Hicks.
Martha D. 6, 11, 1825 (m. to Albert
  Conard.)
Aaron 10, 6, 1827.
Wm. Owen 4, 25, 1830.

NATHAN AND MARY BALL.

Edith d, 8, 23, 1866.
William d. 8, 6, 1857.
Ann d. 8, 22, 1846 (wife of William).

AARON AND SARAH JANE BALL.

{ Aaron 10, 26, 1792; d. 11, 22, 1856.
{ Sarah J. (wife of Aaron).
Eleazer J. 7, 14, 1816; d. 10, 30, 1828.
John 7, 31, 1818.
Harvey S. 1, 28, 1821.
William 7, 28, 1823; d. 10, 27, 1859;
  m. Sarah Shaw.
Eliza Ann 12, 24, 1825 (m. to David
  Roberts).
Joseph J. 3, 19, 1830.
Sarah 7, 28, 1834 (m. to Charles Mason).

JOHN AND SARAH ANN BALL.

{ John 7, 31, 1818.
{ Sarah Ann 3, 29, 1819 (wife of John).
Elizabeth J. 12, 4, 1840.
Mary Ellen 12, 21, 1841.
Jane 3, 16, 1844.
Charles S. 9, 11, 1845.
Saml. Carey } 2, 13, 1848.
Edwin }
Ann S. 11, 29, 1849.

JOHN AND HANNAH P. BALL.

Hannah P. 12, 16, 1798; d. 7, 1, 1865.
Thomas P. 6, 10, 1819; d. 11, 25, 1862;
  m. Martha Hicks.
Gilbert 1, 17, 1821; d. 4, 14, 1863.

Mary 3, 14, 1823 (m. Samuel Styer).
Lewis S. ———

WILLIAM AND SARAH BALL.

{ William 7, 28, 1823 ; d. 10, 27, 1859
(son of Aaron and Sarah J.)
{ Sarah 12, 3, 1826.
Ellwood 3, 24, 1849.
Sidney Ann 2, 16, 1853.
Ella 5, 30, 1860.

GEORGE W. AND SUSAN P. BROWN.

{ George W. 12, 10, 1806.
{ Susan P. 2, 19, 1809.
Thomas P. 9, 28, 1832 ; d. 9, 12, 1852.
Michael 6, 7, 1834.
James V. Potts 8, 2, 1836.
William Vail 4, 15, 1841.
Emma Rebecca 4, 5, 1844.

SAMUEL AND ABIGAIL (GREEN) CAREY.

{ Samuel d. 8, 19, 1864.
{ Abigail 3, 18, 1797 ; d. 8, 21, 1854.
Jane G. 1, 24, 1827 ; m. Samuel Kinsey.
Hannah 8, 22, 1828 ; d. 9, 10, 1828.

EDWARD AND HANNAH R. COOPER.

{ Edward 10, 29, 1815 (son of Chilion
and Rachel, Wrightstown).
{ Hannah R. 4, 7, 1824.
Rachel 7, 7, 1842.
Henry 5, 25, 1845.

WILLIAM AND LYDIA EDWARDS.

Lydia R. 4, 14, 1783 ; d. 1, 5, 1866,
widow of William and daughter of
Israel Roberts.
Ann R. 10, 4, 1817 ; m. Joseph John-
son.
Algernon 6, 6, 1822.
Mary H. 3, 29, 1827 ; d. 2, 26, 1867 ;
m. Milton Johnson.

George W. Evans d. 9th mo., 1864.

JAMES AND HANNAH (SHAW) FOULKE.

{ James 8, 2, 1790 ; d. 4, 8, 1866 ; son
of John and Letitia.
{ Hannah S. 3, 7, 1793 ; d. 5, 28, 1859.
Abby Ann 10, 1, 1816 ; d 2, 24, 1859.
Stephen 1, 3, 1819.
Sarah 4, 30, 1822.
John 10, 12, 1830.

STEPHEN AND MATILDA (PENROSE) FOULKE.

{ Stephen.
{ Matilda P. 6, 15, 1815.
Esther T. 6, 6, 1847 ; d. 1, 26, 1848.
Penrose 6, 16, 1849.
Hannah Martha 3, 20, 1851 ; d. 8, 15,
1864.
Ann Matilda 10, 6, 1853.

SAMUEL M. AND ANN (EDWARDS) FOULKE.

William E. 12, 23, 1816.

JOSHUA AND CAROLINE (GREEN) FOULKE.

{ Joshua 10, 12, 1797, son of Edward
and Ann.
{ Caroline 2, 6, 1805.
Missouri G. 6, 14, 1826 ; d. 3, 26, 1867 ;
m. Milton Roberts.
Cornelia 7, 12, 1828 ; m. David R. Jam-
ison.
Matilda G. 12, 27, 1830 ; m. David R.
Jamison.
Jane 9, 2, 1837 ; m. Lewis Roberts.
Edward 10, 17, 1839 ; d. 8, 7, 1848.
Alice 12, 26, 1847 ; d. 7, 6, 1848.

EDWARD AND MATILDA (GREEN) FOULKE.

{ Edward 5, 26, 1792 ; d. 2, 16, 1859,
son of Edward and Elizabeth.
{ Matilda G. 1, 20, 1809.
Elizabeth 1, 31, 1833 ; m. J. B. Edwards.
Joseph W. 10, 31, 1834 ; d. 2, 3, 1868.
William G. 1, 5, 1837.
Martha R. 7, 4, 1839.
Evan 6, 18, 1842 ; d. 3, 19, 1852.
Mary G. 9, 6, 1844 ; d. 10, 11, 1865.
James 9, 3, 1847.
Agnes 3, 29, 1855 ; d. 11, 29, 1862.

BENJAMIN G. AND JANE (MATHER) FOULKE.

{ Benjamin G. 7, 28, 1813 ; son of
Caleb and Jane G.
{ Jane M. 3, 24, 1817.
Caleb 12, 3, 1839 ; d. 10, 20, 1865.
Charles M. 7, 25, 1841.
Job Roberts 2, 23, 1843.
Anna S. 9, 9, 1846.
Jane 11, 24, 1848 ; d. 3, 20, 1853.
Eleanor 12, 3, 1850.

WILLIAM AND ALICE (THOMAS) FOULKE.

{ William 6, 5, 1828, son of Everard
  and Fanny.
  Alice.

Susan J. 2, 20, 1855.
Mary Ella 9, 20, 1856.
Jane T. 2, 20, 1858.
Alice Lulu 1, 26, 1864

CHARLES AND CATHARINE (EDKINS)
FOULKE.
(Stroudsburg.)

{ Charles 2, 26, 1801.
  Catharine 3, 17, 1809.

Frances Ann 4, 22, 1832.
Sarah Jane 6, 11, 1834; d. 9, 27, 1848.
Susan E. 10, 6, 1836.
Joseph 10, 24, 1838.
Hannah M. 10, 11, 1840.
Samuel L. 9, 4, 1842.
Martha E. 5, 6, 1845.
Mary   } 3, 9, 1848; d. 3, 15, 1848.
Elizabeth } 3, 9, 1848.

ZACHARIAH AND ESTHER FLAGLER.
(Stroudsburg.)

{ Zachariah 1, 26, 1795; son of John Z.
  Esther 3, 22, 1803.

John A. 1, 28, 1823.
Mary M. 11, 19, 1825.
Phebe 8, 9, 1827.
Enoch 1, 20, 1838; d. 4, 24, 1845.

Franklin E. 2, 5, 1857.
Wm. Chapman 3, 16, 1861.
James Walter 6, 16, 1865.
(Surname Green. Names of parents
not given.)

MARIS AND ELIZABETH GARRETT.

Mary 2, 28, 1848.
Kinsey 8, 21, 1849.
Elma 2, 11, 1851.
Amy Ida 10, 23, 1852.
Margaret W. 10, 10, 1854.
Charles M. 7, 22, 1856.
Granville 6, 5, 1859.
Lizzie K. 10, 23, 1860.
Josephine } 11, 4, 1861
George W. }

RICHARD R. AND SARAH F. GREEN.

{ Richard R. 8, 21, 1825 (son of William and Mary).
  Sarah F. 12, 15, 1827.

Mary Emma 1, 22, 1849.
William W. 9, 6, 1850; d. 10, 15, 1865.

WILLIAM AND SARAH HICKS.

{ William 2, 10, 1821 (son of John and
  Martha).
  Sarah W. 5, 16, 1823.

Anna Martha 1, 17, 1847.
Charles Edwin 6, 27, 1848.

Mary Hicks 8, 7, 1821; d. 4, 14, 1855
(wife of Penrose).

JOEL AND ABIGAIL R. HEACOCK.

{ Joel 3, 26, 1794; d. 3, 17, 1853 (son
  of Jesse and Tacy).
  Abigail R. 4, 16, 1808.

Joel Levi 10, 2, 1843.

JAMES M. AND MARY ANN JACKSON.

{ James M. 9, 11, 1797 (son of Hugh
  and Rebecca).
  Mary Ann 1, 6, 1806.

Sarah F. 12, 15, 1827 (m. Richard R.
Green).
Samuel K. 10. 9, 1829.
Elizabeth J. 6, 2, 1832; d. 9, 26, 1864.
James Ellwood } 10, 15, 1834.
Edwin Atlee   }
William Morris 4, 7, 1837.

BENJAMIN AND TACY L. JOHNSON.

William S. 3, 15, 1832.
Matilda Ann 10, 15, 1834.
Clayton F. 4, 7, 1837.
Eli S. 6, 15, 1839.
Evan R. 3, 18, 1843.

Susan F. Johnson 9, 18, 1791; wife
of David.
Evelina E. Johnson d. 10, 3, 1854; wife
of Milton.
Mary G. Johnson d 3. 9, 1869, aged 75
years 20 days; widow of Casper.

NATHANIEL AND ELIZABETH KINSEY.

{ Nathaniel d. 11, 28, 1865; son of
  John and Elizabeth.
  Elizabeth M.

Ann 1, 11, 1845.
John E. 9, 25, 1847.
Howard 7, 12, 1849.
Letitia 7, 9, 1852.
Elizabeth 3, 15, 1860.

SAMUEL AND MARTHA (CUSTARD) KINSEY.

Martha F. 2, 3, 1817 ; d. 12, 7, 1860 (wife of Samuel).
Charles F. 1, 18, 1845.
Emma Letitia 6, 30, 1847 ; d. 8, 17, 1848.
George C. 7, 25, 1849.
John Woodward 10, 21, 1853.
Emma Irene 1, 27, 1856.
William 10, 23, 1858 ; d. 11, 1, 1858.

JOHN C. AND HANNAH B. LESTER.

John C. 4, 28, 1809 (son of John and Abigail).
Hannah B.
Charles Mather 6, 30, 1836.
Mary Jane 3, 13, 1838.
Abby W. 9, 17, 1843.
Cynthia 1, 10, 1841 ; d. 6, 15, 1844.
Sarah M. 4, 26, 1846.
John 11, 2, 1848.
William W. 3, 5, 1851.
Anna 5, 24, 1854.

SAMUEL J. AND SUSANNA MATHER LEVICK.

Samuel J. 8, 30, 1819 ; son of Ebenezer and Elizabeth.
Susanna M. 8, 2, 1819.
Jane F. 3, 10, 1842 ; daughter of Saml. J. and Ellen (first wife).
Lewis Jones 10, 15, 1845.
Charles M. 9, 23, 1847.
Samuel J., Jr., 2, 17, 1849.
William E. 1, 30, 1853.
James Morris 8, 28, 1858.

JOHN J. AND JANE W. MOORE.

John J. 11, 17, 1819.
Jane W.
Alfred 12, 16, 1845.
Ellen 7, 8, 1848.
Arthur 8, 19, 1858.

EVAN AND REBECCA PENROSE.

Evan 4, 2, 1782 ; d. 2, 11, 1864 (son of John and Ann).
Rebecca 3, 2, 1789 ; d. 1, 5, 1852.
Jane 2, 27, 1808 ; d. 12, 18, 1853.
Aaron 12, 28, 1809.
Evan 5, 8, 1813.

Margaret Miller d. 8, 3, 1859 (wife of William).

Jane Maus d. 10, 19, 1866 ; daughter of William and Ann.

Hannah F. Mather d. 7, 4, 1799 (wife of Bartholomew).

AARON AND MARYETTA (FOULKE) PENROSE.

Aaron 12, 28, 1809 ; son of Evan and Rebecca.
Maryetta 7, 30, 1811 ; d. 4, 26, 1851.
Benjamin F. 5, 25, 1839.
Caroline F. 6, 3, 1841.
Rebecca 4, 14, 1845
Aaron, Jr., 3, 29, 1851.

JOHN J. AND PAULINA (ROBERTS) PENROSE.

Paulina 3, 25, 1806.
Evan R. 10, 24, 1845.

OBADIAH AND ABIGAIL PALMER.

James 3, 10, 1804.
Elizabeth 1, 15, 1807.
Abigail d. 4, 20, 1811 (daughter of Jos. and Susanna Van Vliet).

OBADIAH AND SARAH V. PALMER.
(Stroudsburg.)

Obadiah 5, 15, 1780.
Sarah V. (second wife) 9, 1, 1784.
John V. 5, 29, 1814.
Charles Stroud 2, 11, 1818.
Ann Van Vli t 3, 10, 1820.
Samuel Henry 2, 16, 1822.
Susan Drake 4, 14, 1824.

SAMUEL AND PHEBE PHILLIPS.

Samuel 1, 21, 1823 (son of Moses and Christiana).
Phebe 5, 21, 1827.
Alice W. 11, 21, 1846.
Charles W. 4, 12, 1848.
Josephine 3, 21, 1852.
William 3, 21, 1858.
Hannah 10, 1, 1860.
Moses 4, 28, 1862.

MOSES AND CHRISTIANA (CAREY) PHILLIPS.

Moses 12, 24, 1792.
Christiana 3, 28, 1784.
Hannah 6, 15, 1815.

Mary C. 9, 20, 1817.
William 3, 24, 1820.
Samuel 1, 21, 1823.
Sarah 8, 15, 1825.
Thomas C. 4, 27, 1828.
Elizabeth 12, 27, 1830.
Ellen 9, 11, 1835.
Lewis 3, 11, 1837.
Rachel 1, 18, 1838.

JOHN AND MARY ANN PALMER.

{ John 4, 9, 1794.
{ Mary Ann 3, 13, 1801.
James T. 4, 25, 1825.
William E. B. 1, 20, 1828.
Phebe H. 1, 22, 1832.
Sydenham W. 2, 28, 1835.
Anne 9, 10, 1838.
John T. 7, 4, 1840.
Jane E. 11, 25, 1844.
Turner 4, 10, 1848.

LEVI AND PHEBE ROBERTS.

{ Levi 10, 21, 1759; d. 1, 4, 1846, son
{ of Abraham and Peninah.
{ Phebe 8, 2, 1766; d. 3, 30, 1850.
Elizabeth 2, 11, 1803.
Abigail 4, 16, 1808.

EVAN AND ABIGAIL ROBERTS.

{ Evan 4, 20, 1775; d. 3, 26, 1849, son
{ of David and Phebe.
{ Abigail 9, 11, 1771; d. 8, 12, 1854.
William 9, 6, 1800; d. 8, 4, 1865.
Hannah 3, 17, 1802.
Paulina 3, 25, 1806.
Maria 3, 14, 1809.

Martha Roberts d. 4, 18, 1855, widow of
Abel.
Sarah E. Roberts 11, 9, 1802; d. 11, 3,
1853, wife of Enos.

JOSEPH F. AND MARTHA RAWLINGS.

Thomas Ellwood 9, 26, 1840.
Richard M. 12, 31, 1841.
Charles 5, 15, 1843.
Amos R. 4, 17, 1845, dec'd.
Emma 9, 30, 1849; d. 4, 25, 1852.
Martha R. ———; d. 4, 29, 1852.
Amos 12, 24, 1852.
Joseph 9, 11, 1856.

JOHNSON AND JANE (PENROSE) STRAWN.

{ Johnson 4, 4, 1811; d. 8, 28, 1858,
{ son of Thomas and Mary.
{ Jane P. 2, 27, 1808; d. 12, 10, 1853.
Evan Penrose 9, 6, 1834; d. 10, 5, 1838.
Joseph P. 8, 16, 1836; d. 8, 8, 1858.
Thomas 4, 9, 1838.
Mary Ann 4, 18, 1841; m. Joseph W.
Foulke.
Johnson 10, 15, 1849.

ELI W. AND MARGARET (PENROSE) STRAWN.

{ Eli W. 1, 25, 1822, son of Wm. L.
{ and Jane.
{ Margaret P. 9, 11, 1821.
Henry P. 10, 30, 1845.
Mary P. 9, 26, 1847.
Rebecca Jane 7, 20, 1851; d. 7, 13, 1854.
William L. 7, 1, 1855.
Eli 2, 6, 1858.

Jane Strawn d. 2-mo., 1859, widow of
Wm. L.
Jane F. Strawn 1, 25, 1793.

SAMUEL AND SIDNEY (FOULKE) SHAW.

{ Samuel 2, 26, 1784; d. 2, 6, 1863,
{ son of William and Sarah.
{ Sidney 12, 30, 1791; d. 12-mo., 1862.
James 8, 4, 1824.
Sarah 12, 3, 1826; m. William Ball.
William 10, 14, 1829.
Ann 6, 6, 1832.
Edward 9, 20, 1835.

Clementine Schneurman 10, 30, 1810,
wife of Henry.

WILLIAM AND HANNAH M. SHAW.

{ William 10, 14, 1829, son of Samuel
{ and Sidney.
{ Hannah M.
Morgan 10, 15, 1857.
Samuel 12, 22, 1859.
Anna 3, 20, 1862.
Morris 5, 31, 1865.
Elizabeth M. 3, 14, 1867.

EDWARD AND MARY R. SHAW.

{ Edward 9, 20, 1835.
{ Mary R.
J. Wilmer 12, 29, 1869.

JERVIS AND JANE THOMAS.

{ Jervis 9, 9, 1808, son of Samuel and
   Elizabeth.
{ Jane 7, 23, 1811 ; d. 2, 24, 1859.
Alice G.
William G. d. 7, 21, 1864.

THOMAS AND ABIGAIL WRIGHT.

{ Thomas d. 6, 26, 1852, aged 64 y., 4,
   mo.. 1 d.
{ Abigail d. 10, 6, 1869, 75 yrs., 6 m.
Ann.

WILLIAM D. AND PHILENA WALTON.

Sydenham 4, 30, 1812.
Edward H. 9, 19, 1813.
Charles J. 9, 8, 1815 ; d. 5, 25, 1855.
Wm. P. 10, 6, 1817.
James P. 6, 30, 1820.
Davis D. 10-mo., 1822.
Hannah 3, 15, 1825.
Phebe P. 5, 21, 1827.

SYDENHAM AND HANNAH (PHILLIPS) WALTON.
(Stroudsburg.)

{ Sydenham 4, 30, 1812, son of William
   D. and Philena.
{ Hannah 6, 15, 1815.
Wm. D. 2, 17, 1839.
Mary 11, 21, 1841.
Sarah 4, 26, 1844.

Eliza Wintermute 9, 3, 1811, wife of
   William.

ISRAEL S. AND MATILDA ANN (STRAWN) ZORNS.

{ Israel S. 3, 29, 1801, son of Jacob and
   Hannah.
{ Matilda Ann 1, 17, 1811.
Chalkley S. 4, 9, 1834.
Hannah Elma 7, 28, 1835.
Jane Alice 2, 12, 18—.

CHARLES T. AND CATHARINE H. ZORNS.

{ Charles T. 12, 2, 1810, son of Jacob
   and Hannah.
{ Catharine H. 11, 20, 1813.
Jacob Evans 3, 14, 1833.
Samuel E. 2, 22, 1835.
Margaret 8, 27, 1836.

ROBERT AND SARAH (THOMAS) ASHTON.
(Springfield).

Robert 10, 15, 1725, son of Peter and
   Mary, born in Ireland ; d. 10, 22,
   1816, aged 91 years.
Peter 8, 16, 1760 ; d. 12, 30, 1821.
Mary 8, 4, 1761 ; d. 2, 15, 1786.
Margaret 3, 24, 1765.
Samuel 7, 17, 1766.
Robert 4, 1, 1768.
Sarah 5, 10, 1770.

SAMUEL AND JANE (ROBERTS) ASHTON.
(Springfield).

Phebe 3, 28, 1796.
Eleanor 6, 22, 1798.
Thomas 9, 22, 1799.
Sarah 7, 15, 1801.
Elizabeth Roberts 8, 27, 1803.
Abigail 7, 26, 1807.

AARON AND MARGARET BALL.

Hannah 6, 4, 1787 ; d. 3, 2, 1847.
Rebecca 3, 2, 1789 ; d. 1, 5, 1852 (m.
   Evan Penrose).
William 11, 9, 1790 ; d. 2, 19, 1863.
Aaron 10, 26, 1792 ; d. 11, 22, 1856.

Catharine Ball d. 6, 5, 1819.
Gainor Ball d. 6, 11, 1836.
Lewis Ball d. 2, 3, 1824.

Josiah Dennis d. 11, 14, 1819 ; upwards
   of 71 years, Haycock.
Josiah Dennis d. 2, 27, 1834.
Alice Dennis d. 4, 22, 1835.
Sarah Dennis d 4, 5, 1815 ; upwards of
   93 years, Haycock.
Isaac Burson d. 3, 21, 1815 (Springfield).

GEORGE AND HANNAH CUSTARD.

Martha F. 2, 3, 1817 ; d. 12, 7, 1860.
Joseph 4, 12, 1819; d. 11, 25, 1842.
Hannah F. 12, 25, 1789 ; d. 2, 11, 1859.

WILLIAM AND MERIBAH EDWARDS.
(Milford.)

Margaret 2, 28, 1768.
Samuel 3, 4, 1770.
Nathan 2, 20, 1772 ; d. 10, 17, 1855.
William 4, 18, 1774.
Martha 7, 6, 1776 ; d. 5, 8, 1804 (wife of
   Enoch Penrose).
Mary 9, 10, 1778; d. 9, 15, 1779
Joel 7, 3, 1780.
Caleb 10, 23, 1782.

Thomas 9, 28, 1784.
Amos 10, 4, 1786.
Hannah 7, 3, 1788; d. 9, 26, 1801.
Ann 2, 11, 1790; d. 12, 28, 1816; m.
  Samuel M. Foulke.
Meribah d. 9, 8, 1794.
Susanna d. 2, 26, 1818 (age upwards of
  69 years, daughter of Abel Roberts).
William Edwards d. 4, 10, 1818, at 69.
Abigail Edwards d. 6, 16, 1826.

NATHAN AND LYDIA (ROBERTS) ED-
WARDS.
(Milford.)
{ Nathan 2, 20, 1772; d. 10, 17, 1855.
{ Lydia 10, 2, 1775; d. 5, 25, 1852.
Mary 1, 25, 1801; d. 1, 7, 1803.
Sarah 11, 9, 1802.
Tacy 1, 13, 1805; d. 2, 26, 1864.
Martha 4, 19, 1807.
John Edwards d. 4, 23, 1844.

JOHN AND MARY EDWARDS.
Ann Amanda 12, 5, 1842.

WILLIAM AND ELIZABETH FOWLER.
Daniel 9, 22, 1799.
Jane B. 12, 7, 1801.
William 8, 16, 1806.
Mary Ann 8, 8, 1808.
Eliza 9, 4, 1811.
Elizabeth Fowler d. 11, 21, 1812, aged
  about 38 years (Stroudsburg).

THEOPHILUS AND HANNAH FOULKE.
{ Theophilus d. 7, 28, 1798; 37 years.
{ Hannah L. 2, 2, 1767; d. 7, 4, 1850.
Antrim 3, 21, 1793.
Sarah 1, 10, 1797.

HUGH AND SARAH (ROBERTS) FOULKE.
Martha 7, 1, 1789.
Joseph 9, 7, 1791.

JOHN AND RACHEL (GREASLEY) GRIF-
FITH.
Jane 7, 2, 1783.
Hannah 1, 12, 1785.
John Greasley 1, 12, 1789.
Thomas 3, 3, 1791.
Abraham 7, 9, 1793.
William 6, 30, 1795.
Rachel Griffith d. 8, 9, 1841.
Mary Lloyd d. 3, 7, 1813 (Springfield),
  aged 85 years.

JAMES R. AND GRACE GREEN.
Barton R. 5, 22, 1819; d. 11, 16, 1825.
Ann (second wife) 11, 23, 1797.
Chapman 6, 17, 1824; d. 5, 19, 1836.
Hannah 1, 19, 1827; d. 9, 21, 1829.
Caroline 2, 1, 1829 (m. Israel Stokes).
James Barton 11, 10, 1831.

GEORGE AND ANN (PENROSE) HICKS.
{ George 6, 12, 1770; d. 8, 20, 1847
{   (son of Wm. and Hannah).
{ Ann 6, 22, 1779.
Rachel 4, 26, 1800.
Penrose 5, 9, 1802 (m. Mary Edwards
  and Elizabeth Foulke).
William 11, 21, 1803.
Peninah 1, 25, 1806; d. 11, 12, 1821.
Martha 10, 9, 1807.
Speakman 10, 4, 1809 (m. Alice L.
  Strawn).
Hannah 8, 1, 1811.
Nathan P. 9, 7, 1813.
Evan P. 10, 20, 1815.
Anne R. 11, 28, 1817.
Tacy 11, 3, 1820; d. 11, 6, 1821.

William Hicks d. 2, 19, 1810, aged 78 y.

GEORGE AND HANNAH (FOULKE)
IDEN.
Anne 9, 27, 1782.
Elizabeth 2, 29, 1784.
Thomas 7, 25, 1785.
John 6, 16, 1787.
Greenfield 7, 6, 1789 (m. Beulah Green).
Paulina 5, 5, 1792.
Julia 8, 25, 1794.
Jacob 6, 26, 1798.

ISAIAS AND MARGARET (BALL) JAMI-
SON.
{ Isaias d. 9, 27, 1826.
{ Margaret d. 4, 28, 1840.
Joseph 5, 22, 1799; d. 6, 13, 1829.
Margaret 9, 1, 1800; d. 3, 10, 1831.
Mary 11, 15, 1802.

JOHN AND ABIGAIL (WILSON) LESTER.
John C. 4, 28, 1809.
Jane 6, 4, 1811; d. 8, 27, 1837.

SHIPLEY AND MARGARET (NIXON)
LESTER.
Abel 10, 11, 1792.
Morris 4, 26, 1794; d. 6, 10, 1801.
Samuel 12, 8, 1795; d. 4, 10, 1798.

William 9, 29, 1797.
Albert 8, 15, 1799.
Jane 1, 5, 1802; d. 10, 6, 1809.
Hannah 7, 23, 1804.
Mary Ann 9, 15, 1806.
Shipley 8, 2, 1809.

THOMAS AND MARY (STOKES) LESTER.
{ Thomas Lester d. 3, 22, 1828.
{ Mary Lester d. 4, 3, 1803, daughter of
{ John Stokes.
Peter 7, 17, 1797.
Jane 10, 20, 1799; d. 7, 12, 1801.
Mary d. 4, 3, 1803.
Hannah (second wife, daughter of Benj.
  Green) d. 4, 12, 1826, aged 47 years.
Evan Green 9, 29, 1806.
Benjamin 1, 14, 1808.
Sarah Ann 10, 30, 1810.
Mary 5, 17, 1812.
Margaret 7, 22, 1814; d. 6, 29, 1816.

MARK AND MARY WILSON.
Stephen Brock 3, 3, 1829.
Shipley 1, 3, 1831.
Elizabeth 10, 22, 1833.

RICHARD AND SARAH (FOULKE)
MOORE.
Sarah 1, 10, 1797; d. 10, 25, 1852.
John Jackson 11, 17, 1819.
Hannah 7, 29, 1821.
Henry 4, 21, 1826; d. 1, 14, 1831.
Sarah Letitia 11, 8, 1831; d. 1, 7, 1838.

WILLIAM AND MARTHA (ROBERTS)
NIXON.
Hannah 11, 13, 1800.
Sarah 3, 16, 1802.
Samuel 4, 7, 1805.
Edward Roberts 2, 5, 1808; d. 3, 1,
  1808.

PETER AND MARGARET (FOULKE)
LESTER.
Anna F. 3, 12, 1821.
Mary S. 9, 14, 1823.

ENOCH AND MARTHA (EDWARDS) PEN-
ROSE.
{ Enoch Penrose d. 8, 22, 1842, aged 75
{   years.
{ Martha 7, 6, 1776; d. 5, 8, 1804.
Meribah 11, 17, 1802; d. 12, 5, 1841.
Esther (second wife), d. 2, 28, 1842.
Martha 8, 6, 1813.
Matilda 6, 15, 1815; d. 3, 7, 1848.
Anne R. 11, 1, 1816; d. 8, 6, 1852 (m.
  Samuel Shaw).
John T. 1, 7, 1820.

NATHAN AND HANNAH PENROSE.
Martha 6, 6, 1795.
Lavinia 10, 5, 1798; m. William Hea-
  cock.
Nathan 11, 24, 1800.
Tacy 3, 18, 1808.
Washington H. 9, 17, 1809.
William 10, 18, 1812.

THOMAS AND RACHEL (HILLMAN) PEN-
ROSE.
Lydia 2, 5, 1797.
Hannah 12, 16, 1798; d. 7, 1, 1865.
Ann 7, 6, 1801.
John 3, 24, 1804.
Elizabeth 7, 27, 1806.
Clementine 10, 30, 1810; wife of Thomas.
Rachel Penrose d. 4, 5, 1855.

SAMUEL AND JANE ROBERTS.
{ Samuel 5, 4, 1782; d. 3, 14, 1856,
{   son of David and Elizabeth.
{ Jane 5, 24, 1789.
James 8, 28, 1824.
Barton 12, 3, 1825.
Asenath 10, 25, 1832.
Elizabeth Roberts d. 1, 1, 1843.

AMOS AND MARTHA RICHARDSON.
(Rockhill.)
Rebecca 3, 7, 1796.
Jane 2, 27, 1798.
Kezia 2, 20, 1800; d. 10, 20, 1844.
John 12, 4, 1802; d. 9, 4, 1822.
Sarah }
Anne } 3, 5, 1805.
Martha d. 12, 25, 1809.

DAVID AND ELIZABETH (STOKES)
ROBERTS.
Albina Newton 5, 25, 1805.
Stokes Lancaster 1, 4, 1808.

JONATHAN AND MARY M. SHAW.
William 2, 4, 1821; d. 2, 14, 1829.
Samuel 9, 12, 1828; d. 10, 30, 1859.
Jane 6, 10, 1830; d. 8, 12, 1832.
Stephen 9, 14, 1836; d. 1, 17, 1837.
Mary M. Shaw d. 10, 23, 1836, aged 42
  years, 6 months, 14 days.

HUGH AND ELIZABETH (ROBERTS)
FOULKE.
{ Hugh 9, 8, 1793; d. 4, 3, 1853; son
{   of Israel and Elizabeth.
{ Elizabeth 2, 11, 1803; d. 5, 12, 1858
Amos R. 5, 26, 1822; d. 4, 21, 1853.
Barton L. 11, 18, 1823; d. 8, 18, 1856.
Phebe R. 1, 27, 1825; d. 12, 22, 1832.

Jordan 10, 9, 1826; d. 6, 21, 1836.
Elizabeth 3, 13, 1828; m. Penrose Hicks.
Thomas M. 2, 13, 1830; d. 2, 9, 1861.
Sarah E. 6, 1, 1831; d. 4, 19, 1844.
Franklin 5, 5, 1833; d. 6, 24 1835.
Abigail Jane 7, 1, 1835; d. 3, 10, 1845.
Franklin 7, 24, 1838; d. 3, 18, 1860.
Jane R. 6, 9, 1842; d. 1, 24, 1860.
Susan J. 6, 7, 1844.

Moses Shaw d. 9, 6, 1826, aged 68 years.

WILLIAM AND MARY (FOULKE) SAMUELS.
(Saucon.)
Jane 1, 18, 1794.
Jesse 3, 17, 1795.
Mary 8, 10, 1800.
William 8, 7, 1806.

SAMUEL AND ELIZABETH THOMAS.
Amanda 7, 3, 1807.
Jervis 9, 9, 1808.
Louisa 6, 2, 1810.
Thomas 10, 29, 1811.
Edward 3, 27, 1813.
Hannah 1, 6, 1815.
Benjamin 3, 27, 1817.
Mary Thomas d. 12, 19, 1831, aged 76 years.

DANIEL AND MARTHA (GREEN) WALTON.
Jane 6, 24, 1789.
Mary 2, 6, 1791; d. 11, 12, 1796.
Edith 12, 13, 1792; d. 11, 19, 1796.
David 1, 24, 1795.
Lydia 6, 25, 1799; d. 1800.

MOSES AND JANE (LESTER) WILSON.
(Milford.)
Shipley 7, 27, 1798.
Mark 8, 27, 1802.

EDWARD AND JEMIMA (STROUD) BURSON.
(Stroudsburg.)
Samuel 10, 15, 1812.
Ann 6, 4, 1814; d. 4, 10, 1823.
Elizabeth 9, 4, 1818; d. 3, 23, 1819.
John W. 8, 21, 1820.
Lydia 5, 17, 1822.

WILLIAM AND MARY (ROBERTS) GREEN.
{ William 11, 10, 1776; d. 9, 24, 1851; son of Benjamin and Jane.
{ Mary.
Caroline 2, 6, 1805; m. Joshua Foulke.

Elizabeth T. 12, 9, 1806; m. John Mc-Cray.
Matilda 1, 20, 1809; m. Edward Foulke.
Jane R. 7, 23, 1811; d. 2, 24, 1829; m. Jervis Thomas.
Grace 1, 13, 1814; d. 2, 26, 1814.
Grace 2, 27, 1815; m. Eleazer Shaw.
Mary 7, 13, 1817; d. 11, 3, 1869; m. Samuel Carey.
Alice 4, 14, 1820; m. Davis Walton.
Richard R. 8, 21, 1825; m. Sarah F. Jackson.

CALEB AND SARAH (PENROSE) EDWARDS
Margaret 1, 17, 1813; d. 3, 13, 1856.
William P. 11, 30, 1815; d. 3, 2, 1831.
Amos 7, 12, 1817.
Benjamin 12, 7, 1818; d. 7, 28, 1822.
Sarah (wife of Caleb) 11, 21, 1788; d. 1860.

FRANCIS AND JOANNA EDKINS.
Catharine Palmer 3, 7, 1809.
Jane Kinsey 10, 5, 1810.
Deborah 9, 20, 1812.
Mary Brooke 8, 16, 1814.
William d. 8, 17, 1852.
Susan 5, 22, 1820.
Sallie 5, 16, 1823.
Joanna P. 5, 20, 1825.
Martha 10, 23, 1827.
George 12, 18, 1829.
Eliza 12, 19, 1834.

CALEB AND JANE FOULKE.
Jane (wife of Caleb) d. 7th-mo., 1866.
Caroline 10, 2, 1808; d. 12, 11, 1809.
Caroline 2, 25, 1810; d. 12, 17, 1838.
Maryetta 7, 30, 1811.
Benjamin 7, 28, 1813.
Eleanor 3, 12, 1816.

EVERARD AND FANNY FOULKE.
Watson 9, 10, 1826.
William 6, 5, 1828.
Jona. Ingham 3, 20, 1830.
Thomas D.

DAVID AND MIRIAM (SHAW) FOULKE.
Miriam (first wife) d. 11, 14, 1814, aged 32 years; daughter of John Shaw.
Israel 10, 27, 1814.
Mary R. (second wife).
John R. 4, 10, 1818.

JESSE AND TACY HEACOCK.
{ Jesse d. 9, 30, 1841.
{ Tacy d. 2, 10, 1823.
John 8, 28, 1786.

Jonah 2, 18, 1788.
William 1, 19, 1790.
Ann 12, 27, 1791; m. Samuel M. Foulke.
Joel 3, 26, 1794; d. 3, 7, 1853.
Margaret 3, 27, 1796; m. (1) John Good, (2) Jonathan Carr.
Jesse 6, 12, 1798; d. 9, 30, 1841; m. Elizabeth Rees.
Joseph 8, 26, 1800; d. 3, 22, 1883; m. Esther Hallowell.
Enos 12, 20, 1802; m. Sarah Foulke.
Nathan 4, 27, 1806; m. Elizabeth Hallowell.
Aaron 7, 27, 1808.

ELISHA AND LYDIA HOAG.
Hervey 8, 20, 1806; d. 5, 14, 1811.
Joel 7, 14, 1809.
Joanna 5, 9, 1811.
Hervey 7, 11, 1813.

JOHN G. AND ABIGAIL GRIFFITH.
Edward K. 9, 24, 1816; d. 2d-mo., 1864.
Margaretta 12, 6, 1818.
Jane 12, 29, 1820.
Hannah 1, 25, 1823.
Abigail d. 11, 10, 1856.

HENRY AND HANNAH JOHNSON.
William 3, 30, 1785.
Benjamin 5, 20, 1787.
Jane 2, 26, 1790.
Sarah 4, 7, 1793.
Lydia 4, 1, 1795.
Guy 8, 28, 1796.
Hannah 4, 24, 1798.
Henry 9, 2, 1799.
Abigail Johnson d. 10, 16, 1827.
Casper Johnson d. 12, 20, 1832.
Deborah Johnson d. 7, 13, 1836.

SAMUEL AND ELIZABETH (CHAPMAN) IDEN.
James Chapman 1, 5, 1813.
Eleanor 11, 25, 1815.

THOMAS AND RACHEL IDEN.
Charles Parry 3, 25, 1818.

JONAH AND ABIGAIL HEACOCK.
Elizabeth M. 3, 17, 1814.
Phebe W. 3, 19, 1818.
Warner 4, 16, 1821.
Jesse W. } 6, 25, 1825.
Tacy   }

ENOS AND SARAH HEACOCK.
Hannah T. 3, 17, 1828.
Hugh F. 1, 29, 1831.
William 12, 2, 1833.

Tacy Ann 6, 15, 1836; d. 4, 25, 1838.
Enos Ellwood 6, 5, 1843.

SAMUEL M. AND ANN HEACOCK FOULKE.
Ann Foulke (first wife) 2, 11, 1790; d 12, 28, 1816.
William E. 12, 23, 1816. (See page 47.)
Ann, second wife, daughter of Jesse Heacock.
Tacy H. 2, 9, 1822.
Margaret H. 11, 22, 1823.
Jesse H. 4, 5, 1826.
Sarah H. 11, 5, 1827.
Joseph 7, 29, 1829.
Edith 7, 2, 1831.
Mary Ellen 4, 7, 1834; d. 5, 15, 1836.

ABRAHAM AND MARY GRIFFITH.
Samuel 2, 27, 1819; d. 9, 14, 1820.
Rebecca W. 10, 5, 1820; d. 11, 18, 1820.
Violetta L. 12, 25, 1821.

ABEL AND MARGARET LESTER.
Samuel 7, 29, 1824.
Sarah 6, 24, 1826.
Mary Jane 3, 1, 1828; d. 1, 1, 1830.
Jeremiah W. 7, 11, 1829.
Howard 7, 9, 1831.

JOHN AND MARTHA HICKS.
{ John Hicks d. 8, 14, 1830, aged 54 yrs,
{ Martha d. 8, 22, 1861.
Wilson 7, 15, 1811.
Jesse 11, 21, 1812.
Margaret 3, 1, 1814; d. 9, 6, 1823.
Ann Eliza 2, 14, 1816.
Phebe 6, 4, 1818.
John   } 2, 10, 1821.
William }
Elias 5, 9, 1823.
Martha W. 3, 4, 1825; m. Thos. P. Ball.
Joseph 3, 21, 1831; d. 5, 12, 1840.

EMMOR AND LYDIA KIMBER.
Teresa J. Kimber 9, 19, 1819.

ISAAC AND MARTHA WILLIAMS.
Clayton N. 11, 28, 1821.

SAMUEL AND PATIENCE SLEEPER.
Rebecca 7, 25, 1796.
Keturah 2, 17, 1801.
Aves 1, 13, 1804.
Budell 7, 29, 1806.

JOSEPH AND HANNAH SHAW.
Olivia 2, 4, 1797.
Ann 7, 19, 1800.

Guli 6, 23, 1804.
Israel 4, 22, 1809.
Rebecca 3, 11, 1815.
Hannah 10, 15, 1818.

JOHN AND ELIZABETH (BALL) SHAW.
{ John Shaw d. 3, 17, 1839, aged 55.
{ Elizabeth Shaw d. 8, 18, 1837.
Nathan 8, 10, 1805; d. 10, 31, 1833.
Edith 5, 23, 1807.
Nixon 2, 15, 1809.
William 12, 19, 1811; d. 4, 9, 1825.
Lewis 12, 27. 1814.
John 5, 28, 1819; d. 2, 25, 1838.
Hopson 4, 6, 1823; d. 7, 16, 1831.

JOHN AND ANN WELDING.
(Stroudsburg.)
Clementina 12, 19, 1808.
Lydia Ann 10, 4, 1810.
Snsanna Burson 1, 27, 1813.

EBER AND ANN (SHAW) WALTON.
Joseph 12, 19. 1825.
Mary 12, 6, 1827.

ABNER AND SARAH (SHAW) DALBEY.
Abner Dalbey d. 9, 28, 1823.
Moses S. 3, 24, 1816.
Levi 7, 8, 1817.
Mary S. 11, 12, 1818.
Abner H. 3, 28, 1820.
Sarah 2, 17, 1822.
Joel R. 1, 6, 1824; d. 6, 4, 1824.

DANIEL AND SARAH IDEN DOWNING.
Ann Elizabeth 7, 8, 1825.
Sarah 5, 24, 1827.
Susanna 12, 18, 1828.
Henry Randall 2, 23, 1831.

WILLIAM AND LAVINIA (PENROSE)
HEACOCK.
Evelina 4, 30, 1821.
Nathan Barclay 4, 10, 1825.

BENJAMIN AND MARY BATTY.
George 9, 18, 1832.

ABRAHAM AND ELIZABETH FLAGLER.
Thomas B. 8, 21, 1823.
Isaiah B. 5, 10, 1825.
Ann 2, 8, 1827.
Charles 7, 18, 1829.
Catharine Ann 10, 6, 1832.

JAMES AND MARGARET MICHENER.
Samuel 10, 15, 1822.
Rebecca 9, 4, 1824.
Sarah 10, 4, 1826.

SLAYTER (parents' names wanting).
Abraham 6, 21, 1810.
Catharine 1, 23, 1811.
William 3, 11, 1814.
Elisha 6, 20, 1816.
Marcus 9, 27, 1818.
Elizabeth 8, 9, 1822.
Lucinda 3, 2, 1824.

EVAN AND SARAH FOULKE.
Olivia 3, 27, 1796; d. 5, 13, 1832.
Charles 2, 26, 1801.
Asenath 2, 26, 1808.
Susanna L. 10, 5, 1810.

AARON AND MARY CROASDALE.
Evan 7, 12, 1827.
William 5, 15, 1829.
Susan 5, 6, 1831.
Jane 6, 30, 1833.

DAVID J. AND CAROLINE F. AMBLER.
{ David J. 3, 22, 1837; son of Andrew
{   and Mary.
{ Caroline F. 6, 3, 1841; daughter of
    Aaron Penrose.
Ella 3, 27, 1864.

SAMUEL AND ANNA R. SHAW.
William Henry 9, 6, 1856.
Allen 3, 19, 1859.

INDEX TO BIRTHS AND DEATHS.

DEATHS SINCE 1870.

Caroline Ambler 9, 13, 1891; 50 years.
Paxson Blakey 7, 10, 1882.
Susan P. Brown 4, 16, 1892; 82 years; Stroudsburg.
Mary L. Bullock (wife of Joshua) 4, 15, 1891; 77 years.
Sarah J. Ball 12, 29, 1877; 86 years.
Margaret Dalbey 1, 16, 1892.
Amos Edwards 4, 10, 1872. (William and Meribah.)
Amos Edwards 1, 22, 1892; 74 years. (Caleb and Sarah.)
Rachel Foulke 10, 15, 1883; 80 years. (Benjamin and Martha.)
Kezia Foulke 12, 31, 1884; 80 years.
Hannah Foulke 2, 22, 1894; 94 years.
Caroline Foulke 2, 18, 1888; 83 years.

Joshua Foulke 9, 23, 1888 ; 90 years.
Benjamin G. Foulke, 8, 14, 1888 ; 75 years.
Esther Flagler 11, 21, 1870; 67 years ; Stroudsburg.
Zachariah Flagler 10, 14, 1870 ; 75 years ; Stroudsburg.
Phebe Flagler 12, 3, 1890; 63 years; Stroudsburg.
Charles Foulke 1, 3. 1883 ; 82 years ; Stroudsburg.
John A. Flagler 1, 30, 1876; 53 years; Stroudsburg.
Catharine Foulke 12, 16, 1890 ; 83 years; Stroudsburg.
Frances Ann Foulke 7, 25, 1888 ; 56 years ; Stroudsburg.
Richard R. Green 7, 22, 1892 ; 66 years.
Ann Green 1, 20, 1878; 80 years.   (Widow of James R.)
Hannah Griffith 1, 16, 1892 ; 68 years.
Abigail R. Heacock 3, 21, 1882 ; 73 years.   (Wife of Joel.)
Ann Hicks 7, 4, 1872.   (Wife of George.)
Penrose Hicks 7, 11, 1886 ; 84 years.
James M. Jackson 9, 28, 1870; 73 years.
Mary Ann Jackson 9, 28, 1893; 87 years, 8 months.   (Wife of James M.)
Susan F. Johnson 4, 17, 1883.   (Wife of David.)
Samuel Kinsey 8, 23, 1888; 66 years.
John Woodward Kinsey 1, 21, 1872.
John C. Lester 1, 19, 1873; 65 years.
Hannah B. Lester 9, 15, 1875.
Mary Jane Lester 7, 14, 1872; 34 years.
Sarah M. Lester 4, 23, 1874; 28 years.
John Lester 1, 15, 1874; 26 years.
William W. Lester 6, 13, 1870; 19 years.
Anna Lester 1, 30, 1875 ; 21 years.
Samuel J Levick, Jr., 7, 28, 1880; 31 years.
Richard Moore 4, 30, 1875.
John Jackson Moore 10, 6, 1895 ; 75 years, 10 months.
Jane W. Moore 2, 25, 1873.
Bartholomew Mather 2, 7, 1872 ; 87 years.
Ann Morgan 4, 1, 1877.
Aaron Penrose 4, 14, 1883 ; 73 years.
Paulina Penrose 2, 24, 1871.
Clementine Penrose 9, 12, 1881.
John V. Palmer 7, 27, 1875; 61 years; Stroudsburg.
Charles Stroud Palmer 10, 4, 1886 ; 68 years ; Stroudsburg.
Thomas C. Phillips 2, 21, 1881 ; 52 years.
Maria Roberts 4, 18, 1886 ; 77 years.
Rachel Roberts 5, 27, 1871.   (Daughter of Abel and Martha.)
Clementine Schneurman 2, 17, 1890 ; 79 years.
Edward Thomas 8, 2, 1883 ; 70 years.
Eliza Wintermute 9, 29, 1872 ; 61 years ; Stroudsburg.
Rebecca Richardson 2, 20, 1879 ; 82 years.
Jane Richardson 3, 21, 1877 ; 79 years,
Ann Richardson 10, 4, 1873; 65 years.
Philena Walton 5, 16, 1870 ; Stroudsburg.
William P. Walton 7, 24, 1880 ; 61 years; Stroudsburg.
James P. Walton 10, 15, 1874; 54 years; Stroudsburg.
Davis Walton 2, 14, 1888 ; 65 years; Stroudsburg.
Hannah Walton 8, 16, 1891 ; 66 years ; Stroudsburg.
Phebe P. Walton 5, 17, 1885 ; 58 years ; Stroudsburg.
Matilda Ann Zorns 12, 30, 1884 ; 73 years.
Chalkley S. Zorns 3, 4, 1870.
Israel S. Zorns 7, 10, 1895; 94 years.
Jane Alice Zorns 3, 8, 1876; 23 years.

REMOVALS.

2, 21, 1743. Peter Ball to Buckingham.
4, 16, 1743. John Stokes from Burlington.
8, 20, 1743. Griffith David, wife and children from Buckingham.
12, 16, 1743. William Shadaker and wife from Chesterfield.
3, 17, 1744. Margaret Thomas from Abington.
7, 20, 1744. Thomas Head from Buckingham.
2, 18, 1745. Jonathan Heacock from Chester.
9, 21, 1745. John Morgan from Chester.
6, 21, 1746. Thomas Foulke from Gwynedd.
12, 19, 1746. Patrick Ogilby from Abington.
1, 17, 1748. Joseph Ray and wife to Gwynedd.
2, 21, 1748. Thomas Wilson from Middletown.
3, 19, 1748. Ann Griffith from Buckingham.
4, 16, 1748. Joshua Scattergood from Burlington.
4, 16, 1748. William Hogue, wife and sons from Opequan.
5, 21, 1748. James Morgan and wife to Darby.
6, 18, 1748. Abel Roberts to Gwynedd.
3, 18, 1749. Hugh Hilles from Gwynedd.
4, 15, 1749. Thomas Wilson to Middletown.
10, 21, 1749. Thomas Lancaster from Buckingham.
10, 21, 1749. James Burson from Buckingham.
11, 18, 1749. Benjamin Gilbert to Falls.
2, 19, 1750. Griffith Davies, wife and children to Abington.
2, 19, 1750. John Stokes and wife to Burlington.
6, 16, 1750. Samuel Gaskill and wife from Burlington.
6, 15, 1751. Joshua Scattergood, wife and family to Middletown.
8, 17, 1751. Abner Rogers and wife from Burlington.
9, 10, 1751. Abel Roberts and wife from Gwynedd.
9, 10, 1751. Edmund Phillips, wife and children to Goshen.
1, 16, 1752. (N. S.) Isaac Walton and wife from Abington.
10, 19, 1752. Samuel Bevan and wife from Chesterfield.
1, 17, 1754. Thomas Ashton to Wrightstown.
2, 21, 1754. Joseph Unthank to North Carolina.
2, 21, 1754. Samuel Pierson to North Carolina.
5, 16, 1754. Benjamin Lancaster and wife to Gwynedd.
6, 19, 1754. Thomas Jennings from Haddonfield.
9, 18, 1754. Thomas Carrington from Abington; for himself, wife, children and
            wife's daughter, Esther Walton.
12, 18, 1755. William Chilcott from Gwynedd.
2, 19, 1756. John Ashton from Exeter.
3, 18, 1756. Samuel Iden from Abington.
3, 18, 1756. Thomas Jennings, wife and children to Little Egg Harbor.
5, 20, 1756. Thomas Carrington, wife and children to Abington.
12, 16, 1756. Thomas Lancaster and family to Gwynedd.
11, 17, 1757. George Hicks, Jr., to Middletown.
8, 17, 1758. Job Hughes from Exeter.
11, 16, 1758. Joseph Hoge to Virginia.
5, 17, 1759. William Hoge to Virginia.
10, 18, 1759. Thomas Stalford from Ireland.
10, 18, 1759. Thomas Edwards to Goshen.
1, 17, 1760. Samuel Iden to Fairfax, Virginia.
9, 18, 1760. Robert Burr from Burlington.
8, 20, 1761. Joseph Austin and Susanna, his wife, from Abington.
9, 17, 1761. John Chapman, wife and children to Wrightstown.

11, 19, 1761. John Morgan and wife to Kennett.
9, 16, 1762. Rebecca Ogilby to Philadelphia.
11, 18, 1762. William Burr from Philadelphia.
5, 19, 1763. Edward Evans from Gwynedd with wife, Jane, and children, Catherine, Jane, Joel and Sarah.
4, 19, 1764. Robert Blackledge to Philadelphia.
5, 17, 1764. John Greasley, wife and family to Abington.
5, 17, 1764. Job Hughes to Exeter.
6, 21, 1764. Robert Tompkins and wife Elizabeth from Abington.
10, 18, 1764. John Scarborough and wife from Buckingham.
6, 19, 1766. Benjamin Tompkins, wife and two children from Abington.
2, 19, 1767. Michael Clark to Uwchlan.
10, 15, 1767. Sarah Chapman to Wrightstown.
2, 18, 1768. Robert Blackledge with wife Joanna and children Elizabeth and Thomas from Philadelphia.
2, 16, 1769. Isaac Griffith and family to Gunpowder, Md.
12, 21, 1769. Samuel Clark, Jr., to Uwchlan.
1, 18, 1770. Hannah Michener to Buckingham.
3, 15, 1770. Thomas Stalford, wife and children to Sadsbury.
3, 15, 1770. John Ball, Jr., to Gunpowder.
3, 15, 1770. Jane Adams to Nardwick, N. J.
8, 16, 1770. Joseph Shaw to Gunpowder with wife Rachel and children, George and David.
10, 18, 1770. Moses Lancaster from Philadelphia.
12, 20, 1770. Amos Dennis to Kennett.
4, 18, 1771. John Stokes, Jr., from Burlington, for himself, wife Susanna and son William.
4, 18, 1771. James Chapman from Philadelphia.
5, 16, 1771. William Shaw to Exeter.
6, 20, 1771. Moses Lancaster, his wife, Rachel and daughter Meribah to Abington.
4, 15, 1773. John Greasley and family from Abington.
9, 16, 1773. Amos Dennis from Kennett.
11, 18, 1773. Moses Walton to Uwchlan.
2, 16, 1775. Joseph Ball, Jr., and wife to Gunpowder, Md.
9, 21, 1775. Jesse Penrose to Exeter.
4, 18, 1776. David Carr to Buckingham.
11, 21, 1776. Benjamin Gilbert from Abington, for himself, wife Elizabeth and children, Jesse, Rebecca, Abner and Elizabeth.
12, 16, 1779. Joseph Speakman, wife and children to Wrightstown.
4, 20, 1780. Rachel Shaw and children, George, David, Samuel and Ann from Gunpowder. Md.
6, 21, 1781. Ezekiel Green to Hopewell.
12, 20, 1781. Moses Rea to Uwchlan.
12, 20, 1781. James Burson to Wrightstown.
2, 21, 1782. Isaac Roberts to Uwchlan.
3, 21, 1782. John Morgan to Chester.
4, 18, 1782. Jonathan Heacock from Chester.
6, 20, 1782. Sarah Burson and children, Mary and Stephen Twining from Wrightstown.
6, 20, 1782. Mary Adamson and children, Thomas, James and Sarah to Hopewell, Virginia.
9, 19, 1782. Solomon Hoge, wife Esther and children to Fairfax.
11, 21, 1782. Elizabeth Gilbert and children, Rebecca, Abner and Elizabeth to Horsham.
7, 15, 1784. Jacob Verrity from Wrightstown.
1, 20, 1785. Isaac Kirk to Wrightstown.
8, 18, 1785. Jesse Gilbert to Horsham.

6, 21, 1787. Jonathan Heacock, wife and children to Haverford.

7, 19, 1787. Benjamin Walton to Westland.

5, 29, 1788. Joseph Dennis, wife Deborah, and children, Ann, Joseph and Deborah to Niagara.

5, 29, 1788. Ezekiel Dennis, wife and children, Abigail, Hannah, Tamar, John, Mary, Joel, Kezia, Susanna and Charles to Niagara.

5, 21, 1789. Jonas Kirk from Buckingham.

4, 21, 1791. Judah Foulke, wife and children to Exeter.

9, 15, 1791. Eli Kennard, Elizabeth his wife and children William, Thomas, Hannah and Joseph from Buckingham.

10, 20, 1791. James Walton and family to Exeter.

1, 26, 1792. Evan Lloyd to Gwynedd.

3, 15, 1792. John and Moses Shaw and families to Abington.

7, 18, 1793. Samuel Green, wife and children to Exeter.

4, 17, 1794. John Shaw, Phebe his wife, and children, Phebe, Miriam and John from Abington.

4, 17, 1794. Moses Shaw, Mary his wife, and children, Deborah, Sarah, Mary and William from Abington.

4, 17, 1794. Joseph Shaw, Jr,. from Abington.

7, 17, 1794. Isaac Kirk to Bush R., S. C.

8, 21, 1794. Jacob Ritter to Philadelphia.

3, 19, 1795. Silas, Joel, John and James McCarty to Exeter.

6, 18, 1795. Evan Roberts from Gwynedd.

7, 16, 1795. Mary Tyson from Horsham.

10, 15, 1795. Samuel Morris, Rachel his wife, and children, Eizabeth More Morris, Thomas More Morris and Samuel Morris from Buckingham.

4, 21, 1796. Abraham and Nathan Walton and families to Westland.

8, 18, 1796. Joseph Lewis, Jr.. to Abington.

2, 16, 1797. Thomas Ball to Westland.

6, 15, 1797. John Ball, wife and children, Joel, Joseph, Margaret, Jesse, Sarah, James, Susanna and Iden to Westland.

6, 15, 1797. Thomas Roberts from Philadelphia.

7, 20, 1797. Samuel Shaw, wife and children, John, Thomas, Letitia, Susanna and Margaret to Westland.

8, 17, 1797. Mary and Sarah Burson to Wrightstown.

8, 17, 1797. Joel Cadwallader to Abington.

9, 21, 1797. Moses Wilson from Catawissa.

10, 19, 1797. Hannah Beans to Buckingham.

3, 15, 1798. Job Strahen to Redstone.

3, 15, 1798. Stephen Twining to Wrightstown.

2, 15, 1798. John Stephenson to Mt. Holly.

5, 17, 1798. Cadwallader Child from Buckingham.

7, 19, 1798. Thomas Chapman from Wrightstown.

5, 16, 1799. Rachel Foulke to Gwynedd.

10, 17, 1799. Cadwallader Child to Horsham.

2, 20, 1800. Thomas Roberts to Buckingham.

8, 21, 1800. Abel Nixon to Darby.

9, 18, 1800. Sarah Dennis to Catawissa.

2, 19, 1801. Samuel Penrose, wife and children, William, Everard, Benjamin and Margaret to Horsham.

11, 19, 1801. Jesse Hicks and family to Catawissa.

11, 19, 1801. Moses Lancaster, Jr., to Philadelphia, Northern District.

11, 2, 1802. Thomas Roberts from Catawissa.

2, 17, 1803. Joel Cadwallader to Abington.

4, 28, 1803. Judah Foulke, Sarah his wife, and minor children, Samuel, Eleanor, Mary Ann, Thomas, Elizabeth, Jane and Amelia from Muncy.

11, 17, 1803. Joseph Shaw from Gunpowder.

1, 17, 1805. John Iden to Horsham.
3, 21, 1805. Susanna Penrose and minor children, Elizabeth, Enos, Jane and Benjamin to Buckingham.
4, 25, 1805. Rowland Foulke from Buckingham.
7, 18, 1805. Evan Green to Sadsbury.
2, 6, 1806. William Walton from Gwynedd.
2, 6, 1806. Thomas Green to Muncy.
2, 6, 1806. Joel Edwards, wife and child to Muncy.
5, 15, 1806. Jonah Heacock, a minor, to Gwynedd.
5, 15, 1806. Townsend Speakman to Springfield, New Jersey.
6, 19, 1806. Jane Foulke to Gwynedd.
6, 19, 1806. Committee appointed to visit Daniel Stroud's family, believe it safe to receive his children into membership, and concur in having their names entered on the minutes, as follows:
      Charles Stroud, born 1793.
      McDowel Stroud, born 1795.
      William Stroud, born 1797.
      Jacob D. Stroud, born 1799.
      James Hollinshead Stroud, born 1800.
      Susan Stroud, born 1804.
3, 19, 1807. Nathan Roberts and family to Gwynedd.
10, 15, 1807. Moses Roberts, wife Jane and children Ann, Ruth, John and Joseph to Gwynedd.
4, 27, 1809. Jesse Foulke, wife and children to Muncy.
4, 27, 1809. Samuel Gummere, Rachel his wife and minor children Samuel and Rachel from Horsham.
11, 16, 1809. Elizabeth Evans to Gwynedd.
11, 16, 1809. John Iden to Gwynedd.
12, 21, 1809. Maberry McVaugh from Horsham.
12, 21, 1809. Aaron Ball to Buckingham.
1, 18, 1810. Samuel Hicks to Muncy.
3, 18, 1810. Townsend Speakman of Upper Springfield, New Jersey.
5, 17, 1810. Samuel Foulke from Abington.
5, 17, 1810. Obadiah Palmer, Jr., Abigail his wife and minor children James and Elizabeth from Marlborough.
7, 19, 1810. Samuel Sleeper, wife Patience and minor children Rebecca, Keturah, Aves, Buddell and Jacob from Butternuts, New York.
7, 19, 1810. James Bell, wife Susanna and minor children Joseph, Mary, John and James from Gwynedd.
11, 2, 1810. Mordecai Churchman, wife Sarah and minor children Hannah, Margaret and Charles to Southern District, Philadelphia.
1, 4, 1811. Ann Morgan to Gwynedd.
1, 4, 1811. Josiah Heacock to Muncy.
3, 29, 1811. Edward Roberts and wife to Uwchlan; also James Roberts.
3, 29, 1811. Israel Lancaster, wife and children to Horsham.
5, 31, 1811. Abigail Barker and daughter Elizabeth Drinker Barker from Philadelphia, Southern District.
11, 29, 1811. Samuel Gummere to Upper Evesham.
1, 3, 1812. Samuel Nixon and family to Uwchlan.
5, 29, 1812. John Welding and Ann his wife and two minor children Lydia Ann and Clementine from Wrightstown.
7, 3, 1812. Enoch Penrose to Exeter.
10, 30, 1812. Eber, Abraham, Rachel and Amos, minor children of Abraham Walton, from Wilmington.
10, 30, 1812. Abraham Chapman Ashton to Scipio, N. Y.
12, 4, 1812. David Coddington to Marlborough, N. Y.
1, 1, 1813. Hannah Kinsey to New Garden.

1, 1, 1813. Elizabeth Burson and daughter Elizabeth to Buckingham.
10, 1, 1813. Samuel Gummere and wife to Upper Springfield, N. J.
12, 31, 1813. Aaron Ball from Buckingham.
2, 4, 1814. David Roberts, wife Eliza and children to Upper Springfield, N. J.
3, 4, 1814. Isaac Phillips to New Garden.
4, 1, 1814. Israel Roberts, wife and three children to Radnor.
6, 3, 1814. John Burson to Philadelphia, Southern District.
9, 2, 1814. Sarah Foulke from Gwynedd.
9, 2, 1814. Moses Roberts, Jane his wife and minor children to Uwchlan.
11, 4, 1814. Francis Edkins, Joanna his wife and minor children, Catharine, Jane and Deborah from Muncy.
11, 4, 1814. Hannah Dutton and minor son Benjamin to Uwchlan.
11, 4, 1814. Abigail Griffith from New Garden.
3, 3, 1815. Joseph Green to Sadsbury.
3, 31, 1815. William T. Baldwin to Sadsbury.
3, 31, 1815. Edward Foulke to Cincinnati.
4, 28, 1815. Thomas D. Foulke, Jr., to Abington.
6, 30, 1815. Massey Brock from Philadelphia.
6, 30, 1815. John Flagler and son Zachariah from state of New York.
6, 30, 1815. Samuel Row from Oswego, N. Y.
12, 1, 1815. Jonathan Evans, wife Elizabeth and minor children, Thomas, George and Caleb.
12, 11, 1815. Antrim Foulke to Gwynedd.
5, 3, 1816. Jonathan Evans and family to Gwynedd.
8, 30, 1816. Edward Foulke from Abington.
11, 29, 1816. Thomas Roberts to Radnor.
7, 4, 1817. Richard Moore from Gwynedd.
1, 30, 1818. Joseph Watson, a minor, from Buckingham.
4, 3, 1818. Joseph Griffith to Uwchlan.
7, 31, 1818. James Wilson, a minor, to care of Muncy.
9, 9, 1818. Judah Foulke and family and Thomas Foulke to Miami, Ohio.
4, 2, 1819. Emmor Kimber, Jr., from Philadelphia.
9, 3, 1819. Jonathan Heacock, Jr., from Radnor.
3, 31, 1820. David Foulke, wife and son John to Abington.
4, 28, 1820. Nathan Penrose, wife Hannah and minor children, Nathan, Tacy, Washington and William to Yonge street, Upper Canada.
8, 4, 1820. Henry Johnson to Gwynedd.
12, 29, 1820. Harvey Smith to Wrightstown.
3, 2, 1821. Josiah Heacock, wife and minor children, Elizabeth M., Phebe W. and Warner to Abington.
5, 4, 1821. Isaac B. Williams and wife Martha from Kingwood, N. J.
6, 1, 1821. Emmor Kimber, Jr., wife Lydia and minor child Teresa J. Kimber to Philadelphia.
9, 28, 1821. Amos Jones and minor children from Buckingham.
11, 2, 1821. William Ferris, a minor, from Wilmington.
3, 1, 1822. Isaac B. Williams, wife Martha and child Clayton N. to Kingwood.
5, 3, 1822. Samuel Foulke to Bradford.
5, 31, 1822. Cadwallader Foulke, a minor, from Plainfield.
5, 31, 1822. Jesse W. and Joseph Heacock to Abington.
5, 31, 1822. Jonathan Heacock to Darby.
11, 1, 1822. James Linton and minor children, John, Morton, Phebe H., Mary and Sallie Ann from Roaring Creek.
4, 4, 1823. John Brock, wife Massey and minor daughter Mary W., to Buckingham.
4, 4, 1823. Abraham Griffith, wife Mary and minor daughter Violetta L., to Stroudsburg; returned 1, 2, 1824.
4, 4, 1823. Jacob Iden from Buckingham.

4, 4, 1823.	Enoch Penrose, wife Esther and minor children, Martha, Matilda, Ann R. and John T. to Exeter.
7, 4, 1823.	Eber Walton from Middletown.
7, 4, 1823.	John Welding from Stroudsburg.
7, 4, 1823.	Agnes Foulke to Exeter.
10, 31, 1823.	Amos Jones toBuckingham.
1, 30, 1824.	Cadwallader Foulke to Gwynedd.
4, 2, 1824.	Abraham Griffith, wife Mary W. and three minor children to Short Creek, Ohio.
4, 2, 1824.	Martha Heacock to Salem, O.
6, 4, 1824.	Samuel Carey from Buckingham.
4, 1, 1825.	Thomas Iden, wife Rachel and minor children to Scipio, N. Y.
6, 3, 1825.	Daniel Downing, wife Sarah and minor children, Margaret L., Eleanor F. and Jane from Stroudsburg.
12, 2, 1825.	George, son of Jonathan Evans, to Gwynedd.
8, 4, 1826.	Judah Roberts to Buckingham.
8, 4, 1826.	Phebe Foulke to Green Street, Philadelphia.
11, 3, 1826.	Samuel Foulke from Clear Creek.
11, 3, 1826.	Mordecai Churchman and wife Sarah to Southern District, Philadelphia.
12, 1, 1826.	John Thomson to Buckingham.
8, 3, 1827.	Henry and Thomas Lukens from Gwynedd.
1, 4, 1828.	James Wilson from Muncy.
4, 3, 1829.	Peter Lester, wife Margaret and minor children Anna F. and Mary S. to Buckingham.
4, 3, 1829.	William K. Slayter, wife Sarah and minor children to Marlborough, Ohio.
4, 3, 1829.	Eber Walton, wife Ann and child Joseph to Gwynedd.
5, 1, 1829.	Benjamin Lester to Sadsbury.
4, 30, 1830.	Amos B. Shaw to Buckingham.
4, 30, 1830.	Enoch Penrose, wife Esther and minor children Martha T., Matilda, Anna R. and John T. from Exeter.
10, 29, 1830.	Washington Penrose from Roaring Creek.
2, 4, 1830.	William Pickering, wife Tabitha and minor daughter Macre to Green Street, Philadelphia.
6, 3, 1831.	William Heacock, wife Lavinia and* minor children Evaline and Nathan Barclay, to Buckingham.
11, 4, 1831.	Evan G. Lester to Gwynedd.
11, 4, 1831.	John Hudson to Scipio.
2, 3, 1832.	Horace Ferris, wife Mary to Cherry Street, Philadelphia.
2, 3, 1832.	Daniel S. Fowler to Buckingham.
5, 4, 1832.	Benjamin Beatty, wife Mary and minor children Susanna L., Lydia, Phebe L., Isaac Newton, Benjamin Wilson and Ruth L. to Queensbury, New York.
1, 3, 1833.	James Michener and family to Deerfield, Ohio.
1, 3, 1833.	David Michener to Deerfield, Ohio.
1, 31, 1834.	Abraham Flagler, wife Elizabeth and children Thomas B., Isaiah, Nancy and Charles to Oswego, New York.
2, 28, 1834.	Edward Foulke to Uwchlan.
4, 4, 1834.	Everard Foulke and family to Buckingham; being himself, wife Fanny W. and minor children John Watson, Jonathan Ingham, Thomas D.
4, 4, 1834.	Samuel Foulke to Green Street, Philadelphia.
10, 31, 1834.	Moses Wilson, wife Jane, and Mark L. Wilson, wife Mary and minor children Stephen B., Shipley and Elizabeth to Milford, Indiana.
1, 30, 1835.	William Stokes to Buckingham.
7, 31, 1835.	Jesse Iden and wife Ann to Whitewater, Indiana.
6, 3, 1836.	Shipley Lester to Whitewater.

6, 3, 1836. John Heacock, wife Christiana and minor children Rachel and Jesse to Milford, Indiana.

3, 3, 1837. Lewis B. Shaw, wife Esther and daughter Pamelia to Gwynedd.

6, 2, 1837. Daniel L. Downing and family to Whitewater.

8, 4, 1837. John Palmer, wife Mary Ann and minor children Eliza Ann, Mary Ann, James T., William E., Catharine P., Phebe H. and Sydenham W. from Marlborough.

9, 1, 1837. Richard Lukens to Springboro, Ohio.

9, 29, 1837. Isaac Morgan to Chester.

2, 2, 1838. John Jones, a minor, from Radnor.

5, 4, 1838. Jane M. Foulke from Gwynedd.

5, 4, 1838. Samuel M. Foulke, wife Ann and minor children Tacy H., Margaret H., Jesse H., Sarah, Joseph and Edith to Milford, Indiana.

11, 2, 1838. Abel Lester, wife Margaret and minor children Samuel, Sarah, Jeremiah W., Howard, Benjamin Williams, Mary Margaret to Alum Creek, held at Owl Creek, Ohio.

11, 2, 1838. Parry Lukens to Springboro.

5, 3, 1839. Evan Foulke, wife Sarah ; Morris Foulke, wife Mary and son Edward to Deerfield, Ohio.

4, 3, 1840. James M. Jackson, wife Mary Ann and minor children Sarah Fisher, Samuel King, Elizabeth Jones, James Ellwood, Edwin Atlee and William Morris Jackson from Cherry Street, Philadelphia.

4, 3, 1840. Joseph Thorn, wife Edith Ann and minor children Ellwood E. and Joseph Howard Thorn from Cherry Street, Philadelphia.

4, 30, 1841. Benjamin Flagler to Stanford, New York.

4, 30. 1841. Joseph Thorn, wife Edith Ann and minor children Ellwood E. and Joseph Howard to Horsham.

4, 30, 1841. Amos S. Jackson and Clayton Garwood, a minor, with Joseph Thorn to Horsham.

6, 4, 1841. Samuel J. Levick from Green Street, Philadelphia.

7, 30, 1841. Richard Roberts, wife Catherine and minor children Charles, Thompson and Benjamin Franklin to Abington.

9, 3, 1841. Elias Hicks to Buckingham.

11, 4, 1842. George Atherton and wife Sarah to Cherry street, Philadelphia.

6, 2, 1843. Edward Cooper, wife Hannah and minor daughter Rachel from Wrightstown.

3, 1, 1844. John Jones to Radnor.

3, 29, 1844. Washington Penrose to Cherry street, Philadelphia.

1, 31, 1845. Enos Heacock, wife Sarah and minor children Hannah F., Hugh F., William and Enos Ellwood to Milford, Ind.

5, 30, 1845. Samuel Kinsey from Goshen.

4, 3, 1846. Thomas Wright, wife Abigail and minor children Ann and Thomas from Exeter.

7, 3, 1846. Joseph F. Rawlings, wife Martha P. and minor children Thomas Ellwood, Charles M. and Amos R. Rawlings to Solebury.

6, 2, 1848. Bartholomew Mather from Abington.

8, 4, 1848. Samuel K. Jackson, a minor, to New York.

8, 4, 1848. Elizabeth Lear to Buckingham.

8, 4, 1848. William E. Foulke to Milford, Ind.

12, 29, 1848. Benjamin Johnson, wife Tacy and minor children William S., Matilda Ann, Clayton F., Eli S. and Evan R. to Salem, Ohio.

12, 29, 1848. Edward Cooper, wife Hannah and minor children Rachel, Henry and James to West, Ohio.

6, 1, 1849. Samuel Newton Thompson, wife Susan D. and minor children Mary Anna and Cora Cecilia to Roaring Creek.

6, 1, 1849. Joseph H. Taylor to Cherry street, Philadelphia.

8, 30, 1850. Elias Edkin to Muncy.

5, 30, 1851. William H. Ball and wife Martha to Horsham.
7, 2, 1852. Isaac W. Richards to New York.
7, 2, 1852. Harvey S. Ball to Cherry street, Philadelphia.
9, 2, 1853. Henry J. Moore to Uwchlan.
7, 4, 1856. Nathan P. Hicks to Horsham.
7, 4, 1856. Charles Zorns and wife Catharine to Green street, Philadelphia.
7, 31, 1857. Antrim F. Morgan from Uwchlan.
7, 31, 1857. Samuel J. Levick, an approved minister, his wife Catharine M. and five minor children Jane F., Lewis J., Charles M., Samuel J. and William E. Levick from Philadelphia.
2, 26, 1858. Joseph Morgan to Uwchlan.
2, 23, 1859. Maris Garret, wife Elizabeth and minor children Mary, Kinsey, Elma, Amy Ida, Margaret W. and Charlotte from Goshen.
1, 3, 1862. David J. Ambler from Gwynedd.
5, 1, 1863. Thomas P. Marshall from Chesterfield.
9, 30, 1864. Samuel L. Foulke to Race street, Philadelphia.
3, 31, 1865. Charles M. Foulke to Philadelphia.
6, 30, 1865. William G. Foulke to Philadelphia.
6, 7, 1866. Joshua Bullock, wife Mary L. and minor child Mary Alice, and also Edward L. and Anne E. Bullock from Mount Holly.
6, 28, 1867. Paxson Blakey, wife Letitia and minor children Elizabeth S., Thomas J. and Mary Letitia from Middletown.
8, 30, 1867. Amos S. Jackson and minor daughter Emily W. from Horsham.
11, 29, 1867. James M. Hibbert and Mary R., his wife, and minor son James E. from Baltimore.
11, 29, 1869. John Ball, wife Sarah Ann and minor children Edwin and Anna S, from Green street, Philadelphia.
5, 29, 1868. Hannah Burson from Woodbury, N. J.
10, 2, 1868. Charles S. Ball to Race street, Philadelphia.
7, 30, 1869. Ann Green to Burlington.
12, 3, 1869. Harriet B. Roberts from Radnor.
2, 4, 1870. William Howard Merritt from Nine Partners.
3, 4, 1870. Amos S. Jackson to Philadelphia.
4, 1, 1870. Samuel L. Foulke from Philadelphia.
4, 1, 1870. Sarah B. Mason to Buckingham.
4, 29, 1870. Alfred Moore to Philadelphia.
6, 3, 1870. Edwin A. Jackson and Jane L. Jackson to New York.
6, 3, 1870. William Hicks to Fishing Creek.
7, 29, 1870. William G. Foulke to Philadelphia.
7, 29, 1870. Edwin A. Jackson, wife Jane L. and minor Jane J., to New York.

MARRIAGES.

8, 21, 1743. Samuel Foulke and Ann Greasley.
2, 17, 1744. Abel Roberts and Gainor Morris.
3, 10, 1744. Joseph Green and Catharine Thomas.
3, 9, 1745. Jonathan Heacock and Susanna Morgan.
       1746. Isaac Lester and Eleanor Thomas.
4, 11, 1747. Charles Dennis and Sarah Morgan.
4, 23, 1748. John Thomas and Elizabeth Lewis.
       1748. John Zetley and Rachel Griffith.
10, 14, 1749. Edward Thomas and Alice Roberts.
9, 14, 1750. Thomas Roberts and Letitia Rea.

5, 20, 1752. Joseph Dennis, Jr., and Hannah Lewis.
10, 17, 1752. Samuel Thomas and Phebe Lancaster.
10, 12, 1752. William Hogue, Jr., and Esther Ewen.
5, 2, 1754. David Roberts and Phebe Lancaster.
10, 10, 1754. Thomas Foulke and Jane Roberts.
10, 14, 1755. John Foulke and Mary Roberts.
11, 17, 1756. John Greasley and Jane Foulke.
12, 9, 1756. George Hoge and Elizabeth Blackledge.
12, 9, 1756. Abraham Roberts and Katharine Lester.
5, 12, 1757. William Foulke and Pr scilla Lester.
6, 15, 1757. William Blackledge and Ann Lewis.
11, 3, 1757. Benjamin Fell and Sarah Rawlings.
11, 10, 1757. Theophilus Foulke and Margaret Thomas.
11, 17, 1757. Joseph Rakestraw and Rachel Ogilby.
5, 11, 1758. Thomas Blackledge and Margaret Wright.
11, 2, 1758. John Morgan and Mary Gaskill.
5, 10, 1759. Jonathan Penrose and Martha Penrose.
6, 20, 1759. Joseph Rawlings and Ann Hilles.
6, 21, 1759. Thomas Foulke appointed Recorder of Marriage Certificates.
11, 8, 1759. Robert Ashton and Sarah Thomas.
10, 9, 1760. William Thomas and Ann Foulke.
11, 13, 1760. William Hicks and Hannah Shaw.
7, 2, 1761. Thomas Casner and Ann Thomas.
6, 11, 1761. Everard Roberts and Ann Hole.
10, 7, 1762. John Lester, Jr., and Jane Antrim.
1, 13, 1763. Thomas Ashton and Mary Chapman.
5, 12, 1763. Thomas Stalford and Elizabeth Wright.
8, 3, 1763. William Burr and Ann Edwards.
11, 10, 1763. Abraham Ball and Ann Adamson.
11, 23, 1763. Isaac Samuels and Eleanor Lester.
12, 8, 1763. James Walton and Margaret Lewis.
11, 8, 1764. John Penrose and Ann Roberts.
5, 1, 1766. William Clark and Hannah Lloyd.
4, 24, 1766. William Edwards and Meribah Gaskill.
11, 4, 1766. David Walton and Margaret Green.
6, 4, 1767. Joseph Shaw and Rachel Griffith.
5, 11, 1769. Samuel Nixon and Susanna Roberts.
5, 18, 1769. Robert Fisher and Martha Edwards.
6, 8, 1769. Thomas Strahen and Mary Heacock.
10, 12, 1769. Lewis Lewis and Mary Burson.
10, 12, 1769. Abraham Walton and Rachel Heacock.
10, 19, 1769. George Michener and Hannah Carr.
11, 30, 1769. John Chapman and Hannah Antrim.
11, 1, 1770. John Roberts and Martha Edwards.
11, 8, 1770. William Penrose and Mary Roberts.
1, 9, 1772. Randall Iden and Eleanor Foulke.
3, 25, 1773. John Thomson and Abigail Roberts.
9, 16, 1773. William Heacock and Miriam (1st cousins, contrary to order of Friends).
11, 3, 1774. John Hallowell and Martha Roberts.
12, 8, 1774. Edward Fell and Mary Penrose.
11, 9, 1775. Benjamin Green and Jane Roberts.
11, 30, 1775. Amos Roberts and Margaret Thomas.
2, 29, 1776. Isaac Burson and Elizabeth Blackledge.
11, 14, 1776. Joseph Speakman and Catharine Dennis.
3, 27, 1777. William Shaw and Sarah Carr.
10, 9, 1777. Samuel Penrose and Sarah Roberts.
5, 6, 1779. James Green and Martha Foulke.

4, 22, 1779.	Jeremiah Williams and Mary Blackledge.
10, 7, 1779.	Abraham Roberts and Peninah Thomas.
9, 30, 1779.	Edward Roberts and Marah Lewis.
11, 11, 1779.	Asher Foulke and Alice Roberts.
11, 25, 1779.	Samuel Shaw, Jr., and Susanna Rea.
6, 1, 1780.	Moses Shaw and Mary Carr.
11, 17, 1780.	George Williams and Abigail Lancaster.
11, 30, 1780.	Amos Dennis and Jane Heacock.
11, 1, 1781.	Edward Foulke and Elizabeth Roberts.
1, 24, 1782.	George Iden and Hannah Foulke.
6, 6, 1782.	Israel Roberts and Anne Foulke.
11, 14, 1782.	Israel Foulke and Elizabeth Roberts.
1, 2, 1783.	John Griffith and Rachel Greasley.
11, 25, 1784.	Joseph Rawlings and Ann Heacock.
5, 5, 1785.	John Greasley and Margaret Roberts.
4, 28, 1785.	Hugh Foulke and Sarah Roberts.
5, 26, 1785.	Jesse Hicks and Margaret Ball.
6, 8, 1786.	Eli Kennard and Elizabeth Blackledge.
10, 20, 1786.	Joseph Custer and Amelia Foulke.
11, 2, 1786.	Jonathan Griffith and Sarah Burson.
11, 20, 1786.	Judah Foulke and Sarah McCarty.
10, 2, 1788.	Daniel Walton and Martha Green.
3, 26, 1789.	Benjamin Foulke and Martha Roberts.
10, 15, 1789.	Joseph Heston and Anne Thomas.
10, 29, 1789.	John Foulke and Letitia Roberts.
5, 5, 1791.	Nathan Roberts and Margaret Ashton.
11, 24, 1791.	Shipley Lester and Margaret Nixon.
12, 6, 1792.	Samuel Shaw and Elizabeth Ball.
4, 25, 1793.	William Samuels and Mary Foulke.
11, 28, 1793.	Josiah Dennis and Alice Wilson.
4, 9, 1795.	Samuel Ashton and Jane Roberts.
3, 26, 1795.	Lewis Lewis and Abigail Roberts.
4, 30, 1795.	Amos Richardson and Martha Penrose.
6, 4, 1795.	Levi Roberts and Phebe McCarty.
11, 26, 1795.	George Shaw and Rachel Penrose.
3, 31, 1796.	Thomas Penrose and Rachel Hillman.
12, 22, 1796.	Thomas Lester and Mary Stokes.
8, 31, 1797.	Jacob Beans and Hannah Iden.
11, 2, 1797.	Moses Wilson and Jane Lester.
2, 22, 1798.	Israel Lancaster and Hannah Nixon.
4, 26, 1798.	Isaiah Jamison and Margaret Ball.
12, 27, 1798.	Hugh Foulke and Sarah Lester.
4, 4, 1799.	George Hicks and Ann Penrose.
5, 2, 1799.	William Edwards and Susanna Nixon.
1, 2, 1800.	William Nixon and Martha Roberts.
11, 26, 1801.	Enoch Penrose and Martha Edwards.
12, 3, 1801.	Timothy Smith and Rachel Stokes.
4, 1, 1802.	Abel Penrose and Keziah Speakman.
1, 5, 1804.	George Child and Ann Iden.
3, 22, 1804.	David Roberts and Elizabeth Stokes.
11, 22, 1804.	John Shaw and Elizabeth Ball.
5, 2, 1805.	Abel Penrose and Abigail Foulke.
11, 28, 1805.	Thomas Lester and Hannah Green.
2, 27, 1806.	John Lester and Abigail Wilson.
6, 20, 1806.	Daniel Conard and Sarah Roberts.
4, 23, 1807.	Evan Penrose and Rebecca Ball.
11, 26, 1807.	Caleb Foulke and Jane Green.

11, 24, 1808.	Joseph Conard, Jr., and Maria Roberts.
9, 28, 1809.	William Fussell and Jane Foulke
10, 5, 1809.	Jonathan Evans and Elizabeth Iden.
11, 30, 1809.	Thomas Thorp and Mary Foulke.
10, 11, 1810.	Mayberry McVaugh and Lydia Gummere.
11, 20, 1810.	Samuel Iden and Elizabeth Chapman.
11, 15, 1810.	Morgan Morgan, Jr., and Ann Custard.
12, 6, 1810.	Isaac Parry and Mary Nixon.
4, 4, 1811.	Caleb Edwards and Sarah Penrose.
10, 4, 1811.	David Foulke and Miriam Shaw.
10, 10, 1811.	Edward Burson and Jemima Stroud.
11, 12, 1812.	Nathaniel Kinsey and Hannah Griffith.
7, 8, 1813.	Obadiah Palmer and Sarah Van Vliet.
10, 21, 1813.	George Custard and Hannah Foulke.
4, 6, 1815.	Abner Dalby and Sarah Shaw.
4, 20, 1815.	William Heacock and Lavinia Penrose.
10, 12, 1815.	Samuel M. Foulke and Ann Edwards.
10, 5, 1815.	Thomas Jackson and Jane Griffith.
10, 19, 1815.	James Foulke and Hannah Shaw.
12, 7, 1815.	Greenfield Iden and Beulah Green.
11, 14, 1816.	John Johnson, Jr., and Elizabeth Foulke.
2, 27, 1818.	Abraham Griffith requests certificate to proceed in marriage with Mary Michener, Stroudsburg.
5, 14, 1818.	John Ball and Hannah Penrose.
12, 10, 1818.	Samuel M. Foulke and Ann Heacock.
1, 7, 1819.	Richard Moore and Sarah Foulke.
6, 10, 1819.	Charles Stroud and Susan Burson.
4, 6, 1820.	Jonathan Shaw and Mary Miller.
5, 18, 1820.	Daniel Downing and Sarah Iden.
5, 25, 1820.	Peter Lester and Margaret Foulke.
2, 11, 1821.	Abel Lester requests certificate to proceed in marriage with Margaret Williams, Kingwood.
3, 8, 1821.	Hugh Foulke, Jr., and Elizabeth Roberts.
8, 31, 1821.	John Lester requests certificate to proceed in marriage with Mary Stackhouse, Byberry.
4, 4, 1822.	Thomas Stradling and Mary Jamison.
11, 14, 1822.	James R. Green and Ann Foulke.
11, 14, 1822.	Samuel Shaw and Sidney Foulke.
9, 9, 1824.	Samuel Carey and Abigail Green.
3, 10, 1825.	Eber Walton and Ann Shaw.
5, 12, 1825.	Joshua Foulke and Caroline Green.
6, 4, 1829.	John Hampton Watson and Hannah Lester.
5, 14, 1829.	Andrew Ambler and Mary Johnson.
5, 20, 1830.	Jervis Thomas and Jane R. Green.
5, 30, 1830.	John Good and Margaret Heacock.
3, 17, 1831.	Benjamin Johnson, Jr., and Tacy L. Strawn.
6, 9, 1831.	Charles Foulke and Catharine P. Edkins.
12, 15, 1831.	Edward Foulke, Jr., and Matilda Green.
3, 7, 1833.	Israel S. Zorns and Matilda Ann Strawn.
10, 10, 1833.	Johnson Strawn and Jane Penrose.
11, 14, 1833.	Thomas Wright and Abigail Foulke.
11, 12, 1835.	Eleazer C. Shaw and Grace R. Green.
3, 22, 1838.	Aaron Penrose and Maryetta Foulke.
4, 5, 1838.	Sydenham Walton and Hannah M. Phillips.
10, 17, 1839.	Joseph F. Rawlings and Martha P. Roberts.
3, 4, 1841.	Samuel J. Levick and Ellen Foulke.
12, 16, 1841.	John F. Edwards and Mary Ball.

10, 16, 1842.	Joel Heacock and Abigail Roberts.
10, 5, 1843.	William M. Levick and Hannah Moore.
3, 14, 1844.	Samuel Kinsey and Martha F. Custar. The first who were married at a private house instead of the meeting-house.
12, 12, 1844.	Eli W. Strawn and Margaret Penrose.
11, 13, 1845.	Stephen Foulke and Matilda Penrose.
1, 6, 1846.	William Hicks and Sarah W. Edkins.
1, 8, 1846.	Thomas P. Ball and Martha W. Hicks.
2, 12, 1846.	Albert Conard and Martha D. Ball.
9, 9, 1847.	Penrose Hicks and Mary Edwards.
10, 13, 1847.	Joseph Paul and Mary Foulke.
3, 21, 1848.	William Ball and Sarah Shaw.
3, 15, 1848.	Richard R. Green and Sarah F. Jackson.
8, 23, 1848.	Davis D. Walton and Alice Green.
9, 12, 1848.	Israel L. Stokes and Caroline Green.
10, 10, 1849.	John A. Flagler and Phebe H. Palmer.
12, 4, 1848.	Bartholomew Mather and Hannah Foulke.
5, 15, 1851.	Samuel Shaw and Anna R. Penrose.
3, 16, 1854.	William Shaw and Hannah Morgan.
4, 6, 1854.	William D. Foulke and Alice G. Thomas.
3, 12, 1856.	Samuel Carey and Mary Green.
3, 6, 1862.	David J. Ambler and Caroline F. Penrose.
11, 13, 1862.	Penrose Hicks and Elizabeth Foulke.
2, 10, 1863.	Joseph W. Foulke and Mary Ann Strawn.
5, 28, 1863.	Thomas P. Marshall and Sophie B. Mickle.
3, 8, 1866.	Samuel Kinsey and Jane G. Carey.
9, 17, 1868.	T. Ellwood Lippincott and Abigail W. Lester.
3, 11, 1869.	Speakman Hicks and Alice L. Strawn.
6, 9, 1869.	Edwin A. Iden and Jane A. Levick.
8, 18, 1869.	William M. Jackson and Anna M. Davis.
3, 24, 1870.	Richard M. Johnson and Mary P. Strawn.
6, 13, 1872.	S. J. Levick, Jr., and Annie E. Bullock.
10, 10, 1872.	Joseph Primrose and Martha Foulke.
2, 11, 1873.	Theodore Wolf and Elizabeth Foulke.
2, 12, 1874.	Jesse Thatcher and Elizabeth Blake.
10, 14, 1875.	Allen J. Flitcraft and Emma Roberts.
3, 27, 1890.	Morris Shaw and Jane G. Johnson.

INTERMENTS AT RICHLAND.

The records contained in this chapter prove how great the care bestowed by Friends on such matters. The following list of interments at Richland covers a period of fourscore years.

8, 2, 1818.	William Hicks.	8, 28, 1823.	Ann Rawlings.
11, 6, 1821.	Tacy Hicks.	9, 6, 1823.	Margaret Hicks.
11, 11, 1821.	Peninah Hicks.	9, 11, 1823.	Edith Jenkins.
9, 4, 1822.	John Richardson.	9, 24, 1823.	Septimus Heacock.
1, —, 1823.	Tabitha Thomas.	9, 27, 1823.	Abner Dalby.
1, —, 1823.	Susan Lester.	9, 27, 1823.	Rachel Wood.
2, 10, 1823.	Tacy Heacock.	10, 3, 1823.	Joseph Shaw.
2, 16, 1823.	Joseph Shaw.	12, 28, 1823.	Mary Morgan.
6, 24, 1823.	Peninah Roberts.	2, 3, 1824.	Lewis Ball.
5, —, 1823.	Gulah Jones.	8, 22, 1824.	Joseph Penrose.

9, 26, 1824.	Israel Foulke.
10, 8, 1824.	David Burson.
12, 7, 1824.	Abel Penrose.
3, 11, 1825.	Elizabeth Roberts.
4, 9, 1825.	William Shaw.
9, 6, 1825.	Tacy Heacock.
11, 16, 1825.	Barton R. Green.
11, 24, 1825.	Casper Johnson.
12, 11, 1825.	Elizabeth Penrose.
2, 27, 1826.	Hannah Martin.
4, 12, 1826.	Hannah Lester.
6, 16, 1826.	Abigail Edwards.
7, 5, 1826.	Gainor Heacock.
9, 5, 1826.	Moses Shaw.
9, 24, 1826.	John Shaw.
9, 27, 1826.	Isaiah Jamison.
10, 31, 1826.	Margaret Penrose.
1, 29, 1827.	John Stokes.
2, 6, 1827.	James Bryan.
3, 13, 1827.	Ann Foulke.
8, 28, 1827.	John Martin.
9, 3, 1827.	Mary Strawn.
9, 5, 1827.	Everard Foulke.
10, 16, 1827.	Abigail Johnson.
2, 5, 1828.	David Roberts.
4, 12, 1828.	Philip Zorns.
5, 23, 1828.	Benjamin Green.
9, 22, 1828.	Mary Tyson.
9, 23, 1828.	Enoch Walton.
9, 26, 1828.	Margaret Lewis.
10, 3, 1828.	Myra Dalby.
10, 30, 1828.	Eleazer Ball.
2, 14, 1829.	William Shaw.
2, 18, 1829.	Robert Penrose.
3, 27, 1829.	Thomas Rawlings.
6, 13, 1829.	Joseph Jamison.
9, 20, 1829.	Rachel Lancaster.
9, 21, 1829.	Hannah Green.
1, 1, 1830.	Mary Jane Lester.
3, 23, 1830.	William Edwards.
5, 1, 1830.	Phebe Shaw.
9, 2, 1830.	Eliza Burson.
8, 14, 1830.	John Hicks.
10, 18, 1830.	Oliver Strawn.
12, 8, 1830.	Ann Foulke.
1, 14, 1831.	Henry Moore.
2, 28, 1831.	Ann Maus.
3, 2, 1831.	William Edwards.
3, 10, 1831.	Margaret Jamison.
5, 22, 1831.	John Lester.
6, 28, 1831.	Mary Williams.
7, 16, 1831.	Hobson Shaw.
8, 1, 1831.	John Lancaster.
8, 14, 1831.	Martha Foulke.
10, 31, 1831.	Mary Morgan.
12, 1, 1831.	Catharine Dalby.
12, 6, 1831.	Jesse Decoursey.
12, 17, 1831.	Elizabeth Foulke.
12, 19, 1831.	Mary Thomas.
1, 4, 1832.	John Jamison.
4, 27, 1832.	William Penn Carey.
5, 13, 1832.	Levia Foulke.
6, 11, 1832.	Thomas Foulke.
7, 27, 1832.	James Green.
8, 12, 1832.	Jane Shaw.
9, 23, 1832.	Elizabeth Roberts.
10, 2, 1832.	John S. Roberts.
12, 2, 1832.	Casper Johnson.
4, 30, 1833.	Mary Shaw.
7, 8, 1833.	Eleanor Iden.
12, 22, 1832.	Phebe Foulke.
4, 24, 1832.	Shipley Lester.
9, 26, 1833.	Harriet Shaw.
8, 2, 1833.	Israel Shaw.
10, 31, 1733.	Nathan Shaw.
2, 26, 1834.	Josiah Dennis.
2, 27, 1834.	Jeremiah Williams.
—, —, 1834.	Lydia Carey.
—, —, 1834.	Mary Ann Heller.
—, —, 1834.	Ann Loyd.
11, 5, 1834.	Rachel Shaw.
12, 27, 1834.	Samuel Jamison.
2, 19, 1835.	Rebecca Shaw.
5, 2, 1835.	Jane Foulke.
4, 23, 1835.	Alice Dennis.
6, 25, 1835.	Franklin Foulke.
11, 22, 1835.	Joseph Penrose.
4, —, 1836.	Deborah Johnson.
5, 15, 1836.	Mary Ellen Foulke.
5, 26, 1836.	Chapman Green.
6, 11, 1836.	Gainor Ball.
6, 21, 1836.	Jordan Foulke.
10, 23, 1836.	Mary Shaw.
1, 18, 1837.	Stephen Shaw.
4, 20, 1837.	Benjamin Johnson.
4, 20, 1837.	Abel Roberts.
8, 17, 1837.	Elizabeth Shaw.
5, 30, 1837.	Susanna Stokes.
8, 27, 1837.	Jane Lester.
1, 7, 1837.	Sarah Letitia Moore.
2, 23, 1838.	John Shaw.
4, 27, 1838.	Tacy Ann Heacock.
4, 28, 1838.	James Griffith.
10, 5, 1838.	Evan P. Strawn.
10, 28, 1838.	Nathan Ball.
12, 26, 1838.	Caroline Foulke.
3, 19, 1839.	John Shaw.
6, —, 1839.	Joseph P. Roberts.
7, 20, 1839.	Jane Jamison.
11, 24, 1839.	Edward Foulke.
12, 29, 1839.	Samuel Miller.
3, 7, 1840.	Ann Wilson.
4, 5, 1840.	John Foulke.
5, 30, 1840.	Margaret Jamison.

5, 10, 1840.	William Strawn.	
5, 14, 1840.	Joseph Hicks.	
9, 30, 1840.	Nixon Shaw.	
5, 1, 1841.	Ann Penrose.	
5, 20, 1841.	Jane Green.	
5, 31, 1841.	Ann Maus.	
5, 3, 1841.	Sarah Maus.	
7, 10, 1841.	Esther Speakman.	
10, 2, 1841.	Jesse Heacock.	
12, 4, 1841.	Meribah Penrose.	
1, —, 1842.	Edith Childs.	
3, 2, 1842.	Hester Penrose.	
3, 5, 1842.	Phebe Wilson.	
5, 21, 1842.	Elmina Blake.	
5, 3, 1842.	Martha Jane Blake.	
8, 13, 1842.	Ellen Levick d.	
8, 22, 1842.	Enoch Penrose.	
10, 28, 1842.	Joseph Custard.	
1, 1, 1843.	Elizabeth Roberts.	
10, 13, 1843.	Rachel Roberts.	
11, 18, 1843.	Mary Green.	
4, 15, 1844.	Sarah Foulke.	
4, 23, 1844.	John Edwards.	
7, 26, 1844.	Miles Strawn.	
10, 22, 1844.	Keziah Richardson.	
2, 3, 1844.	Martha Strawn.	
3, 12, 1845.	Abigail Jane Foulke.	
4, 6, 1845.	Rachel Penrose.	
12, 7, 1845.	Martha Green.	
1, 2, 1846.	William Wilson.	
1, 7, 1846.	Levi Roberts.	
6, 22, 1846.	Hugh Foulke.	
12, 30, 1846.	Catherine Foulke.	
2, 21, 1847.	Emma King.	
2, 16, 1847.	Rachel Carr.	
4, 19, 1847.	Mary Foulke.	
5, 3, 1847.	Hannah Ball.	
5, 17, 1847.	Samuel Thomas.	
6, 27, 1847.	Judah Roberts.	
8, 20, 1847.	George Hicks.	
11, 2, 1847.	Judith Edwards.	
3, 7, 1848.	Martha Penrose.	
5, 4, 1848.	Miriam Segal.	
5, 24, 1848.	John Penrose.	
5, 24, 1848.	Jane Penrose.	
11, 20, 1848.	Abel Strawn.	
3, 26, 1849.	Martha Richardson.	
4, 7, 1849.	Enoch Strawn.	
3, 26, 1849.	Evan Roberts.	
12, 10, 1849.	Mary Penrose.	
2, 12, 1850.	Amos Richardson.	
4, 2, 1850.	Phebe Roberts.	
7, 4, 1850.	Hannah Foulke.	
9, 5, 1850.	Leonard Thomas.	
10, 26, 1850.	Lydia Green.	
4, 26, 1851.	Maryetta Penrose.	
8, 26, 1851.	Mary Dalby.	

9, 25, 1851.	William Green.	
1, 5, 1852.	Rebecca Penrose.	
1, 29, 1852.	Joseph Fussel.	
2, 22, 1852.	Caleb Foulke.	
3, 22, 1852.	Deborah Roberts.	
5, 25, 1852.	Lydia Edwards.	
6, 26, 1852.	Thomas Wright.	
10, 19, 1852.	John Ball.	
10, 25, 1852.	Sarah Moore.	
1, 23, 1853.	Samuel Edwards.	
3, 17, 1853.	Joel Heacock d.	
4, 3, 1853.	Hugh Foulke d.	
4, 22, 1853.	Amos R. Foulke d.	
8, —, 1853.	Enoch Roberts.	
11, 6, 1853.	Sarah Roberts.	
12, 21, 1853.	Jane Strawn.	
1, 11, 1854.	Jesse Roberts.	
1, 15, 1854.	Elizabeth Johnson.	
2, 12, 1854.	Peninah Foulke.	
2, 13, 1854.	Edward Griffith.	
2, 17, 1854.	William Miles Ball.	
3, 12, 1854.	Reuben Lester.	
4, 17, 1854.	Susan Roberts.	
7, 14, 1854.	Rebecca Jane Strawn.	
7, 30, 1854.	Mary Hicks.	
8, —, 1854.	Abigail Roberts.	
9, 28, 1854.	Abigail Carey.	
10, 3, 1854.	George Custard.	
10, 5, 1854.	Eveline Johnson.	
10, 21, 1854.	Letitia Foulke.	
12, 1, 1854.	Lydia Decoursey.	
12, 3, 1854.	Thomas Penrose.	
11, 23, 1854.	John Roberts.	
4, 7, 1855.	Mary Jane Shaw.	
4, 17, 1855.	Mary Hicks.	
4, 19, 1855.	Benjamin Heller.	
4, 21, 1855.	Martha Roberts.	
8, 17, 1855.	Sarah Roberts.	
8, 30, 1855.	Jane Jamison.	
10, 19, 1855.	Nathan Edwards.	
12, —, 1855.	Ellen Roberts.	
1, 15, 1856.	Anne Roberts.	
2, 4, 1856.	William Miller.	
3, 17, 1856.	Samuel Roberts.	
4, 3, 1856.	Margaret Foulke.	
8, 12, 1856.	Caroline Ball.	
8, 18, 1856.	Virginia Johnson.	
8, 20, 1856.	Barton Foulke.	
11, 12, 1856.	Martha Heasly.	
11, 13, 1856.	Abigail Griffith.	
11, 24, 1856.	Aaron Ball.	
12, 30, 1856.	Mary Jane Johnson.	
1, 15, 1857.	Thomas Strawn.	
2, 11, 1857.	Eveline Edwards.	
3, 17, 1857.	Enos Roberts.	
4, 2, 1857.	Cornelia Jamison.	
4, 25, 1857.	Charles Foulke.	

4, 30, 1857,	Bartholomew Roberts.
7, 2, 1857.	Joseph Van Buskirk.
8, 31, 1857.	Caroline Ball. (Infant.)
12, 8, 1857.	Jane Edwards.
1, 30, 1858.	John Griffith.
4, 7, 1858.	Evan Penrose. (Infant.)
4, 28, 1858.	Sarah Dalby.
5, 12, 1858.	Elizabeth R. Foulke d.
6, 29, 1858.	Joel Roberts.
8, 9, 1858.	Joseph Strawn.
8, 13, 1858.	Benjamin Lester.
8, 19, 1858.	George Penrose. (Inf.)
8, 28, 1858.	Johnson Strawn d.
8, 29, 1858.	Abigail Shaw d.
9, 30, 1858.	Sarah Carr.
1, 8, 1859.	Cornelia Jamison. (Inf.)
1, 9, 1859.	Jonathan Shaw.
2, 14, 1859.	Hannah Custard.
2, 19, 1859.	Edward Foulke.
2, 27, 1859.	Jane Thomas.
2, 27, 1859.	Abby Ann Foulke.
2, 28, 1859.	Jane Strawn.
3, 4, 1859.	Catharine Teany.
4, 29, 1859.	Mary Paul.
5, 30, 1859.	Hannah S. Foulke.
7, 13, 1859.	David Roberts d.
8, 3, 1859.	Margaret Miller d.
8, 10, 1859.	Martha Edwards d.
10, 29, 1859.	William Ball.
10, 30, 1859.	Morgan Morgan.
11, 2, 1859.	Samuel Shaw d.
1, 10, 1860.	Deborah Wood d.
1, 25, 1860.	Jane R. Foulke d.
2, 22, 1860.	Edgar Linderman. (Inf.)
3, 18, 1860.	Franklin Foulke d.
8, 3, 1860.	Abraham Segal.
8, 21, 1860.	Manasses Ochs.
8, 28, 1860.	Sarah Edwards.
12, 5, 1860.	Martha Kinsey d.
1, 1, 1861.	Elizabeth Thomas.
2, 10, 1861.	Thomas Foulke.
3, 11, 1861.	Ann Roberts.
4, 7, 1861.	Sarah Jane Roberts.
5, 20, 1861.	John T. Penrose.
8, 25, 1861.	Martha Hicks.
11, 12 1861.	Ida Ochs.
1, 15, 1862.	Rachel Roberts' child.
3, 18, 1862.	William Roberts.
10, 7, 1862.	Caleb Edwards.
10, 23, 1862.	Caroline Roberts.
11, 28, 1862.	Thomas P. Ball.
11, 29, 1862.	Edward Shaw.
12, 1, 1862.	Agnes Foulke.
12, 3, 1862.	Clayton Foulke.
12, 9, 1862.	Sydney Shaw.
12, 17, 1862.	David Johnson.
1, 2, 1863.	John Foulke.

2, 8, 1863.	Samuel Shaw.
2, 16, 1863.	Benjamin Foulke.
2, 22, 1863.	William H. Ball.
4, 17, 1863.	Gilbert Ball.
9, 6, 1863.	Ann Franklin.
9, 17, 1863.	Fell's child.
9, 27, 1863.	Josephine Garret. (ch.)
10, 12, 1863.	Mary Fell.
10, 27, 1863.	Philina Garret. (ch.)
12, 20, 1863.	Martha Hicks.
2, 14, 1864.	Evan Penrose.
2, 28, 1864.	Tacy Edwards.
6, 27, 1864.	Mary Deal.
7, 23, 1864.	William G. Thomas.
8, 8, 1864.	Penrose Hicks, son of Speakman Hicks.
8, 18, 1864.	Hannah M. Foulke, daughter of Stephen Foulke.
8, 19, 1864.	Dr. Samuel Carey d.
8, 16, 1864.	James Levick, son of Samuel J. Levick.
9, 28, 1864.	Lizzie Jackson.
9, 15, 1864.	George Evans.
11, 15, 1864.	Elizabeth Roberts.
1, 2, 1865.	Maris Garrett's child.
1, 10, 1865.	Jane Roberts.
5, 6, 1865.	Jacob Teany.
5, 30, 1865.	Frederick Gears.
7, 1, 1865.	Hannah P. Ball d.
7, 28, 1865.	Ellwood Miller.
8, 17, 1865.	Alice Jamison d.
8, 24, 1865.	William P. Roberts d.
10, 13, 1865.	Mary Foulke.
10, 17, 1865.	William Green.
10, 22, 1865.	Caleb Foulke.
11, 27, 1865.	Mary Deal's child.
12, 1, 1865.	Nathaniel Kinsey.
1, 5, 1866.	Lydia Edwards.
3, 8, 1866.	Martha Foulke.
4, 11, 1866.	James Foulke.
5, 20, 1866.	William Maus d.
5, 22, 1866.	Sallie Miller.
6, 20, 1866.	James Ringgold. (Col.)
6, 23, 1866.	Edith Ball.
7, 26, 1866.	Ann and Elizabeth Mason.
8, 5, 1866.	Alice Linderman.
10, 19, 1866.	Jane Maus.
2, 26, 1867.	Mary E. Johnson.
3, 26, 1867.	Missouri Roberts.
5, 8, 1867.	Margaret Edwards.
5, 17, 1867.	Lizzie Wright.
9, 27, 1867.	Sarah Richardson.
10, 12, 1867.	Edward Shaw's child.
1, 5, 1868.	Cynthia Dennis.
1, 9, 1868.	Owen Ball.
2, 5, 1868.	Joseph Foulke.

2, 25, 1868.	Joseph Foulke's child.
3, 12, 1868.	Mary Johnson.
3, 15, 1868.	Henry Strawn.
2, 28, 1868.	Abigail Wildman.
9, 5, 1868.	John Strawn.
9, 30, 1868.	Henry Dotts.
10, 9, 1868.	John Burson's child.
11, 26, 1868.	Martha Foulke.
5, 11, 1869.	Jeffries' child.
9, 19, 1869.	William Van Buskirk.
10, 10, 1869.	Abigail Wright.
11, 6, 1869.	Mary Carey.
11, 18, 1869.	Sarah Foulke.
2, 8, 1870.	Hannah Hicks, daughter of Evan.
2, 19, 1870.	Lewis Roberts' child.
4, 12, 1870.	A grandchild of Joseph Lancaster.
4, 21, 1870.	Child of John Jamison.
6, 15, 1870.	William Lester.
9, 30, 1870.	James Jackson.
10, 20, 1870.	David Jamison's son.
10, 27, 1870.	Anna Foulke.
11, 9, 1870.	Sidney Strawn.
12, 24, 1870.	Catharine Erwin.
1, 5, 1871.	Jane Jackson's child.
2, 24, 1871.	Paulina Penrose.
3, 4, 1871.	John Foulke.
4, 17, 1871.	Mary Walton.
5, 27, 1871.	Rachel Roberts d.
5, 31, 1871.	Child of Jesse Foulke.
7, 13, 1871.	Hannah K. Pugh.
8, 22, 1871.	Evan R. Penrose.
8, 29, 1871.	Thomas Morris' child.
1, 12, 1872.	Jane Roberts.
1, 25, 1872.	John Kinsey.
2, 4, 1872.	Samuel Foulke.
2, 14, 1872.	Bartholomew Mather.
4, 10, 1872.	Amos Edwards.
6, 12, 1872.	Samuel C. Bradshaw.
7, 3, 1872.	Clarissa Morgan.
7, 4, 1872.	Ann Hicks.
7, 14, 1872.	Ann Penrose.
7, 14, 1872.	Mary Jane Lester.
10, 24, 1872.	Hamilton's child.
10, 27, 1872.	Mary Roberts.
12, 30, 1872.	John Burson's child.
1, 22, 1873.	John Lester.
2, 11, 1873.	James Shaw.
2, 25, 1873.	Jane W. Moore d.
4, 10, 1873.	Ann Richardson d.
11, 1, 1873.	Washington Ball.
3, 16, 1874.	Samuel Johnson's child.
3, 18, 1874.	Lydia Penrose.
4, 23, 1874.	Sallie Lester d.
1, 30, 1875.	Anna Lester d.
3, 20, 1875.	Wilson Dennis d.

5, 2, 1875.	Edwin Johnson's child.
4, 30, 1875.	Richard Moore d.
6, 3, 1875.	Wilson Roberts.
7, 26, 1875.	Elizabeth Foulke.
8, 11, 1875.	Martha Ball d.
9, 16, 1875.	Hannah Lester d.
10, 21, 1875.	Edwin Thomas.
1, 9, 1876.	William Cox's child.
9, 16, 1876.	Mary Ann Heacock d. (Infant.)
2, 28, 1876.	Franklin Deal d.
3, 8, 1876.	Jane Alice Zorns.
3, 15, 1876.	Sallie Meredith d.
3, 25, 1876.	Joseph Heacock.
4, 5, 1876.	James Burson
5, 7, 1876.	Olivia Strawn.
7, 25, 1876.	James Hoot.
8, 22, 1876.	Ellen Foulke.
12, 25, 1876.	Edwin Jackson's child.
1, 14, 1877.	Ellen Ball d.
3, 21, 1877.	Jane Richardson d.
4, 1, 1877.	Ann Morgan d.
11, 29, 1877.	Matilda Foulke d.
12, 27, 1877.	Charles Penrose d.
12, 28, 1877.	Sarah Ball d.
3, 21, 1882.	Abigail R. Heacock d.
3, 23, 1882.	Annie Roberts d.
10, 4, 1882.	Milton Johnson.
12, 28, 1882.	William Edwards.
3, 31, 1883.	Daniel Edwards.
4, 18, 1883.	Aaron Penrose.
4, 21, 1883.	Burroughs Michener.
4, 22, 1883.	Susan Johnson.
5, 10, 1883.	Joseph Johnson.
6, 17, 1883.	Henry Boyer.
7, 12, 1883.	Hannah Mann.
8, 2, 1883.	Edward Thomas d.
9, 14, 1883.	James Vanhouten.
10, 19, 1883.	Rachel Foulke.
2, 15, 1884.	Margaret Carr d.
3, 5, 1884.	Hannah Roberts d.
7, 10, 1884.	Joel W. Strawn.
9, 28, 1884.	Rachel Strawn.
9, 28, 1884.	Alice L. Hicks d.
12, 30, 1884.	Matilda S. Zorns d.
1, 6, 1885.	David Kenderdine d.
4, 12, 1885.	Kate Smulling.
4, 14, 1885.	Jane Strawn d.
4, 19, 1885.	Mary Ann Finley, *nee* Grear.
8, 25, 1885.	Deborah Moore d.
1, 2, 1886.	Keziah Foulke d.
3, 30, 1886.	Lizzie Kinsey, wife of George.
4, 18, 1886.	Maria Roberts d.
5, 6, 1886.	Stephen F. Penrose d.
7, 13, 1886.	Rollo. (Child.)

7, 14, 1886. Penrose Hicks.
8, 14, 1886. Cora Kinsey, child of George.
12, 9, 1886. Benjamin Roberts, son of Jesse Roberts.
1, 6, 1887. Eliza Ann Roberts.
6, 11, 1887. Annie Fillman, *nee* Foulke.
9, 4, 1887. Matilda Foulke d.
12, 25, 1887. Hucillia Edwards d.
2, 18, 1888. Caroline G. Foulke d.
3, 1, 1888. Joseph Morgan.
3, 27, 1888. Benjamin Roberts.
8, 14, 1888. Benjamin G. Foulke d.
8, 28, 1888. Samuel Kinsey.
9, 23, 1888. Joshua Foulke d.
11, 3, 1888. Nathan Hedges' wife. (Colored).
12, 28, 1888. Evan Penrose.
1, 3, 1889. Evan Paxson.
3, 14, 1889. David R. Jamison d.
5, 12, 1889. Henry Franklin. (Col.)
8, 14, 1889. Algernon Edwards d.
4, 6, 1890. Isaac Tomlinson.
10, 15, 1890. Joseph Fillman. (Inf.)
12, 12, 1890. Joseph R. Lancaster d.
1, 11, 1891. Annie Johnson d.
7, 20, 1891. Fred. Strawn d., son of C. F. Strawn.
11, 10, 1891. Elizabeth McRay.
12, 28, 1891. Anthony Johnson.
1, 16, 1892. Hannah Griffith d.
1, 22, 1892. Amos Edwards d.
1, 31, 1892. Margaret Dalby.
7, 22, 1892. Richard R. Green d.
6, 25, 1893. Maria Roberts.
7, 3, 1863. Bertha Linderman d.
7, 29, 1893. Mary Johnson d.
9, 28, 1893. Mary Ann Jackson d.
10, 20, 1893. Eli Strawn d.
11, 13, 1893. Angeline Stackhouse.
1, 22, 1894. Helen Johnson d.
1, 25, 1894. Joseph Hill.
2, 22, 1894. Hannah Mather d.
3, 6, 1894. Matilda G. Jamison d.
7, 1, 1894. Zachariah Mast.

8, 31, 1894. A. H. Degrote.
12, 19, 1894. Joseph Foulke.
3, 6, 1895. Alice Heacock.
3, 10, 1895. Israel S. Zorns d.
10, 6, 1895. John J. Moore d.
11, 4, 1895. Harry Bush d.
2, 22. 1896. Ann Wright.
3, 1, 1896. Dr. Chas. F. Meredith.
8, 11. 1896. Sarah Taney.
8, 30, 1896. Morgan Shaw's child.
12, 5, 1896. Hugh Foulke.
12, 12, 1896. Charles Cadwallader.
4, 10, 1897. Ellwood Ball.
4, 14, 1897. Wm. L. Strawn's child.
6, 28. 1897. Child of Samuel Bleam.
11, 6, 1897. Sarah Foulke.

———

7, 28, 1894. Robert Bockius, Richhill.
8, 8, 1894. Elizabeth Heacock, Delaware county.
9, 22, 1894. Annie Hicks Whitaker d., Philadelphia.
9, 30, 1894. Mary Hibberd d., Md.
10, 9, 1894. Joseph Hill d.
10, 10, 1895. Mrs. John Blank d.
2, 24, 1896. Edwin A. Jackson d., New York.
2, 25, 1896. Simon Springer, Sellersville.
3, 31, 1896. Samuel Gettman, Rockhill.
9, 21, 1896. Albert Paist d.
10, 5, 1896. Susanna Wolf.
10, 6, 1896. Washington Cressman.
1, 17, 1897. John Ball d., Philadelphia.
1, 25, 1897. Reading B. Slack d.
1, 28, 1897. Catharine Seigel, N. J.
2, 23, 1897. David R. Johnson d.
4, 1, 1897. Isaiah Flitcraft.
4, 9, 1897. Jacob Seigel d., Phillipsburg, N. J.
5, 6, 1897. Wm. Heacock d., Philadelphia.
9, 17, 1897. Ezekiel Thomas d.

VI.

ORIGINAL DOCUMENTS.

Under this head are given a number of original documents, most, or all of them, now in print for the first time. They are introduced at this point rather than in connection with the genealogical chapters further on in order to prevent a break in the continuity of the narration in connection with each family. The reader will perceive a reason for the use of each. Morris Morris' narrative of the convincement of his father is from the original paper in his handwriting in the possession of Eleanor Foulke, of Quakertown. It traces with such clearness and simplicity the various stages of persecution as to give an excellent idea of the motives inducing Friends to leave their old homes in England, Wales and elsewhere, and seek new ones in Pennsylvania. Evan Morris' story is that of many another of his time. The wills, inventories and other papers illustrate the customs and modes of life of our forefathers more clearly, perhaps, than could pages of description, revealing much of value as to eighteenth century life to a generation on the verge of the twentieth.

CONVINCEMENT OF EVAN MORRIS.

There is something on my mind to be set in writing what is in my memory concerning the convincement of my father, Evan Morris.

He was born in a small town called Grikhoth in Carnarvonshire [Wales] in the year 1654, of honest, religious parents, according to the manner of the Church of England. My father was brought up very strictly in that way, and when he was about the age of twenty-two years, he married my mother, a sober, religious woman, in the same profession. He was of a cheerful temper, given something to poetry and verses and singing, which seemed to be very pleasant to his companions in the loose way they lived ; but after he was married four or five years it pleased the Lord to lay a concern upon him for the salvation of his soul, which brought him at times very low in his mind, insomuch as my mother was afraid he was going melancholy, he being by nature of very cheerful temper to show so much chagrin.

I can remember, being then about five or six years of age, that he took mother in his arms and desired her to be easy. He must go somewhere, but he knew not where. So took his horse and proceeded about four and twenty miles to a town called Dolgelly, and was walking the street, very low in his mind. Then he saw a kinsman of his, so he went to him and asked him if he knew aught of those people called Quakers. He said, "The man who is the chief of them is in the town now." He asked him if he would go with him to the man. He was willing, so father asked the Friend if he would go with him to a tavern to drink a part of a mug of beer.

"No," said the Friend, "I have no occasion of drink." Then he desired his kinsman, being as he was acquainted with him, to tell him he wanted to have some discourse with him about his religion.

Then the Friend asked him where he came from. Father said, "Wales." The Friend asked him if he knew any of their Society. He said "No." Then he asked how he came to inquire for them, for they were despised by the world. He answered him that by searching the word of God (he meant the scriptures).

The Friend repeated to him the first of John concerning the Word that was in the beginning and was God.

So the Friend invited him home with him which was not far from the town, and there was a meeting at his house the next day in which Father was very much broken and tendered, insomuch that he spoke publicly of that he found of love of truth in his heart, as I was informed.

So the Friends would have him to stay with them till First-day, this meeting being the Fifth [day].

Father told Friends that he could not well stay, for he had left his wife in a very concerned condition for him, not knowing fully the occasion of it. The Friend that had spoke with him first (his name was Owen Lewis, a very well known minister) that if she knew the occasion of it she would not be troubled at it, for the husband was a better husband to the wife and the wife a better wife to the husband for coming to the truth of God.

So in parting Father told the Friend that he understood that they did not use the custom and fashion of bowing and taking off the hat, as he had been brought up in. The Friend told [him] that he must endeavor to come to the root of the matter in himself and he would gradually come through that. So Father told him that he was fully convinced that it was the truth and through the Lord's assistance he hoped that should be able to stand ground.

So they parted. As he was going home he met a Justice of the Peace of his acquaintance. Though it came close upon him to stand, but when he came to the man he only asked how he did, but the man looked at him with a stern look and said: "What a devil is come to you?" so passed along. So when he came home the noise went about that Evan Morris had turned a Quaker. So he that was Deacon or Bishop of Bangor came to the Parish Church as they called it on purpose to preach against the Quakers, and in his sermon told his hearers as Korah, Dathan and Abiram withstood Moses so the Quakers withstood Christ, and as the earth swallowed them so hell would swallow the Quakers. So my poor mother was [at] their worship and came home crying, in a sorrowful condition. Father asked her what was the matter with her. The matter was to so hear of a man being lost forever. So she told what the Bishop said concerning the Quakers.

Father desired her to be easy—he was but a man. So father heard of a man pretty near of that [who] pretended to be something of a Friend but a weak one, and got some acquaintance with him. They appointed to meet every other First-day at the houses of each and kept a meeting, and some of the neighbors met with them. There was no meeting of Friends in the county where he lived, but the priest of the parish became very angry and stirred the magistrates to apprehend them, but the other poor man was too weak to stand persecution, [he] shrank and could not stand his ground. So Father was apprehended and the oath of allegiance tendered to him. So he refused to take it. A mittimus was got and a prison was his portion, where he was called every quarter session and the oath tendered to him, he refusing to take it.

They asked him many ensnaring questions which by divine assistance he was made able to answer, but I can remember one that I have heard him tell of that the Judge told him that if he would put his hand on his breast and then on the bar and say [he] had good will to the king he should have his liberty. He not giving any answer presently they told the jailor to take him away to the jail. He was not used to be concerned with the law, but it opened in his mind that those that did so were apprehended for some treason against the king. Many that were standing by wondered that he could not do that for his liberty.

He told them that he could put his hand that he had no ill will against the king, but not in any form as if he had been guilty of any treason against the king which they knew false.

He had many disputes with the Bishop of Bangor and many other great men. I can remember that I have heard him say that he had pinched the Bishop so close that he grew angry and told him that he would be a witness against him in this world and in the world to come before the throne of Christ, which was a very presumptuous saying.

After the death of King Charles the Second, James came to be king. He gave liberty of conscience to those that were prisoners on the king's account. Then Father having his liberty the officers came for their fees. Father told them that he did not know that [he] owed them anything. They said that they were employed and they should be paid. He told them that those who employed them should pay them. Then they said the law gave it [to] them and [they] must have [it].

"Well," Father said, "I have suffered the law and have no freedom to give any [thing]." Then they seized his bed and furniture with other things that [were] worth two or three times the value of the fees. So when he came to the place where he had lived before, the priest of the parish was so bitter against him that he said that but either he or Evan Morris should live in the parish. Father had no real estate of his own. He went to his father to live for he had some thought of going to Pennsylvania. But while he tarried there his brother died. There were but two of them so his father desired him to stay for they could not tell how it stood in the brother's concerns, for they were both of the same trade of skin dressing and glovers, so that he could not well be easy but stay to see how his affairs were, and found there was a good deal of debt on him. So [he] set to work to dress up the skins, making them in gloves and took them to the market, and paid all the debts left by his brother. So he left his father and mother clear of the cumber of it. Then he removed to Dolgelly that he might be near Friends' meetings and waited an opportunity to come to Pennsylvania, and tarried there about three years till a number of Friends from the place called Bala in Merionshire were about going—so provided himself to go with them. So they and we went to Liverpool; so had a vessel there bound to Maryland. The passengers agreed with the Captain to bring them to the Horekill. It was a troublesome time at sea, being in King William's war with France, and many of the French privateers at sea, but, through the help of the Almighty God we got clear of them and had a pretty good passage considering it was in the fall of the year. Most of the passengers were Friends, so we had meetings once or twice a week, except it was exceeding stormy; and the Captain was very civil. He commanded the sailors to be very still meeting while. So we landed in about ten weeks at the Horekills, where we and most of the passengers remained some time and had meetings.

There were a good many Friends living there then but Hugh Roberts and Robert Owen came up by land and ordered settlements for themselves at Merion. So in the spring they hired a vessel and came down to us and we came up Schuylkill for the most part of the passengers had a mind to settle at Merion. So Father stayed at the sea. There was a meeting house there at that time where all the Friends in the house came, so he bought a house and lot and lived there about five years and followed his trade of gloving and skin dressing, and having a public testimony for truth traveled abroad some times to Chester county and other places about the province and more amongst his country folks, for he was more perfect in the Welsh tongue then.

At the end of about five years I seemed to have more mind to a plantation than the gloving trade, so Father seemed to stay willing and came to hear of a plantation at Abington to be sold with three hundred acres of land. So he bought it and sent me to work at it which seemed to be pretty hard at first, not having been used to hard work, but it came pretty natural at last. Father followed something of his trade of making gloves, not being much used to husbandry, and went sometimes to visit some meetings abroad, till he was about the age of fifty-four years, having met with exercise from some Friends which seemed pretty hard for him to bear.

So it happened to be the time of our Yearly Meeting at Burlington. I had a mind to be at the meeting, so went, not thinking, but stayed all the meeting. But after the first day something of a concern came on my mind that I must go home. So came home. It was pretty late in the night when I came home. My wife told Mother that Father was very unwell with a pain on one side of his face and throat.

So in the morning I went soon to see him; found him sitting by the fire in a sweet frame of mind and telling that he had some unusual pain in his throat. I asked him if I should go to a Doctor for him. He said "No." I sat with him some considerable time. He said that he found himself full of love to all men, and he had nothing but good will to all, for he seemed to be full of the love of God in his heart.

He spoke much of the goodness of God to him. After considerable time with him I went home, for I had not long gone to live there at my own place. He expected his daughter and son-in-law to come and live with him, as he intended to give them the plantation where he lived: So Mother was saying that he walked about all the day and at night brought the things home for the man that lived with them was gone to the Yearly Meeting. When he came in and sat by the fire awhile [he] said that he seemed to be sleepy and said to Mother he was willing to go to bed.

Mother said she would come soon after him. She went in a short time. He lay asleep as she thought, so she slept a little, but waked suddenly and found him sitting upon the bedside. * * * * * He fell backward and breathed no more. We imagined a quinsy he had in his throat had burst and strangled him, which was a great surprise to us, being so unexpected to us, and a melancholy surprise to poor Mother, being alone with him in the house. He was buried at Friends' grave-yard at Abington.

So this account is given by his son

MORRIS MORRIS.

[It should be mentioned that there has been no adherence to antiquated modes of spelling, use of capitals, etc., in the preceding reproduction of "Evan Morris' Convincement." The language of Morris Morris has been followed, however, very closely. In the will of John Roberts, which follows, the exact language, use of capitals, etc., are reproduced.]

WILL OF JOHN ROBERTS.

I, John Roberts, of Lower Milford Township, in the County of Bucks, in the State of Pennsylvania, being well in health and of sound mind and memory thanks be given to god Therefor calling to mind the mortality of my Body and Knowing that it [is] appointed for all men once to Die Do make this my last will and testament in writing in manner and form following that is to Say

First. It is my will and I do order that all my Just Debts and funeral Expenses Shall be paid and Discharged.

Item I Give and bequeath unto Mary Roberts my Beloved wife, one full half of all the Household goods and other Effects which she had at the time of our Marriage which may remain to be in my Possession at the time of my Decease Together also with one-half of all the money that can be recovered of Debts Due to her at the time of our Marriage, to hold, to her and her heirs & assigns forever and it is my will that my said wife Shall have the use and benefit of the other Half of the said household goods and other Effects During her Natural Life if She remains so long my widow, and also have the use of a cupboard & a Brass Kettle so long as she lives on the Premises herein willed to her and after her Decease or Marriage which may first happen all the said Goods & Effects that may be then remaining Shall be Equally Divided among my five Daughters hereinafter named.

I give and devise unto my son John Roberts and to his heirs and assigns all my Lands & Tenement situate in Lower Milford Township in the County of Bucks in the State of Pennsylvania to hold to him and to his heirs and assigns forever.

It is my will Nevertheless that in case my said son John Roberts Should happen to Die Seized of the said Lands and Tenement & without Lawful Issue that then the said Land & Tenement Shall Derive to my two Sons Edward Roberts and William Roberts and to their heirs and assigns forever to be held by them as Tenants in common and not as Joint Tenants. It is my will that in that case the Land Shall be appraised and one-third part of the Value of the said Land shall be Equally Divided among my five Daughters Namely Anne Penrose, Mary Penrose, Jane Green, Martha Worrough & Sarah Foulke, and paid to them by my two sons, Edward Roberts and William Roberts.

I will and order that my Son John Roberts Shall pay the sum of Twenty-five pounds into the hands of my Executors to be added to the Money arising out of my Personal Estate. It is my will & I Do order that my son John Roberts shall pay his Brother William the Sum of Eighty pounds in the Space of Eighteen Calendar Months after my Decease which Sum of Eighty pounds I Give unto my son William.

It is my will that my wife Mary Roberts shall Hold Occupy and enjoy the Store Room and the Room adjoining to it in the Brick house at her option, & also as Much of the Cellar and Springhouse as may be Necessary for her use Together also with one-half of the Garden for and During her Natural life if she remains so long my widow.

And She Shall have full Privilege to take apples or any other fruit out of the orchard for her own use.

It is my will that my son, John Roberts, or the Possessor or occupier of the said Lands Shall keep a Cow & a riding horse for my said wife and provide for her Sufficient of firewood ready Cut for use & Brought as near to the House as conveniently may be during her Natural life if she remains so long my widow & give unto her every year During her life or widowhood Eight

Bushels of wheat two Bushels of Rye and two Bushels of Indian-corn, Forty pounds of Good beef & Sixty pounds of good pork and also give her one Barrel of cider and half a Barrel of water Cider every year that the orchard Yields Apples Sufficient to admit of it & sow for her one quarter of an acre of Land with flaxseed & at all times Keep her Garden Sufficiently Dunged or Manured.

And in case my said wife should Marry then at the time of her Marriage all her Rights and Privileges in the House & Premises as well as all Claims and Demands that she has against my son John Roberts or the Possessor or occupier of my said Land by virtue of this my Last will shall Cease and Determine.

And it is my will that what I have herein given to my said wife Shall be Taken and Deemed to be in Lieu of her Dower.

I Give unto my son Edward the sum of Thirty pounds, to be Taken out of the Interest due to me upon Bond.

I Give to my son William the sum of Twenty-five pounds to be Taken out of Interest Due to me upon Bond.

I Give to my Son-in-law, John Penrose, the sum of ten pounds in Special Trust for the use of my grandson John Penrose.

I Give all my wearing apparel to my three sons Namely Edward, John and William to be Equally Divided Between them.

I Give my son Edward a Book Called Francis Howgill's Works.

I Give my son John all my Carpenter Tools and Sewell's History or George Fox's Journal at his choice.

I Give my Daughter Martha a Book Called Barclay's Apology And as I have Several more Journals and Histories, it is my will that my son William and my Daughters Anne, Jane, Mary and Sarah may have each of them one of the said Journals and Histories as they may agree to Take.

And it is my will and I Do order that all my household Goods & Movable Effects whatsoever that I have not herein given, bequeathed or disposed of Shall be Sold as Soon as Conveniently may be after my Decease either at public or Private sale at the Discretion of my Executors, and all the Money that may be Left remaining of my Estate after my Just Debts & Funeral and Other Necessary Expenses and the abovesaid Legacies are paid, I Give and Bequeath to my five Daughters to be Equally Divided among them Share and Share alike Namely, Anne Penrose, Mary Penrose, Jane Green, Martha Worrough and Sarah Foulke.

And I Do make ordain Constitute and appoint my Son Edward Roberts and my Son-in-law John Penrose Executors of this my Last Will and Testament And I Do hereby revoke and

Disannul all former Wills and Testaments by me at any time made Ratifying and Confirming this and none other to be my Last will and Testament.

In Testimony whereof I the Said John Roberts have hereunto set my hand and seal this fifth Day of December in the Year of our Lord one Thousand Seven Hundred and Ninety-one. JOHN ROBERTS. [SEAL.]

Signed Sealed published and
  pronounced by the said John
  Roberts as & for his Last
  will and Testament in the
  Presence of us.
  Abraham Ball.
  Nathan Ball.
  David Roberts.

The above will was probated February 24, 1797, by James Hanna, Register of Wills for Bucks, letters testamentary being granted to Edward Roberts and John Penrose.

MEMORIAL OF MARTHA ROBERTS.

A memorial concerning our worthy deceased Friend, Martha Roberts, wife of John Roberts, of Milford, Bucks county.

She was a daughter of our ancient friend, Hugh Foulke and Ann his wife, late of Richland, and being religiously educated, was in her young years an example of virtue and sobriety to her sex; and in the twenty-second year of her age, was married to Wm. Edwards, an approved minister of Richland Monthly Meeting. Her care and zeal for the promotion of religion increasing as she advanced in years, she was, in the year 1749, and twenty-ninth of her age, appointed an elder, being the first woman Friend appointed to that station in the said monthly meeting, after it was erected—in which service and that of an overseer she with a continued zeal and diligence labored for the maintenance of good order and our Christian discipline, and in the year 1754 received a portion of the gospel ministry, in which she engaged under great diffidence and self-abasement, and, growing in her gift, her labor therein was acceptable and edifying, both at home and abroad, as she frequently was concerned to visit the neighboring meetings, and several times visited the meetings of Friends in the back parts of New Jersey, and other distant places.

Her said husband, William Edwards, dying in the year 1764, she remained a widow six years, in which state she conducted with religious circumspection and prudence, with un-abated zeal and care in promoting the cause of truth and right-eousness until the year 1771 she accomplished her second marriage with John Roberts, a member of the same meeting, and continued through the remaining part of her life, as before, to show forth, by example as well as precept, an extensively benevolent and charitable disposition, in visiting and relieving the poor, the sick and distressed, not only of our religious So-ciety, but many others, whom, together with us, she being truly esteemed as a Mother in Israel, her loss is deeply felt amongst.

The last year of her life she was much confined at home by illness, which gradually increasing, brought her body into a very weak state, under which dispensation of Providence she often expressed her satisfaction and full resignation, being fre-quently favored with the enjoyment of spiritual comfort and inward help, as she expressed it, to wait with patience her ap-proaching change, and being preserved sensible to the last, she departed this life as going into a sweet sleep on the 17th of Fourth-month, 1781, and was decently buried the 19th of the same, in the 65th year and 27th of her ministry.

5th-mo. 20, 1781.   Samuel Foulke.

MARRIAGE CERTIFICATES.

The following is a copy of the original marriage certificate of Benjamin and Jane Green, in possession of Mary Emma Green, of Quakertown.

Whereas, Benjamin Green of Richland in the county of Bucks, son of Joseph Green & Catharine his wife late of Spring-field in the said county Deceased, and Jane Roberts daughter of John Roberts of Lower Milford in the county of Bucks aforesaid & his late wife Martha deceased; having declared their Intentions of Marriage with each other before several Monthly Meetings of the People called Quakers at Richland aforesaid, according to the good order used amongst them & having Consent of re-lations and parties concerned their said proposals of Marriage were allowed of by the said Meetings.

Now these are to Certifie all whom it may concern that for the full accomplishing of their said Intentions this Ninth day of the Eleventh month in the year of our Lord One Thousand Seven Hundred & Seventy-five they the said Benjamin Green & Jane Roberts appeared at a Public Meeting of the said people at Richland aforesaid & the said Benjamin Green taking the said

Jane Roberts by the hand did in solemn manner openly declare that he took her the said Jane Roberts to be his wife promising with divine assistance to be unto her a loving and faithful husband until death separate them; and then and there in the same assembly the said Jane Roberts did in like manner declare that she took the said Benjamin Green to be her husband promising with divine assistance to be unto him a faithful and loving wife until death separate them.

And moreover they the said Benjamin Green & Jane Roberts, she according to the Custom of Marriage assuming the name of her husband, as a further confirmation thereof did then and there to these presents set their hands, & we whose names are hereunder also written being present at the solemnization of the said Marriage have as witnesses thereof hereunto set our hands the Day and year above written.

BENJAMIN GREEN.
JANE GREEN.

John Lancaster	James Walton	Margaret Roberts
Will'm Foulke	Thomas Edwards	Phebe Roberts
Sam'l Foulke	Hannah Edwards	Ann Foulke
Thomas Foulke	William Edwards	Amelia Foulke
Jane Foulke	John Thomas	John Roberts
Ann Foulke	Elizabeth Thomas	James Green
Martha Hallowell	John Roberts	Thomas Green
Alice Roberts	Martha Roberts	Martha Roberts, jr
Israel Roberts	Thomas Thomas	Martha Foulke
Everard Foulke	Wm Heacock	Sarah Roberts
Richard Roberts	John Penrose	Elizabeth Roberts
Amos Roberts	Anne Penrose	Anne Thomas
Margaret Thomas	William Penrose	Priscilla Roberts
Samuel Penrose	Mary Penrose	
Isaac Lewis	Edward Roberts	

William Green son of Benjamin & Jane Green was born the tenth day of November 1776.

Hannah Green was born the 29th of September 1778.

Evan Green was born the 10th day of November 1780.

Benj. Green was born the Tenth day of December 1782.

Jane Green was born the 8th of February 1785.

James Green was born the 4 day of March 1787.

Lydia Green was born 20th day of February, 1789.

Joseph Green was born 14th day of February, 1791.

Martha Green was born February ye 14th, 1793.

John Green was born 24th of March 1795.

Abigail Green was born March the 18th 1799.

The following is a copy of the original marriage certificate of William Green and Mary Roberts, in possession of Mary Emma Green, Quakertown:

This is to certify that on the Seventeenth day of April in the year of our Lord One Thousand Eight Hundred and Four, before me David Spinner one of the Justices of the Peace in and for the County of Bucks William Green of Richland Township in Bucks County aforesaid [and Mary Roberts] were legally joined in marriage each of them Declaring themselves free respectively from prior engagement or other lawfull impediments In Witness whereof as well they the said William Green and Mary Green she assuming the name of her said Husband, as I the said David Spinner and other the witnesses present have hereunto Subscribed our Names the day and year aforesaid.

WILLIAM GREEN.
MARY GREEN.

David Spinner.
Samuel Roberts.
Mira McCarty.
Samuel Jamison.
Alice Roberts.
Jesse Roberts.
Caty Spinner.
Catharine Spinner.

William was 27 years 5 months and 7 days old when married.

Mary his wife was 19 years 15 days old when married.

ROBERT AND SUSANNA HEATH.

Philadelphia, 12th-mo 10, 1816.

In a pleasant conversation we had at thy house respecting our ancestors, I mentioned a worthy pair from whom we both descended, who arrived in this country about the year 1701 (See Mary Emlen's Memorial) with five daughters and one son, and thee wishes to be furnished with some account of them and their descendants. I have spent a leisure hour in endeavoring to oblige thee, an esteemed friend and kinsman; although it may not be quite perfect, having nothing but memory to govern me, and it is reasonable to suppose that is much impaired, being in the 78th year of my age, yet I believe it is nearly correct as far as it goes.

The couple alluded to were Robert and Susanna Heath, who arrived from England as above. Their children were: Ann, married to Richard Waln, their descendants were the father of the late Richard and Nicholas Waln, of this city; Joseph, who settled near where Norristown now stands, died without issue; Robert, the father of the present Robert Waln, of this city, and Richard, father of the late Jesse Waln, the daughters, if any, I did not know. Susanna married Morris Morris, of Abington, their children were: Samuel, settled at White Marsh, never married; Joshua (thy grandfather), Daniel, the father of the late Robert Morris (miller) and Ann Humphreys, the wife of Richard Humphreys, of this city, Morris, father of the present Susanna Morris and the late Governor Mifflin's wife, and David, died a young man; their daughters were Sarah, married James Paul, of Abington; Susanna married Thomas Fletcher, of Abington; one married Thomas Evans, of North Wales, and one married Abel Roberts, of Richland; Elizabeth married Thomas Livezey, of Lower Dublin, their children were Susanna (my mother) married Daniel Thomas, of Abington; Rachel, married Thomas Roberts, of Bristol; Martha married Joseph James, brother of the late Abel James, of Philadelphia, Mary, wife of the late Joseph Paul, of Spring Mill; Thomas, father of the present John and Joseph Livezey and Elizabeth married John Shoemaker, of Cheltenham; Hannah first married Worrell, then Sermon, lastly to Husford. I believe her descendants were few. Joseph Sermon, whose widow Mary now lives near Green Street Meeting, was one of her sons; Mary married George Emlen, of Philadelphia. Their children were George, father of the late George and Caleb Emlen, of this city; Hannah married William Logan, and was the mother of the late Doctor Logan, and grandmother of Hannah Smith, wife of James Smith, her other sisters, if any, I do not remember. Richard Heath, their only son, died single. I have understood if he had lived he was to have been married into the Norris family. He was Recorder of Deeds, and, I believe, Clerk of the Court.

I have given thee an account of some of the numerous descendants of a worthy couple, of whom we are a part. If not correct, I suppose it is as near so as can at this time be obtained, believing there are now few, if any, living who have known as many of the different branches as myself, and although there may be many blemishes amongst us, yet I believe as I mentioned to thee the other day, there are as many of respectability as in most other connections (with the exception, if thee please, I then made). If thee should preserve this account it may, perhaps, in a future day, be some consolation to know so many of the branches of that stock with which thou art connected, also in remembrance of thy ancient friend and kindred.

DANIEL THOMAS.

To Joshua Longstreth.

By way of continuing the Heath-Livezey genealogy to the present day in one line at least, that of Thomas Livezey 2d, it may be added that he was born 1st-mo. 25, 1723. He married Martha, daughter of John and Ann Knowles, born 4th-mo. 25, 1723, at Abington, 4th-mo. 2, 1748. He died of paralysis 9th-mo. 11, 1790, and was buried at Germantown.

Samuel Livezey, son of Thomas and Martha, born 1st-mo. 26, 1760, married, at Plymouth Meeting, 11th-mo. 14, 1793, Mary, daughter of James and Rebecca Wood, born 5th-mo. 7, 1769. She died 2d-mo. 2, 1833, and Samuel 9th-mo. 3, 1840, Both were buried at Plymouth Friends' ground. Their children:

Thomas, 10th-mo. 22, 1795, d. 11th-mo. 9, 1802.

Martha, 10th-mo. 13, 1797, d. 12th-mo. 18, 1864; m. Jacob Albertson, father of J. Morton Albertson, of Norristown, deceased.

Rachel, 8th-mo. 9, 1799, d. 4th-mo. 14, 1883; m. Jonathan Maulsby.

Samuel, 8th-mo. 16, 1801, d. 10th-mo. 11, 1860, unmarried.

Thomas, 4th-mo. 19, 1803, d. 10th-mo. 2, 1879; m. Rachel Richardson. Among their children were John, Henry (both unmarried), Edward, decd., who married Mary Balderston; Their children are John, Henry and Martha. Samuel, m. Mary Roberts, and has one child, Thomas H. Livezey; Joseph R., m. Deborah Morgan, and has children; T. Ellwood, m. Mary Childs; their children: Rachel, m. Samuel Ifill, Anna, Thomas, Walter, Emily and others deceased.

William, 7th-mo. 3, 1804, d. 5th-mo. 8, 1805.

Joseph, 11th-mo. 3, 1806, d. 7th-mo. 4, 1844; m. Edith S. Burr. Charles A. Livezey, of Gwynedd, and Joseph Burr Livezey, of Mount Royal, N. J., are among their children.

Mary, 7th-mo. 31, 1808, d. 11th-mo. 5, 1896, m. Lewis Jones.

Ann, 12th-mo. 10, 1812, d. 7th-mo. 1, 1875, m. William Ely.

The children of Joseph R. and Deborah Livezey are Sarah and Morgan. Samuel Livezey, son of Thomas and Martha, was a recommended minister, and traveled much in the exercise of his gift from 1813 to 1838, chiefly within the limits of Philadelphia Yearly Meeting. He did much good among the poor, the sick and the afflicted, particularly among those who were overlooked and neglected by the world.

Rachel R. Livezey, widow of Thomas Livezey, died 6th-mo. 21, 1890, in her eighty-second year.

PETITION FOR GUARDIANS.

The petition for guardians mentioned below was presented to the Bucks county court December 12, 1751:

The Petition of Thomas Lancaster administrator of Thomas Lancaster, his Late Father In the sd. County Yeoman, Deceased was exhibited to the Court and Read Praying that Proper Persons may be appointed Guardians for the Children of the sd. Intestate, that are not arrived at age to Choose for themselves.

And Likewise to Admit those that are Arrived at Age to Choose for themselves, &c. The sd. petitioned likewise Produces the Names and Ages of the sd. Intestate's Children which are as follows, viz:

John Lancaster, born ye 10th of the	12-Month		1732
Phebe Lancaster, "	4th	10	1734
Job Lancaster, "	13th	8	1736
Joseph Lancaster, "	21st	8	1738
Jacob Lancaster, "	27th	3	1740
Isaac Lancaster, "	4th	12	1742
Aaron Lancaster, "	24th	2	1744
Moses Lancaster, "	3rd	10	1746
Elizabeth Lancaster,"	26th	6	1748

And the sd. John Lancaster Aged 19 Years Appears in Court & Chooses Thomas Ross for his Guardian.

And the said Job Aged 15 Years Likewise Appears and Chooses the aforesaid Thomas Ross for his Guardian, which is allowed according To their Respective Choices now made in Court.

And the Court also Appoints the aforesaid Thomas Ross & Wm. Edwards Guardians for the said Joseph, Jacob, Isaac, Aaron, Moses and Elizabeth Lancaster who are all Now Under the Age of 14 Years.

INVENTORIES.

An Inventory of the goods and Chattels of Thomas Roberts late of Lower Milford in ye County of Bucks Deceased, as the same were appraised the 18th day of June 1767 by Samuel Foulke & Joseph Rawlings Two Freeholders of the said County.

	£.	s.	d.
His wearing apparrel............................	5	05	0
his Bed, bed Clothes, Curtains & all appurtens.....	5	10	0
Do some old linnens.............................	0	7	6
Cash	4	7	6
Five Pewter plates...........................	0	5	0
a pair of Tongs..............................	0	3	6
a Close Stool................................	1	0	0
Three Chairs.................................	0	8	0
A Saddle.....................................	0	12	6
A Walnut Chest...............................	1	5	0
A Bond of Nathaniel Allison..................	10	0	0
Ditto of Do................................	10	0	0
Do of Thomas Stalford.................	11	0	0
Do of William Heacock £16 with interest	16	19	6
Do of John Lester £26 with one year's interest	27	11	3
Do of Thomas Roberts Junr £10 with 13 years interest	17	16	0
Do of Do £25 with 8 years interest.....	37	0	0
money due upon a bond of Aaron Feller......	1	10	0
Do Due upon a Bond of John Roberts....	24	3	2
Do Due on a Bond of Thomas Roberts Junr	61	13	2
Do Due on a bond of Richard Roberts....	4	2	4
Due upon a Note Edward Thomas..........	1	16	0
Sum of the Assets.............235	235	19	11
Sum of the Legacies.......... 75	75	15	0
Remainder 160	160	4	11

An Inventory of the goods Chattles Rights & Credits of Edward Thomas late of Richland in Bucks County dec. taken & appraised this Sixteenth day of April Anno Dom. 1782 by us the Subscribers.

	£	s.	d.
Purse & Apparrel..............................	15	14	3
in the Back rom			
Bedstead Bed & Beding........................	10	5	

	£	s.	d.
Case of Drawers.............................	7		
Dressing Table 45s. Looking Glass 40s.........	4	5	
Six Chairs & an Armed Do....................	2	5	
Five plates one dish and two Bowls............		10	
Stand		18	

Front Rom

	£	s.	d.
Desk	5		
Spice Box 10s. Dining Table 30s..............	2		
Tea table 30s. two Windsor Chairs 12s..........	2	2	
Four Chairs 10s. And Irons & fire Shovel 12s.....	1	2	
Bible & other Books 20s. Six plates one dish 7s. 6..	1	7	6
One doz. pewter plates one pewter mug & two spoons	1		
Four glass bottles 5s. spoon mould 7s. 6........		12	6

Front Room Upstairs

	£	s.	d.
Bedsteads Bed & beding.......................	5	15	

Back Room Upstairs.

	£	s.	d.
Bedstead Bed & beding.......................	4		

Garret.

	£	s.	d.
Upper & Soal Leather........................		15	
Flaxseed Sieves & Lumber....................		6	

Stove Room.

	£	s.	d.
Clock	9	10	
Bedstead Bed & Beding.......................	4	10	
Couch	4		
Joint Stool Table 6s. Gun 37s. 6..............	2	3	6
Shoemaker Tools & Lasts 10s. five chairs 13s....	1	3	

Kitchen.

	£	s.	d.
Copper kettle 7s. 6 Iron pots & kettle 37s. 6.......	2	5	
Large brass kettle 50s. Pot rack & chain 4s.......	2	14	
Four flat Irons 12s. Shovel and Tongs 3s.........		15	
Two candlesticks Ladle fleshfork chopping knife & lamp		8	
Hatchel 7s. 6 dough trough 4s. Pewter &c. on the Dresser 22s. 6	1	14	

Cellar.

	£	s.	d.
Churn 18s. cedar tubs & Buckets 10s.............	1	8	
Casks and Tubs...............................	1	7	

Kitchen Loft.

	£	s.	d.
Bedstead Bed & beding.......................	1	15	
Saddle & Saddle Bags.........................		15	
Two long & two small Spinning wheels..........	1		
Check Reel 5s. half bushel 2s...................		7	

	£	s.	d.
Two pair of Iron Hopples 6s. six bags 9s.........		15	
Lumber 12s. horse Gears 22s. 6 Log chain 6.....	2		6
Two pitching Axes 5s. three Rakes 2s..........		7	

[Barn.]

	£	s.	d.
Waggon	4	10	
Grubbing hoe weeding Do. & Shovel............	7	6	
Cutting Box & knife..........................		12	
Two pitch forks one dung fork & nine Cow Chains	1	4	
Plough & Irons 25s. Harrow 20s................	2	5	
Thirteen Old Sheep & three Lambs.............	8		
Wheat & Rye in the Ground....................	8		
Young Sorrel Mare............................	16		
Roan Mare	2	10	
Old Sorrel Mare..............................	12		
Little brown Horse...........................	9		
The Brown Horse.............................	15		
Brown Mare Colt.............................	5		
Roan Colt	3	10	
Red Cow	5		
Do.	5		
Brindle Cow	5	10	
Red Do.	4	10	
Young pied Do...............................	5		
Red Heifer	4		
Red Do.	2	15	
Do.	3	2	6
Two Heifers	4		
Bull & Steer.................................	3	10	
Bull	4		
Three Young Calves..........................	2	10	
Sow and Pigs................................	1	15	
A Bond agt. John Dennis princl. £100 Int. £30..130			
Jonathan Penrose princl. £100 Int. £18 118			
William Thomas princl. £179 Int. £42 19s. 2.....................221	19	2	
Thomas Foulke senr. princl. £20.... 20			
William Foulke princl. £14 Int. £50 4 16	10	4	
Robt. Ashton princl. £100 Int.£6...106			
Thomas McCarty princl. £13 Int. 77s. 11 16	17	11	
Joseph Ball princl. £10.......... 10			

	£	s.	d.

Ebenezer Walker princl. £100......100
A Note against Willm. Heacock Junr. prn. £15... 15
William Thomas prin. £21 Int.
£15 2s. 4..................... 36 2 4
John Dennis prin. £12 Int. £3 12s. 15 12
Book Debt 41s............................ 2 1

JOHN GREASLEY
JAMES CHAPMAN

Personally appeared before me George Weiker one of the Justices of the Peace in and for the County of Bucks the above named John Greasley and James Chapman and tuck their salm affirmation that they have appraised the goods and gadel of Edward Thomas of Richland township leade decesed upon their best schill & Judgement. Witness my hand this 8th-day of May A. D. 1782.

GE. WEICKER.

AN OLD LETTER.

Quakertown, Twelfth-mo. 20, 1831.

Respected Cousins:

I take this opportunity to inform you of the death of your sister, Mary Thomas.

She departed this life on the 19th inst., in a quiet sweet frame of mind, perfectly resigned to meet the awful summons. I was with her in her last moments, and it seemed with me to say: "Blessed are the dead that die in the Lord."

About eight days previous to her decease, she unfortunately fell, and dislocated her hip joint, which caused her a great deal of pain and threw her into a fever. Her cough increased and her sufferings were great for a few days, but she bore it with a great deal of patience and the last two days of her life she appeared very quiet, and died like a person falling asleep.

Aunt Martha and Cousin Lydia are neither of them very well. Cousin Lydia buried her husband on the eighth of this month. He died suddenly of a fever that was prevailing in this place. She feels her loss sensibly. She has two small children. We also feel the loss. They have lived in the house with us since they commenced housekeeping.

Mother and myself are as well as usual. Mother is growing feeble. She desires to be affectionately remembered to thee and thy family, as do Aunt Martha and Cousin Lydia.

I expect thou hast heard of the death of thy sister, Elizabeth [Roberts] Foulke. She departed this life on the 17th inst., and was buried yesterday morning. Excuse my not mentioning it sooner. I expect thou wast informed of her decease by her family.

Please excuse this scrawl. I am in a hurry and have a very poor pen.

Please give my love to thy daughters and accept a large share thyself and wife. From your Cousin

LYDIA GREEN.

Amos and Margaret Roberts.

THE WORRELLS.

The name spelled 'Worrough" in the will of John Roberts, in speaking of his married daughter Martha, and in many contemporary documents, should be Worrell, as appears from the following letter and statement among the papers of Amos Roberts, now in possession of the author, his great grandson (Amos then lived on his farm, Mount Pleasant, near Branchtown, Philadelphia) and from other undoubted authority:

5th-Month 25th, 1810.

Cousin John Worrell:

I have succeeded in getting good places for thy two daughters, Jane & Abigail. I have allotted Jane to Robert Morris Esq., and Abigail to his son-in-law, Jonathan Roberts—two very good places. Thee must know Robert Morris, Uncle Abel Roberts' nephew, living near Frankford. They are very much pleased with the good account I have given them of the girls and are very desirous of their coming and will do right by them. Thee will please send them next Fourth-day or Seventh-day at farthest.

I believe it will be best to send them on Seventh-day, as I will make it my business to come to town and take charge of them and convey them to Robert Morris's. Very respectfully

Thy kinsman,

AMOS ROBERTS.

The above is evidently the rough draft of a letter which was rewritten and mailed to Josiah Worrell. On the same sheet is the following statement:

The following are the ages [of] Jane and Abigail Worrell as I took [them] from the account kept by their father Isaiah [Josiah?] Worrell or their mother who was my first cousin,

Martha Roberts was her maiden name, who deceased the first month last.

Jane Worrell was born first month 31st, 1792.

Abigail Worrell was born twelfth month 24th, 1793.

The above girls were placed by their father under my care.

I placed Jane at Robert Morris Esq.'s 6th-mo 6th not to recive wages until the 7th of 6th-mo., 1810. Abigail I placed at Jonathan Roberts' same time.

WILL OF EDWARD THOMAS.

To all Christian people whom these presents may concern be it known that I Edward Thomas of Richland in the County of Bucks Yeoman being in health & of perfect memory, Considering the uncertainty of time & the mortallity of my Body, do make & put in writing this my last Will & Testament in manner & form as followeth—

First, it is my Will that all my Just Debts & funeral Expenses be carefully paid & discharged.

Secondly, I give & devise unto my Son Samuel Thomas all my Lands & real Estate, consisting of the House & Lot of Ground whereon I dwell Together with my Farm & tract of land thereunto belonging situate in the Township of Richland aforesaid Containing in the whole One Hundred & fifty acres, To Hold to him my said Son Samuel his heirs & assigns forever, and also the rents & profits arising therefrom after my decease, and I do appoint my Trusty Friends Thomas [Thomas] & Thomas Foulke Esqr. to be his Guardians during the time of his minority.

Thirdly, I give & bequeath unto my beloved Wife Alice Thomas the Sum of two Hundred pounds to be at her disposal forever in lieu of Dower. I give her also the free use of one half of the House in which I now live, so long as she remains my widow, and the use of one half of ye Garden & Orchard & half of the pasture ground on the Lott whereon my said Dwelling house stands during her widowhood as aforesaid & no longer.

4thly. I give unto my Daughter Margaret the Sum of One Hundred & Fifty pounds Current money of Pennsylvania.

5thly. I give unto my Daughter Miriam Heacock the sum of One Hundred & fifty pounds currency aforesaid.

6thly. I give unto my Infirm Daughter Mary the like sum of One Hundred & fifty pounds, or the Interest of that sum yearly during her life, but if the said Interest will not be sufficient for her support, it is my will that the principal be made use of for that purpose at the discretion of my Loving Friends Thomas Thomas and Thomas Foulke above named whom I do appoint to take care of her as of her said Legacy, and the remainder thereof if any be after her decease & burial to be equally divided between my surviving children. Nevertheless if it shall please Providence to restore her to her health & faculties she shall have the full Possession and Disposal of the abovesaid Sum, any thing herein to ye contrary notwithstanding.

7thly. I give unto my Daughter Martha the sum of One Hundred & Fifty pounds Current money as aforesaid.

8thly. I will the residue of my Estate, if any be, shall be equally divided amongst all my Children share and share alike.

9thly. My will is & I do hereby order, that if any of my Children shall dye before they arrive to the age of Twenty one years without Issue, the share or shares of such of them so dying shall be Equally divided between all the rest of my surviving Children.

Lastly. I do ordain & appoint my Loving Friends Thomas Thomas & Thomas Foulke above-named to be my Executors of this my last Will and Testament hereby revoking and annulling all other & former Will or Wills Testament or Testaments & Executors by me before this time made or named, ratifying & confirming this & no other to be my last Will and Testament. In Witness whereof I have hereunto set my hand & seal the Twenty third Day of July in the year of our Lord One Thousand Seven Hundred & Seventy Five.

EDWARD THOMAS. [SEAL.]

Sealed signed & de-
clared by the said
Testator to be his
last Will & Testa-
ment in the presence of us
    Samuel Foulke
    John Thomas
    John Foulke

P. S. My brother Thomas Thomas above named being Deceased since the Executing of the above Written Will, I do therefore ordain & appoint my Son Samuel Thomas in his stead to be my Executor in Conjunction with my Friend Thomas Foulke above named. In witness [etc.] the sixth day of May, 1781. EDWARD THOMAS. [SEAL.]

Saml Foulke.

The will was proved May 31, 1782, William Hart being Register.

EDWARD ROBERTS.

Edward Roberts was a native of Merionethshire, Wales, where he was born in Third-month (May), 1687. The reader should remember that the New Year began with March at that time. He came to this country in 1699, with "his cousin, Thomas Lawrence" (according to a tradition handed down in the family). From this circumstance it has been supposed that he was left an orphan at an early age. He settled at Byberry, and early became a member of Abington Monthly Meeting, the nearest at that date.

At the monthly meeting held at Abington 10th-month 27, 1714, the following minute was made:

"Whereas Edward Roberts and Mary Bolton having declared their intentions of marriage with each other before two monthly meetings, enquiry being made by persons appointed and found clear from all others on ye account of marriage did accomplish their marriage in ye unity of ffriends as is signified by their marriage certificate."

As previously mentioned, the journey to the Great Swamp was made in the spring of 1716. Their firstborn child Martha was then about six months old.

At the monthly meeting held at Abington Eleventh-month 28, 1716, the following entry was made on the minutes:

"A certificate was granted Edward Roberts and his wife in order for their removing hence to the Great Swamp."

Persons familiar with the customs of Friends are aware that such certificates are not usually requested until some time after the proposed change has been made. In this case about six months intervened.

It must not be imagined that he went to a new settlement without having made provision for the future, so far as it was possible. He had secured a warrant for 250 acres of land at Great Swamp, from the Commissioners of Property, bearing date Ninth-month 17, 1715, which tract was surveyed and laid out on First-month 13, 1716, "unto Edward Roberts yeoman." Having accomplished so much, he made application to the Commissioners of Property for a patent for the tract, which was given to him, and the original is now in the possession of a descendant, Evan Roberts Penrose, of Quakertown. This deed bears date "November 21, 1716, in the third year of the reign of King George over Great Britain." The patent recites the foregoing facts, and adds: "Know ye that for and in consideration of the aforesaid grant and of the sum of 37£ 10s. the said Commissioners of Property have granted to the said Edward Roberts the said tract of 250 acres of land with all Mines, Minerals, Quarries, Meadows, Marshes, Savannas, Swamps, Cripples, Woods, Underwoods, Timber and Trees, Ways, Waters, Water Courses, Liberties, Profits, Commodities, Advantages, Hereditaments and Appurtenances whatsoever the said 250 acres of land, belonging or in any wise appertaining and lying within the bounds and limits aforesaid (three full and clear fifth parts of all royal mines free from all deductions and reprisals for digging and refining only excepting and hereby reserved) and free right and liberty to the said Edward Roberts his heirs, etc., to hawk, hunt, fish and fowle in and upon the hereby granted lands and premises, yielding and paying therefor to my heirs and survivors at Pennsbury aforesaid at and upon the first day of March in every year from the first survey thereof an English silver half crown for the whole said 250 acres or value thereof in coin current to such persons as shall from time to time be appointed to receive the same, &c., &c."

The circumstances attending their settlement at Great Swamp have been briefly narrated (Chapter I, page 19), including the return to Gwynedd in order to obtain the benefit of such attention and medical care as was necessary in a case of the kind. The cure effected, the couple returned in the same way they had come. A temporary habitation had been built, which was used by the family until 1729, when a substantial stone house was erected, a portion of which remained until 1868. It had a window in the attic, of small panes of glass, and with leaden sash, in the style of colonial days. The date stone in the gable bore the inscription "E & M. R., 1729." The antique window was preserved for some time by Stephen Foulke, the present owner and occupant of the property, but was carried off several years ago by a tenant, when he moved away from the property. The wigwams of the Indians were to be found along the streams which, according to tradition, swarmed with shad and other fish, while the woods abounded with game. The children of Edward and Mary Roberts have been named on page 37, and the dates of birth and also of the death of most of them given. All were born at Richland, as it came to be called in due time, except Martha, mentioned as having been born in Byberry.

THE BOLTONS.

Mary Bolton, wife of Edward Roberts, was the daughter of Everard and Elizabeth Bolton. The Boltons are an ancient English family, its head being possessed of landed estates at the time of the Conquest. These were located in Lancashire and Yorkshire. The name was originally Bodelton, probably from boel, a mansion. The family has traced its ancestry back for many centuries to the Lord of Bolton, who is said to have been bow-bearer to the royal forests of Bowland and Gilsland, and who was the lineal representative of the Saxon earls of Murcia. From this family it is regarded as probable that Everard Bolton sprung. His family were Friends, and they suffered persecution with others of that people on account of their religion.

Everard Bolton and his wife came from Ross in Herefordshire, England, in 1682, and settled in Cheltenham, where Everard became prominent in the business meetings of Friends, he being treasurer of Abington meeting for nearly forty years. He settled on a tract of land a little east of where Milestown now is, his eldest son occupying it in turn.

A monument, which was set to mark the boundary of Everard Bolton's land, is still pointed out, some distance below Abington Friends' School, at the side of the road leading to what has been known as Hallowell's mill, on Tacony creek. It is of native stone, two and a-half feet in height. Few of the early settlers of Cheltenham were better known than he, and his name received very frequent mention in the records of Abington Monthly Meeting. He was appointed a Justice of the Peace, at a Council held in Philadelphia, May 30, 1715. His wife died June 5, 1707, and he married, some time afterwards, Margaret, widow of John Jones. He died in 1727, leaving the following children, all by his first wife:

Everard, born in Ross, England, March 28, 1680. He became a glover and married Mary, daughter of Robert Naylor, of Plymouth, settling in Abington. Their children were Priscilla, Mary, Elizabeth and Samuel.

Elizabeth, born also in Ross, June 26, 1681. She married Ellis Davis, in 1709, and settled in Cheltenham. He died in 1745, and she in August, 1749. Their children were Deborah, 1710; David, 1712; Abel, 1715; Ziba and Hannah, twins, 1718; Lydia, who married John Hurr.

Hannah, born in Cheltenham, December 22, 1684, married Richard Carver, Byberry, in 1708. Their children were Mary, 1709; Ann, 1710; Sarah and John. Richard Carver died in 1727.

Mary, born in Cheltenham, Nov. 4, 1687, married Edward Roberts, as already detailed, in 1714, and removed with him to the "Great Swamp," in 1716. The names of their children are given elsewhere.

Samuel, born October 31, 1689, married Sarah Dilworth. She died in 1732. Rachel Roberts, who died in 1751, named her "trusty friend, Samuel Bolton of Cheltenham," her executor. Samuel and Sarah Bolton had but one child, Hannah, so far as appears, who married John Coombs. He having been absent for many years, she, first obtaining the consent of Friends, married John Clark, in 1745.

Abel, born November 9, 1691; died in his eleventh year.

Sarah, born November 25, 1693, married William Bolton,

and in 1751, Michael Brown. She resided on Front street above Race, Philadelphia, and died there, leaving no children.

Lydia, born September 3, 1695, married John Biddle, in April, 1721. He died June 17, 1750, and she fourteen years later, leaving eleven children, as follows: Elizabeth (Pearson), Sarah, 1723; Hannah (Waterman) 1727, died August 17, 1772; Josiah, 1729; John, 1730; Abigail, 1731; Joseph, 1733; Lydia, 1735; Mary, 1736; John, 1738; Martha, 1741.

Isaac, born June 27, 1697, married Sarah Jones, in 1724. He resided in Philadelphia for several years subsequent to 1722, on the north side of Market street, below Second. In 1750, he removed to Abington, still later buying a large tract of land in Bucks county, where he spent the rest of his days. He called it "The Bolton Farm," which name it still bears, though it passed from the family more than a century ago. He dealt in skins, and his name appears in deeds and other documents as "Isaac Bolton, peltermonger." He became one of the wealthiest men in the province. Isaac and Sarah Bolton had eight children: Margaret, Rachel, Sarah, Rebecca, Jemima, Jesse, Joseph and Everard.

It may be noted here that the executors of Everard Bolton's estate, named in his will, were Isaac Bolton and Edward Roberts, his son-in-law, and the records show that both of them acted in such capacity.

Martha, born May 20, 1703, probably died in infancy.

In this connection it may be mentioned that Priscilla, daughter of Everard Bolton, Jr., married Cornelius Conard, son of Matthias Conard, of Germantown, March 24, 1732. She died November 22, 1765. Their children were Matthew, 1733; Mary, 1735; Everard, 1741; Joseph, 1742; Samuel and John, twins, 1744; Susanna, 1750. Of these Samuel Conard and his wife, Mary, had six children, Sarah, Samuel, Hannah, Ruth, Samuel and Cornelius; John and Sarah, his wife, had six also: Hannah, Priscilla, Benjamin, Esther, Sarah and John. The Conards are of German descent, the first of the family in this country being Dennis Kunders, who settled in Germantown, in 1683. Of the other children of Everard, Mary is mentioned in her father's will, but nothing further is known of her; Elizabeth was born June 26, 1718; Samuel married Mary Livezey, residing first in Abington and afterwards in Byberry, dying September 12, 1757. His children were Mary, who married John Paul, and died in 1796, and Martha.

Samuel Bolton, a descendant of Everard Bolton, born 1771, married Rachel Scull, was a man of inventive genius, an associate of John Fitch, of steamboat fame. Many models of his patented designs were destroyed when the British burned the public buildings, at Washington, 1814. For further interesting particulars of the Boltons the reader is referred to Martindale's "Byberry."

WORK IN THE MINISTRY.

Edward Roberts appeared in the ministry, probably about 1725, meetings at that time being held in the small log structure, which had been erected in 1723.

The "Collection of Memorials" of deceased ministers and others, printed by Joseph Cruikshank, Philadelphia, in 1787, contains the following "testimony from Richland Monthly Meeting in Pennsylvania, concerning Edward Roberts' life and work in the ministry:

"He was born in Merionethshire, in the principality of Wales, in the Third-month, 1687, and came into Pennsylvania about the twelfth year of his age; was early convinced of the principle of truth as held forth by Friends, with whom he joined in communion, and by his godly life and conversation through the course of his time, was nearly united to them.

"His ministry was attended with divine sweetness and energy, [he] laboring faithfully therein to the comfort and edification of the living whilst health and bodily ability continued; being a lively example of humility, plainness, temperance, meekness and charity, and of justice and uprightness in his dealings amongst men, which gained him the love and esteem of people of all denominations.

"He was a tender, affectionate husband and father, earnestly concerned to train up his children and family in the fear of

God, and example and instruct them in the paths of virtue, and also manifested a true zeal for promoting and preserving peace and good order in Society, wherein he was often singularly serviceable.

"His bodily strength gradually diminishing, he was reduced even to a child's state, in which he quietly departed this life without much sickness, on the 25th of the Eleventh-month, 1768, in the eighty-second year of his age; a minister above forty years."

Edward Roberts lived and died on the farm on which he settled in 1716. It is located a mile west of the meeting-house at Quakertown, the site being owned and occupied by Stephen Foulke.

Edward Roberts and his wife lived to an advanced age, he dying Eleventh-month 25, 1768, in his eighty-second year, and she Seventh-month 22, 1784, aged 96 years, 6 months, 9 days. Of their children, Abel lived to be ninety; David eighty-three; Nathan died in his eightieth year; Jane died in her ninetieth year.

The children of Edward and Mary Roberts were:

Martha, b. 8th-mo. 16, 1715, m. John Roberts, son of Thomas and Alice. Her descendants will be given in his line. She died the same year as her father, the date being 1st-mo. 26. Her husband survived her many years, having in all three wives. He died in 1797. His will is given in Chapter VI.

Abel, b. 8th-mo. 23, 1717, m. 2d-mo. 17, 1744, Gainor, daughter of Morris and Susanna Morris, their wedding being the second celebrated after the establishment of Richland Monthly Meeting. Their children were Susanna, m. Samuel Nixon; Sidney, Sarah, Gainor and Abel.

John, b. 11th-mo. 22, 1719, m. Margaret Gaskill, in 5th-mo., 1753. Their children (see p. 38): Hannah, b. 1754; Uriah, 1755, d. 1762; Enoch, 1757; David, 1758; Samuel, 1761, d. 1762; Uriah, 1762; Margaret, 1768; Martha, 1764, m. Benjamin Foulke, d. 1831; Abel, 1770. John died 8th-mo. 8, 1776. The family lived in Milford.

David, b. 1st-mo. 10, 1722, m. 5th-mo. 2, 1754, Phebe Lancaster, daughter of Thomas (a well-known minister) and Phebe

Wardell Lancaster. Their children: Amos, b. 4th-mo. 19, 1758, m. Margaret Thomas, daughter of Edward and Alice, 11th-mo. 30, 1775; Mary, 4th-mo. 19, 1758, d. 8th-mo. 22, 1760; Elizabeth, 7th-mo. 1, 1760, m. Israel Foulke, 11th-mo. 14, 1782; Nathan, Sixth-mo. 29, 1762, d. 5th-mo. 28, 1763; Jane, 12th-mo. 19, 1764, m. Samuel Ashton; Abigail, 2d-mo. 14, 1767, m. Benjamin Johnson; Nathan, 9th-mo. 24, 1769, m. Margaret Ashton, 5th-mo. 5, 1791; David, 9th-mo. 21, 1772, m. Elizabeth Stokes, 3d-mo. 22, 1804; Evan, 4th-mo. 20, 1775, m. Abigail Penrose in 10th-mo., 1799, d. 3d-mo. 26, 1849.

Everard, 3d-mo. 9, 1725, m. Ann Hole, 6th-mo. 11, 1761.

Nathan, 6th-mo. 13, 1727, d. 12th-mo. 10, 1806.

Mary, 10th-mo. 26, 1730, m. 10th-mo. 14, 1755, John Foulke. The latter was a member of the Provincial Assembly from 1769 to 1775, from Bucks county. Their descendants are named in the Foulke line.

Jane, 11th-mo. 3, 1732, m. Thomas Foulke, brother of John, 10th-mo. 10, 1754. Jane d. 7th-mo. 25, 1822.

All the children of Edward and Mary Roberts, named above, married and became the founders of families, with the exception of Nathan.

DAVID ROBERTS' DESCENDANTS.

The family history of Amos, eldest son of David and Phebe Roberts, will be given further on.

Elizabeth married Israel Foulke. He was the son of Samuel and Ann Foulke, and was born 2d-mo. 4, 1760. Israel died Ninth-month 27, 1824. Elizabeth died Twelfth-month 17, 1831, aged seventy-one years.

Four of their offspring, William, Cadwallader, Jane and Deborah, died in childhood. Others were Thomas, David, Hugh, Phebe and Amos Foulke.

Thomas Foulke (born 12-mo. 31, 1784, died 6-mo. 4, 1832) m. Sarah Lancaster, in 1814. She was the daughter of Thomas and Ann Lancaster, of Whitemarsh, and died in 1869, aged seventy-one years. Their children were Anne, Letitia, Sarah,

JEAN BAPTISTE PORÉE

Tacy.   Anne married Edward Thomas, now deceased, of Richland.   Their children: Lancaster, Irvin, Ellwood, Sallie and Edwin, the last-named deceased.   Letitia m. Jehu Roberts (dec'd), of Cheltenham.   Anne L., widow of Robert Croasdale, and Caroline Roberts are daughters.   Sarah m. John Walton and has children.   Tacy m. Charles Knight and has two sons and four daughters.

David Foulke, born 12th-mo. 21, 1786, m. Miriam Shaw, and had two sons, Israel and John R.   David's second wife was Mary Roberts, of Byberry.   Jane, wife of Israel J. Grahame, of Germantown, is a daughter.   She has several children.   A sister married John D. Matthews, of Baltimore, and has children, among them Thomas F. Matthews.

Hugh Foulke (1793-1853) m. Elizabeth Roberts, daughter of Levi and Phebe.   Their children: Amos, Barton L., Phebe R., Jordan, Elizabeth (m. Penrose Hicks); Thomas M., Sarah E., Franklin, Abigail Jane, Franklin 2d, Jane R., Susan J., &c.

Nathan, son of David and Phebe Roberts, m. Margaret Ashton.   His children were Ashton, Theophilus and Guy. Ashton died about 1875.   He had a son, Wilson, long since deceased, whose daughter, Gertrude, m. and removed to Philadelphia.   Ashton's daughter, Annie, married ——— Eastburn and died without children.   Guy Roberts m. Hannah Wilson; he is also deceased, leaving no children.

David Roberts, son of David and Phebe, m. Elizabeth Stokes.   Their children: Stokes L., Albina N., and Elizabeth.

Stokes L. Roberts was born in Richland township, being a descendant of Edward Roberts.   He was educated at Princeton, and soon after receiving his diploma, commenced the study of law in the office of Hon. George M. Dallas, in Philadelphia. Admitted to the Philadelphia bar, he subsequently opened an office at Newtown, being admitted to the Bucks county bar in 1832.   He became active in politics, was elected to the Pennsylvania Assembly in 1838 and 1839.   He was defeated in 1840. Removing to Doylestown soon afterwards, he resumed his law practice.   Stokes L. Roberts was appointed Deputy Attorney-General of Pennsylvania in 1844, and was tendered the consulate at St. Jago de Cuba by President Buchanan, but declined it.

In 1858 he was the Democratic candidate for Congress in the district, but was defeated. He went soon after with his wife, who was Margaret Spangler, of York, Pa., to Europe. In 1872 he was elected to the Judgeship, but resigned the position in a few weeks. The couple never had any children. He died in 1882. His widow is still living in Doylestown, spending her winters usually in France or Italy. After his trip to Europe, he did not again enter very actively into the practice of law. Battle's History of Bucks County, published in 1887, says of him:

"It was not until some years after he had dissolved all connection with the courts and legal proceedings, and after modes and forms of practice had materially changed, that he was elected to the bench of the Bucks county courts. He was suffering with ill-health, and he soon discovered that his condition and the labors and responsibilities of the position did not accord, and resigned, after holding a single term of court. He was a man of unimpeachable integrity; he was uniformly courteous towards the bench and his professional brethren; a zealous advocate and faithful to his client. He was a diligent student, of which the numerous marginal notes and references, to be found in the volumes of his law library, give ample evidence. In his personal relations he was pleasant and genial, and in all respects a polished gentleman."

Stokes L. Roberts' sisters, Eliza M., who m. Judge Ihrie, of Easton, and Albina, who never married, are both deceased, so that there are no living descendants of David Roberts the younger, and that branch of the family is extinct. He resided at Newtown most of his life and died there at an advanced age, as mentioned elsewhere.

Other children of David and Elizabeth Stokes Roberts, in addition to those previously named were Gervase Stogdell Roberts and Charles Bolton Roberts, twins, 6th-mo. 21, 1813. Gervase d. 11th-mo. 10, 1834. Charles d. 12th-mo. 7, 1863.

Evan married Abigail Penrose. He was the youngest child, as Amos was the eldest. Evan's children: William, born Ninth-month 6, 1800, died Eighth-mo. 4, 1865; Hannah, born Third-month 17, 1802; Paulina, born Third-month 25, 1806; Maria, born Third-month 14, 1809. Paulina married John J.

Penrose. Evan Roberts Penrose, well known in Bucks county Republican politics, is their son. The others (all deceased) were unmarried.

THE LANCASTERS.

Ann Chapman, daughter of John Chapman, the first settler in Wrightstown, Bucks county (1684), was a preacher in the Society and went to England, presumably on a religious mission. It is probable that she went on such errands more than once. Returning in May or June, 1712, from one of these religious visits, she brought with her from England a little boy, Thomas Lancaster, his mother, left behind, being a widow with several children. This Thomas Lancaster was the first of his family in this country. He grew up, married Phebe Wardell, and settled in Richland in 1740. In 2d-month, 1750, he obtained a minute to visit Barbadoes, where was a considerable colony of Friends, and Tortola. Towards the latter end of the year, Thomas performed this visit, but he died at sea on his way home.

The following is an extract from the testimony of Richland Monthly Meeting concerning him:

"About ten years of the latter part of his time, he was a member of this meeting. He was found in the ministry, and exercised his gift therein with great fervency and zeal, his life and conversation corresponding therewith.

"In the Second-month, 1750, he laid before our meeting his concern to visit Friends on the islands of Barbadoes and Tortola, which the meeting approved of, and gave him a certificate in order thereto.

"Towards the latter end of said year he performed said visit, and had good service there, as appeared by certificates from Friends on each of the said islands.

"On his return homewards, it pleased Divine Providence to visit him with sickness, of which he died at sea; his removal being deeply felt and lamented by his family and friends at home."

Thomas Lancaster was probably of the same lineage as other Quaker Lancasters, notably those of Whitemarsh, and

James Lancaster, who was a companion of George Fox, in England. This, however, as suggested by Howard M. Jenkins, is only supposition.

The name occurs frequently in the records of Richland Monthly Meeting, elsewhere in this volume, those bearing it being his descendants. A list of his children occurs in their petition for guardians in Chapter VI.

AMOS ROBERTS.

Margaret Thomas, the wife of Amos Roberts, was a granddaughter of Thomas Roberts, one of the settlers at Richland, previously mentioned, her mother, Alice, wife of Edward Thomas, being his daughter. She and Amos were married, as stated, 11th-mo. 30, 1775. As a matter of interest the signers of their certificate as witnesses may be given, its form being practically the same as that of Benjamin and Jane Green, which is given under the head of "Original Documents," Chapter VI. The original, in the handwriting, it is believed, of Samuel Foulke, who was one of the signers, is in the possession of the author, a great-grandson of the couple. The witnesses were:

John Roberts Senr	Sarah Roberts	Jane Foulke
Saml. Foulke	Martha Foulke	William Heacock
Abel Roberts	Ann Foulke	Ann Heacock
John Foulke	Susanna Chapman	William Foulke
John Greasley	Hannah Chapman	Margaret Foulke
Benjamin Green	Saml Elliott	David Roberts
Jane Green	Jane Foulke Junr.	Phebe Roberts
Susanna Iden	Jane L. Mather	Alice Thomas
John Roberts	John Thomas	Miriam Heacock
Jane Roberts	Elizabeth Thomas	Mary Thomas
William Heacock	Thomas Thomas	Martha Thomas
Susanna Worral	Everard Foulke	Eliza Roberts
Susanna Nixon	Amelia Foulke	Rachel Greasley
Martha Roberts	Hannah Foulke	Samuel Thomas
Hannah Hicks	Jane Heacock	
Martha Roberts Jun'r	Thomas Foulke	

It will be seen that they were largely relatives of the couple,

ALICE MATILDA ROBERTS PORÉE

as is usual on such occasions. Among them are both parents
of Amos, whereas only Margaret's mother was present, her
father being absent, probably by reason of sickness. The Roberts, Thomas and Foulke names were well represented, and also
other families, connected by relationship with the bride or groom.
A family record was kept on the back of the certificate, the
earlier entries being in the handwriting of Amos Roberts, as
follows:

Mordecai, 8th-mo. 29, 1776, d. 8th-mo. 31, 1823, aged 47
years, 2 days.

Mary, 3d-mo. 17, 1778, d. 3d-mo. 1, 1857, aged 78 years,
11 months, 15 days.

Alice Matilda, 4th-mo. 28, 1780, d. 1st-mo. 25, 1860, aged
79 years, 8 months, 28 days.

Hugh, 2d-mo. 16, 1782, d. 3d-mo. 28, 1821, aged 39 years,
1 month, 12 days.

Andrew, 1st-mo. 3, 1784.

George, 1st-mo. 9, 1786, d. 11th-mo. 17, 1789, aged 3 years,
7 months, 8 days.

Phebe, 3d-mo. 7, 1788, d. about 1840.

Margaret, 2d-mo. 20, 1790, d. 3d-mo. 21, 1858, in her 69th
year.

Deborah, 4th-mo. 7, 1792, d. 3d-mo. 31, 1858, in her 66th
year.

All the above were natives of Richland, except Deborah,
who was born in Philadelphia county, on the Logan farm, at
Stenton, to which the family had removed in 1791. Among
Amos Roberts' papers is the original lease "between George W.
Logan, M. D., of Stenton, of the one part, and Amos Roberts,
of Bucks county, of the other part." The farm contained a
hundred acres. It was occupied by the family several years, or
until the farm known as "Mount Pleasant," near Branchtown,
was purchased. Deborah Logan witnessed the lease. It was
in honor of her that the youngest child was named. The lease
is dated March 25, 1791. Amos Roberts sold his Quakertown
farm to Enoch Walton, May 17, 1796, for 600 pounds. It contained 60 acres.

Of the children of Amos and Margaret Roberts, Mordecai married. He left a daughter, Laretta, a son, Mordecai, and another son.

Mary, Margaret and Deborah all died unmarried, and were buried at Fairhill Friends' ground.

Andrew married and removed to the state of New York. He died many years ago, and nothing is known as to his descendants, if there are any.

Alice Matilda m. Jean Baptiste Porée. Her descendants are given under the proper head.

Phebe m. ——— Huston. Their children were John H., who left home for Pittsburg, in 1835, to work at his trade of machinist, and whether he left descendants or not is unknown; Theresa, who married ——— James. Both are long since deceased. She left no descendants.

Amos Roberts removed to Philadelphia in 1813, residing first at No. 27 North Fifth street, where his son, Mordecai, kept the Fountain Inn, a livery stable being attached to it. He lived later, for a number of years, at No. 64 South Eleventh street, being for a long time Assessor and Collector, for Walnut and South wards. He died 12th-mo. 11, 1835, and his widow 3d-mo. 15, 1840. The later years of his life, the family residence was No. 52 North Fifth street. Both were buried in the grounds belonging to Arch Street Meeting.

The descendants of Hugh Roberts, son of Amos and Margaret, are by far the most numerous branch of this line. The descendants of Alice and J. B. Porée will be given next, to be followed by those of Hugh Roberts.

———

Nathan, Amos' brother, removed from Richland to Gwynedd, in 1807, a certificate being granted him by the former Monthly Meeting, 3d-mo. 10, of that year. He purchased a farm, near what is now Gwynedd station, North Pennsylvania railroad, belonging later to Jesse Castner, and still more recently to Conard Castner, son of Jesse. The Ashtons are descended from Peter and Mary Ashton, emigrants from Ireland, who settled at Richland. Their son, Robert, of Springfield, born 10th-mo. 15, 1725,

ALEXANDER WALTER PORÉE

m. 11th-mo. 8, 1759, Sarah Thomas. Robert died 10th-mo. 22, 1816, aged almost ninety-one years.

Samuel Ashton, a brother of Margaret (Nathan Roberts' wife), married Jane Roberts, sister of Nathan. Their children were Phebe, 1796; Eleanor, 1798; Thomas, 1799; Sarah, 1801; Elizabeth Roberts, 1803; Abigail, 1807. Ashton Roberts, m. at Gwynedd, 2d·mo. 14, 1815, Sarah Wilson, daughter of Joseph and Ann Wilson, of Bristol, Bucks county.

THE POREES.

The acquaintance of Alice Roberts with J. B. Porée grew out of the somewhat famous marriage of Pierce Butler and the celebrated actress, Fanny Kemble. The Butlers were neighbors of the Roberts family, at Mount Pleasant. Vice Chancellor Porée, of the French Consulate, in Philadelphia, attended the wedding, as did also his future wife. She is said to have been a beautiful woman, a reputation which appears to be fully justified by the silhouette on the opposite page, furnished by her grandson, Ferdinand C. Porée, of Roxbury, Mass. The Frenchman, who was much the older of the two, improved the acquaintance, and the couple were married at Christ Church, Philadelphia, May 5, 1801, the ceremony being performed by Rev. James Abercrombie, Assistant Minister.

The couple took up their residence in Philadelphia, where twin children, Robert Alexander and Francis Victor, were born to them. Both died in infancy, the first April 6, 1802, the second July 31, 1803.

A third son, Ferdinand Charles John Baptiste, was born November 9, 1805, at Philadelphia. He died at Boston, Mass., May 23, 1869.

A fourth son, Alexander Walter, was born March 13, 1818, at New Orleans, whither the couple had removed meantime, the father having received a consular appointment there. He died at New Orleans, unmarried, November 12, 1860.

J. B. Porée died at New Orleans, May 9, 1819. His widow,

Alice Matilda Porée, continued to reside there, dying January 25, 1860.

Ferdinand C. J. B. Porée married Caroline Eliza Gurney, the second daughter of Alpheus Gurney, of North Bridgewater, near Brockton, Mass., and Eliza Gore, daughter of Jeremiah and Thankful (Harris) Gore, of Boston. Their children, all born at New Orleans, were:

Alice Matilda, July 16, 1841, unmarried.

Caroline Eliza, September 30, 1842, unmarried.

Ferdinand Charles, December 31, 1843, unmarried.

Roberts Lancaster, March 29, 1845, died January 8, 1847.

Harriet Augusta, July 22, 1846.

The last-named married Theodore Richmond Skinner, of South Boston, Mass., August 1, 1867, at her father's home, in Boston, Rev. Pelham Williams, of the Church of the Messiah, officiating.

Alice M. Porée was for many years engaged as an assistant librarian in the Boston Public Library. She has recently catalogued the President Adams Library, at Quincy, of nearly 20,000 volumes, and also the Dedham Public Library, as many more.

The children of Harriet Augusta and Theodore Richmond Skinner were Martha and Hattie, twins, December 27, 1868, Martha d. January 27, 1869, Hattie, March 16, 1869. George Alfred, February 19, 1871, Charles Porée, October 16, 1875. A daughter, who lived only a few hours, was born November 4, 1877.

The Porée family is very ancient in France. As far back as 1070 A. D., Gilbertus Porretanus was born. He was known as "Pictarensis," or Gilbert de la Porée, and was chosen Bishop of Poitiers, the capital of Vienna, or Pictou. He was a schoolman, of the Realist order, and wrote several learned treatises.

Caroli, Carolus, or Charles Porée, a French Jesuit, and a rhetorician, lived from 1675 to 1741, and was the author of several sacred dialogues or dramas. A copy of these works, written in French, is in the possession of the family, in Massachusetts.

C. Gabrial Porée, the canonist, was brother to the above-

FERDINAND C. J. B. E. PORÉE

named Charles, and was one of the preceptors of Voltaire, the noted French writer. He was born 1685, died 1770.

Charles and Gabrial were great-uncles of Jean Baptiste Porée, being brothers of his grandfather, Pierre.

Jean Baptiste Porée was a native of Paris, France; son of Pierre and Marie Laura Porée.

He was an inhabitant of the island of Santo Domingo, West Indies, and a Notary of Louis XVI, King of France, for twenty-five years, and also served under the French Republic. He was many years Consul to His Imperial Majesty, Napoleon Bonaparte, of France.

During the rebellion in San Domingo, in 1791 and 1793, Porée was exiled and came to the United States, landing at Newport, R. I., in May, 1793. In the latter part of 1795 he was at Georgetown, Md.; in 1801 Vice Chancellor of the French Consulate at Philadelphia. And it was thus that while on a visit to Pierce Butler, in connection with his marriage to Fanny Kemble, he met Alice Matilda Roberts, daughter of Amos Roberts, of Mount Pleasant, York Road, whom he afterward married.

In 1807, Porée was at Norfolk, Va.; in 1808, in Bordeaux, France; in 1808 and 1809, at Paris, France, where he was received as Vice Consul to the United States, to which he returned in 1810, and located at New Orleans, La. He was in Boston, Mass., in 1813; in New York city in 1815; and died at New Orleans, La., May 9, 1819, about 70 years of age, of apoplexy.

Ferdinand Charles Porée, his grandson, was engaged in the dry goods establishment of C. F. Hovey & Co. when the Rebellion broke out. He enlisted as a private, and was promoted to Second Lieutenant in one year. He served three years in all, participating in many engagements. He was employed twenty-five years in the Boston post office. He spent four years in Florida, where he became interested as owner of an extensive orange grove. The trees were destroyed by the hard frost of February 8, 1895, involving a loss of many thousand dollars.

HUGH ROBERTS.

Hugh Roberts, son of Amos and Margaret Roberts, learned the trade of a miller. He and Sarah Spencer, eldest daughter of Nathan and Rachel Pim Spencer, were married in 1806. He purchased the mill property, with thirty-two acres of land, February 16, 1811, from Susanna Holby, administratrix of William Holby. He is described in the deed as being of Moreland, Montgomery county, he having operated a mill there subsequently to his marriage, for several years. William Holby bought the old mill, April 1, 1797, from the estate of Nicholas Burkhart. Burkhart bought it from Jacob Brown, December 1, 1764, the latter having purchased it from the Lukens family.

The couple lived in the old house on the premises for a few years, and here most of their children were born. The oldest child, Lydia, who died in infancy, was born in 1807. The second daughter, Caroline, 12th-mo. 2, 1809, married in 1835, Charles S. Rorer. She died 2d-mo. 24, 1872. He has been deceased several years. Their children: Clementine, 3d-mo. 20, 1838; Adelaide, 10th-mo. 13, 1839; Bartlett T., 11th-mo. 2, 1841. Clementine Rorer m., 3d-mo. 20, 1865 (her twenty-eighth birthday) Albert French. They live at Hatboro, and have one child, Lottie, who m. Newton Walton, a furniture dealer and undertaker. They have one child, Oscar. Adelaide m. William Hill. They reside in Bucks county, near Pleasantville. Their children: Caroline, m. Charles Shutt, had three children, William, Charles and Adelaide, became a widow and married a second time; Susie, unmarried; Charles, deceased; Clementine m. Lowell Hoover, and has one child, Maria. Bartlett T. Rorer, who is a grocer, at Glenside, m. Emeline Williams; their children: Charles, deceased; Mary W. and Carrie R., teachers; Elizabeth U. and Alice.

Spencer Roberts' line is given elsewhere.

Margaret, 6th-mo. 27, 1813, married Gideon Lloyd; d. 9th-mo. 27, 1891. They removed to Indianapolis, Ind., in 1857. Their children: Spencer, 1846, unmarried; Mary Caroline, unmarried, a dentist of that city, and enjoys the distinction of being

THE OLD ROBERTS MILL

the first regularly graduated woman dentist in America; Washington, married, and has children, Spencer, and others.

Edmund, 6th-mo. 30, 1815, died Fifth-mo. 20, 1866. He also learned the trade of a miller. Was employed for some years at Brandywine Mills.

Alfred, 1817, and Maria, 1819, died in infancy.

Hugh, born Eighth-month 5, 1821. His descendants are given elsewhere.

"Some Account of the Pim Family," by Sarah, widow of Hugh Roberts, dated at Philadelphia, December 20, 1867, may be inserted at this point. She says:

"Thomas Pim purchased a large tract of land in Chester county, midway between the Delaware and Susquehanna rivers.

"He sent for his brother and two sisters—Richard, Sarah and Ann. Richard was the father of Moses and Mary Pim. Sarah married a man in Chester county named Mendenhall, whose daughter's husband was a Cope, of the same place, from whom descended John, Thomas Pim, Israel and Jasper Cope. Hannah died single, after arriving at the years of womanhood. Ann was married to a Thomas Paine, of the Valley, whose daughter married Cornelius Dewees, father of Hannah Sagers, Sarah Shallcross, Ann Wilson, mother of Dr. Ellwood Wilson, and their sister, Mary, who went to Ohio.

"Thomas Pim buried his wife about four years before his death. He had three sons and four daughters—William, Thomas and John. William married a daughter of Thomas Stocker, of the Valley [the name is Stalker on Nathan and Rachel Pim Spencer's wedding certificate], named Mary. They settled on a farm and mill, on the Octorara creek, the boundary between Lancaster and Chester counties. They had one son, William, and three daughters, named Mary, Rachel and Lydia. The three girls married three brothers, sons of Arnold Michener, of Abington—William, John and Rynear. They all moved to New Philadelphia, Ohio.

"Thomas married Mary Pim, his cousin. They had one son and four daughters. Hannah was the wife of Job B. Remington, and mother of Thomas Pim Remington, formerly a mer-

chant of Philadelphia, who died last summer, at his farm, near
that city. There are twin sons, Edward and William, living.

"John Pim's wife was Lydia Pusey, of Delaware county.
They had two sons, Thomas and Israel, and three daughters,
Elizabeth, Rachel and Maria. After his wife's death he sold
his farm and mansion, left him by his father, and removed, with
all his family, except Maria, to Dayton, Ohio. Maria was the
widow of Isaac Baldwin, who died at Coatesville, in Chester
county.

"Hannah, daughter of Thomas Pim, Sr., married Dr. Miller,
of Downingtown, who practised medicine in Northumberland
until his death. His widow, with several of their children, went
to Presque Isle, now Erie, where the family have become numerous and influential in the community.

"Ann, second daughter of Thomas Pim, Sr., married John
Edge, of the Valley. Their oldest son, Thomas Pim Edge. and
his family, are now living on Linden street, Germantown.
George, with his family, remained on his farm, in Chester Valley.

"Sarah, third daughter of Thomas and Frances Pim, married Amos Lee, of Oley, Berks county. They have seven children—two sons and five daughters—Thomas Pim Lee and Amos
Lee; Frances, Ellen, Anne, Sarah and Rachel. Ellen and Sarah
reside on Queen street, Germantown. Anne was the wife of
Benjamin Garrigues, of Jarrettown.

"Thomas married and is still living on the old farm, in Oley,
and Amos, near Norristown.

"Rachel, the youngest daughter of Thomas and Frances
Pim, married Nathan Spencer, near Germantown. They had
two sons and five daughters—Sarah (myself), Abigail, Hephzi-
bah, Maria and Lydia, Thomas Pim and Joseph Spencer. Abi-
gail and Lydia died young. I became the wife of Hugh Roberts.
We had eight children—Lydia, Caroline, Spencer, Margaret, Ed-
mund, Alfred, Maria and Hugh. I married the second time,
Joseph Hirst, of Branchtown Mills. We had four children—
Joseph Josiah, Sarah Ann, Rachel Abigail and Nathan Ellwood.
The last-named died young.

"Hephzibah married Spencer Thomas. They had ten
children—three sons and seven daughters. Anna Maria married

NATHAN AND RACHEL SPENCER'S MARRIAGE CERTIFICATE

Algernon S. Jenkins, of Gwynedd. Howard M. Jenkins is their son. Mordecai remained single. Caroline became the wife of Basil Shoemaker; Lydia, the wife of John Paul; Lemuel married Drusilla Rowlett; Mary became the wife of Harry Brown; Elizabeth never married, and Hannah and Sarah died young. Jonathan married Margaret Phipps, and died soon afterwards.

"Maria married Richard Thomas, a cousin of Spencer. Their children were N. Spencer, Isaac, Edwin L., Hugh and Rachel.

" Thomas Pim Spencer married Ann Kemble, of the Red Lion Tavern, on the Bristol road. They lived together many years, but had no child. Ann died in 1863.

"Joseph Spencer married Cornelia Davidson, of Trenton. They had three children—John, Hannah and Josephine. John and Josephine are dead. Hannah lives in Nevada, with her husband, William Staats, and family. Joseph married a second time, Rachel Brelsford. They had two sons, Zachary and Nathan. He died within the last year [1866]. His sons live in Bucks county.

"I neglected stating that Rachel Lee married Thomas Lightfoot. After living a widow some years she died, leaving children. Moses Pim died a bachelor, at an advanced age. Mary became the wife of Thomas, Jr., father of Richard Pim, and others before mentioned, whose widow and family, twin daughters and others, are living on the East Caln farm, which is a portion of the land purchased by Thomas Pim, soon after arriving here.

"It only now occurs to me I did not mention Mary Ann, only daughter of Job and Hannah Remington. She married a man named Stockton, brother to the New Jersey politician. They made the tour of Europe, and on their return settled in New York city."

John Pim was born at Castle Dunnington, in Leicestershire [England], in 1641, and came, with his parents, into Ireland, in 1655; was convinced of Friends' principles in 1657. They settled in County Caven, and from thence moved to Mountmelick. Being of circumspect life, he gained a good report. He was well-gifted for discipline in the church, suffered imprisonment, on account of tithes, for seven years, in Marybro jail, being tenderly taken care of by his wife, with the other prisoners, she taking a house and residing in Marybro for that purpose.

Richard Pim, father of William, and grandfather of the above John Pim, was a retainer of Sir John Stanhope, ancestor to the Lord of Chesterfield. He carried off a farmer's daughter, sent her to school, and married her. They had a son and two daughters, married to William Neale and Godfrey Cantrell. Richard Pim died in Ireland, and his son William, dying, was buried in his orchard, by his own desire. They went into Ireland in 1655.

William Pledwell, father of the above Mary Pim, went into Ireland, with his wife, in 1655. They were Baptists, settled near Killaloe, and were convinced, with their daughter, Mary, by the ministry of Edward Burrough, a Friend, and the coadjutor of George Fox.

Mary Pledwell, wife of John Pim, was well-gifted in women's meeting, having a good understanding in spiritual matters. During her husband's long confinement, she managed his affairs so well that on his enlargement he found his outward substance increased, at which time he removed, to live at Mountrath, where the meeting was held at their house.

John Pim and Mary Pledwell Pim had eleven children, of whom the eldest was Moses, born 7th-mo. 19, 1664, who married Ann, daughter of Christopher and Philippa Raper.

William Pim, in the next generation, born at Lackah 11th-mo. 15, 1692, married, 11th-mo. 21, 1715, Dorothy Jackson, daughter of Thomas and Dorothy. The family came to Pennsylvania in 1730, and settled in East Caln township, where Dorothy died, 1st-mo. 15, 1732, and her husband, 10th-mo. 11, 1751. He was for many years the clerk of Bradford Monthly Meeting, an elder in the church, and an active, influential citizen.

The Spencers are descended from Samuel Spencer, who came to Philadelphia from Barbadoes, late in the seventeenth century. He married Elizabeth Whitton, and died in 1705, leaving two sons, Samuel and William, from whom the family,

THOMAS P. SPENCER

so numerous in Bucks, Montgomery and adjoining counties, are descended. An old family genealogy runs thus, Samuel, Sr., being 1, William, his son, 2, and Samuel, his other son, from whom Sarah Spencer Roberts was descended, 3.

William's (2) children were: 4 James, 5 Job, 6 Thomas, 7 Samuel, 8 Enoch, 9 Sarah, 10 Ann, 11 Abel.

James' children: 12 Josiah, 13 Enos, 14 William, 15 Seneca, 16 Ezra, 17 Elizabeth, 18 James, 19 Abner.

Enos' child: 20 Enoch M.

Enoch M.'s child: Frances.

William's (14) children: Lydia D. and Elizabeth. Elizabeth intermarried with Peter Shoemaker. Their children: 23 James, 24 Samuel, 25 Thomas, 26 Peter, 27 Spencer, 28 Margaret, 29 Sarah, 30 Elizabeth, 31 Mary and Angeline.

Sarah (29) intermarried with Thomas Hallowell. Their children: 32 Lydia, 33 Sarah, 34 Margaret, 35 Eliza.

Elizabeth (30) married Cadwallader Cooper. Their children: 36 Theophilus, 37 Margaret.

Ezra's (16) children: 38 Hugh, 39 Hannah, 40 Sarah.

James' (18) children: 41 Josiah, 42 Samuel, 43 Hannah, 44 Rachel, 45 Sarah, 46 Elizabeth, 47 Ann, 48 Ruth, 49 George, 50 John.

Josiah's (41) children: 51 Elvira, 52 Cadwallader.

Samuel's (42) children: 53 George T., 54 Albert, 55 Emanuel.

Hannah (43) married Jesse Clime. Their children: 56 Hiram, 57 Sarah Ann, 58 Lydia, 59 Elizabeth, 60 William, 61 Anna Maria.

Rachel (44) married Jacob Rynear. Their children: 62 Spencer, 63 Daniel, 64 Josiah, 65 James, 66 Emeline, 67 Jonathan.

Sarah (45) married William Rynear. Their children: 68 Charles, 69 Ann, 70 Elizabeth.

Elizabeth (46) married Jesse Banes. Their child: 71 Ellen Eliza.

Abner's (19) children: 72 Catharine M., 73 Louis, 74 Moses M.

Job's (5) children: 75 Edward, 76 Job, 77 Mary, 78 Hannah.

Edward's (75) children: 79 Cadwallader, 80 Agnes.

Job's (76) children: 81 Edward, 82 Rebecca, 83 Jacob, 84 William, 85 Hannah, 86 Elizabeth.

Mary (77) married Cadwallader Lloyd. Their children: 87 Job, 88 John, 89 Martha.

Hannah (78) married William Harding. Their children: 90 Charles, 91 Mary.

Thomas' (6) children: 92 Thomas, 93 William, 94 Amos, 95 Mary, 96 Sarah, 97 Margaret.

Thomas' (92) children: 98 Thomas, 99 Mary, 100 Esther.

William's (93) children: 101 Mary, [Sarah, Margaret, Elizabeth].

Amos' (94) children: 102 Thomas B., 103 John G., 104 Charles, 105 William, 106 Sarah and 107, 108 and 109.

Samuel's (7) children: 116 John, 117 Samuel, 118 Margaret, 119 Elizabeth, 120 Ann.

John's (116) children: 121 Samuel, 122 John, 123 Sarah, 124, 125, 126.

Margaret (118) married William (93). Issue traced above.

Sarah (123) married Amos Sagers.

Sarah (96) married Isaac Hallowell. Their children: 128 Benjamin, 129 Mary, 130 Eleanor, 131 Thomas.

Benjamin (128) had children. Mary (129) married William Hallowell. Their child: 133 Elias.

Enoch's (8) children: 134 Mahlon, 135 Sarah, 136 Elizabeth.

Ann (10) married James Ahern. Their children: 137 James, 138 Sarah.

[The record at this point turns to Samuel Spencer (3), whose children were:] 139 Jacob, 140 Nathan, 141 Joseph, 142 John, 143 Edith, 144 Elizabeth, 145 Sarah, 146 Mary.

[It will be seen that it is fragmentary, the names of some children being omitted and what are given not in the order of their ages.]

Jacob's (139) children: 147 Jarrett, 148 Samuel, 149 John, 150 Mary. [Other children, Susanna, Elizabeth, Sarah, died in childhood.]

Jarrett's (147) children: 151 Charles, 152 Samuel, 153 Thomas, 154 Hannah, 155 Ann, 156 Mary.

Charles' (151) children: 157 Elizabeth, 158 Ann, 159 Sybilla.

Samuel's (148) child: 162 Joseph.

John's (149) children: 163 George, 164 Jesse, 165 Jonathan, 166 Edith, 167 Priscilla, 168 Susan, 169 Rebecca, 170 Lydia.

Joseph's (141) son: 171 Nathan.

Nathan (171) married Rachel Pim. Their children: 172 Thomas Pim, 173 Hephzibah, 174 Sarah, 175 Maria, 176 Joseph. Hephzibah married Spencer Thomas (183). Sarah (174) married Hugh Roberts. Their children: 177 Caroline, 178 Spencer, 179 Margaret, 180 [Hugh, Edmund and others].

John's (142) children: 181 Sarah, 182 Elizabeth. [Also Abraham, Sarah, Samuel, Mary, Jacob and Samuel 2d—these six dying, however, in infancy or childhood.]

Sarah (181) married Jonathan Thomas. Their children: 183 Spencer, 184 Mordecai.

Spencer's (183) children: 185 Anna Maria, 186 Mordecai, 187 Elizabeth, 188 Lemuel and others.

Edith (143) married George Shoemaker. Their children: 190 Samuel, 191 Rachel, 192 Abraham. [The last-named married Martha Webster.]

Samuel (190) [married Elizabeth Ellis.] Their children: 193 George, 194 Isaac, 195 Edith, 196 Jonathan, 197 David, 198 Samuel.

Rachel (191) married Samuel Robinson. Their children: 199 Edith, 200 John, 201 George. [Her second husband was Joseph Clark, but the marriage was childless.]

Sarah Spencer, wife of Hugh Roberts, and later of Joseph Hirst, but for more than forty years of her life a widow, was a woman of excellent conversational powers. She was accustomed, during the later years of her life, to go among her children, and other kindred, and relate what had come to her knowledge of recent happenings, here, there and everywhere. When she wrote letters to her children, they partook of the same general character, and were they collected they would form a very

complete history of family affairs for a half-century or more.
She had a copious flow of language, speaking grammatically,
and avoiding colloquialisms and slang. On the occasion of her
visits, she was often in the habit of entertaining, not only the
immediate family, with whom she was staying, but such of their
friends or neighbors also, as were favored with an invitation to
meet her. Nor were her hands idle while her tongue was busy.
She had always in process of completion some exquisite bit of
fancy work "all her own design." She had been educated according to the custom of her day, not only in mere accomplish-
ments, but in what was substantial. Born and raised on the
Spencer farm, near Branchtown, she had come in contact, in her
youth, with many notabilities, the seat of government of the
United States being then at Philadelphia. She had about her a
degree of self-possession that did not desert her in any company,
however exalted, and she could maintain her dignity amid any
surroundings. She had a vein of innocent sarcasm in her com-
position, which afforded much amusement to her grandchildren
and others. Brought up a Friend, she was always one in principle, although in going about, as she often said, she could accommodate herself to whatever religious faith was professed by
her hosts. She felt that she could kneel in formal prayer without
sacrificing a jot of the Quaker principle so dear to her.

She was born 3d-mo. 30, 1788, and died 1st-mo. 22, 1874,
living to a ripe old age, retaining all her faculties to the last, and
passing away, after a useful, as well as a long life,

> " Like one that wraps the drapery of his couch
> About him, and lies down to pleasant dreams."

Sarah Roberts, widow of Hugh Roberts, married, a second
time, Joseph Hirst, a neighboring manufacturer, of English
birth. Their children were: Joseph Josiah, 1823; Sarah Ann,
1825; Rachel Abigail, 1827; Nathan Ellwood, 1829, died in infancy. Joseph J. was brought up by his uncle, Thomas P.
Spencer, who owned a farm in Lower Makefield, Bucks county.
He married Abigail Wharton, daughter of Moses Wharton, who
resided on the adjoining farm.

Sarah Roberts Hirst became a widow in 1831, being known

SARAH S. HIRST

after her second marriage as Sarah S. Hirst. Of the children by her second marriage, Sarah A. and Rachel A. survive.

Joseph and Abigail Hirst settled on a farm near Fallsington, in the fifties. Their children were: Sarah, Phebe Ann, Hannah and Susanna, twins; Mercy, Wharton and Caroline. All are now deceased, except Susanna and Wharton. Joseph died in 1870, having injured his spine by a fall from an apple tree, striking a log in his descent. He lived a few weeks, the lower portion of his body being paralyzed. His widow died a few years later, of consumption. Sarah married Joseph White. She died recently, leaving several children. Phebe Ann also married, leaving two children. Mercy also married.

Sarah A. Hirst was born July 19, 1825. On May 6, 1851, she married Henry Van Horn, born June 18, 1818. He died June 16, 1893, in Philadelphia. Their children: Anna Theresa, Spencer Roberts, Harry (deceased), Ella, William Hirst (deceased). Anna Van Horn married William Selman, April 16, 1873. Their children: Henry Pim, Edith, William. Spencer R. Van Horn married Ida Virginia Smith, June 30, 1879. Their children: Helen Roberts (deceased), Spencer Roberts, Ethel.

Rachel A. Hirst married Casper Souder, Jr., December 23, 1851. He was a well-known literary man, connected with the Evening Bulletin, and other Philadelphia newspapers, being part owner of the Bulletin. Their children: Kate Maria, Leah Bickerton, Rachel Hirst. Kate M. Souder married Theodore A. Langstroth, of Germantown, July 24, 1873. Their children: Katharine Bartram, James Heidel, Charles Souder, Francis Drexel, Theodora Ashmead, Louise Drexel Morell. Leah Bickerton Souder married William Smith Parker, February 3, 1881. He died May 6, 1890, and she died January 23, 1891. Rachel H. Souder married Rev. Thomas A. Gill, D. D., U. S. Navy, June 19, 1883. Their children: Madeline Kate, Thomas Sidney (died July 20, 1890). Casper Souder, Jr., died October 21, 1868. His attainments in his line of work were of a very high order.

THE OLD ROBERTS MILL.

The Roberts mill was the second grist mill in Pennsylvania. It was located on the Wingohocking creek, one mile northeast of the market square, Germantown. It was erected in 1683, by Richard Townsend, a minister among Friends. In a testimony about the year 1727, Richard tells how he came to America on the "Weicome," in company with William Penn, in 1682. He says:

"After some time I set up a mill on Chester creek, which I brought, ready framed, from London, which served for grinding corn and sawing of boards, and was of great use to us. * * *

"As soon as Germantown was laid out, I settled my tract of land, which was about a mile from thence, where I set up a barn and a corn mill, which was very useful to the country round. But there being few horses, people generally brought their corn upon their backs, many miles. I remember, one man had a bull so gentle that he used to bring the corn on his back.

"In this location, separated from any provision market, we found flesh meat very scarce, and on one occasion we were supplied by a very particular providence, to wit: As I was in my meadow, mowing grass, a young deer came and looked on me while I continued mowing. Finding him to continue looking on, I lay down my scythe and went towards him, when he went off a little way. I returned again to my mowing, and the deer again to its observation, so that I several times left my work to go towards him, and he as often gently retreated. At last, when going towards him, and he not regarding his steps whilst keeping his eye on me, he struck forcibly against the trunk of a tree and stunned himself so much as to fall, when I sprang upon him and fettered his legs. From thence I carried him home to my house, a quarter of a mile, where he was killed, to the great benefit of my family. I could relate several other acts of providence of this kind.

"Being now in the eighty-fourth year of my age, and the forty-sixth of my residence in this country, I can do no less than return praises to the Almighty for the great increase and abundance which I have witnessed. My spirit is engaged to supplicate the continuance thereof; and as the parents have been blessed, may the same mercies continue on their offspring to the end of time.

"RICHARD TOWNSEND."

Roberts' Mill was on the north side of Mill street, or, as it was formerly called, the "Road to Lukens' mill." The mill jutted somewhat into the street, and this, together with its antique appearance, still remembered by myself and many others, produced a highly picturesque effect. It ought not to have been torn down at all, but preserved as one of the earliest landmarks of colonial days. Such relics are becoming altogether too rare in our day.

Richard Townsend left only one child, Mrs. Cook, but his brother, Joseph, had numerous descendants of the name, many of whom reside in Eastern Pennsylvania.

As to the name of the creek, it is recorded that the Indian chief, Wingohocking, was a particular friend of James Logan, and, according to the Indian custom, asked him to change names with him. Logan replied that the Indian might have his name (so runs the story), but that, instead of accepting the Indian's, he would give it to the creek, which ran through the estate. Thus it became the Wingohocking, though often called Logan's run, and occasionally Mill creek.

In the days when Richard Townsend erected the mill, as may readily be imagined, the stream had a much greater volume than it had in the later years of the structure. There are frequent references in family letters to the failure of the stream to furnish needed water power. "Spencer is having a bad year at the mill, on account of dry weather," is a complaint many times repeated.

The old Roberts mill possessed peculiar interest for the family, it having been operated by father (Hugh Roberts) and son (Spencer Roberts) for many years, and Hugh Roberts, brother of Spencer, having learned his trade there. It is not out of place to trace its ownership from Richard Townsend to Hugh Roberts. It passed first to John Peters, who sold it to Matthias Lukens, whose daughter, Hannah, became the first wife of Joseph Spencer. Joseph's second wife, however, Abigail West Conrad, was the mother of Nathan Spencer, whose daughter, Sarah, married Hugh Roberts. The property on which the mill was situated was willed by Matthias to his son, John Lukens, the eldest of the family. From John Lukens it passed to Brown, Burkhart and Holby, in succession, and thence to Hugh Roberts, as noted.

It was leased and operated by various tenants during the minority of Spencer Roberts. He purchased it at administrator's sale, in 1835, and operated it until 1858, when he purchased the large steam mill at Mill street and the Reading railroad, from Charles Spencer. It stood, however, as already stated, until 1874. The land adjacent to it was sold, years ago, to an improvement association, and the neighborhood is greatly changed from what it was in the middle of the present century. The mansion erected by Hugh Roberts still stands, but in a very dilapidated condition.

THE JOHNSONS AND AMBLERS.

[This article should have preceded the Amos Roberts line but may be conveniently inserted here.]

Abigail Roberts, daughter of David and Phebe, 2d-mo. 15, 1767, m. 9th-mo. 18, 1788, Benjamin Johnson, a descendant of Casper Johnson, who settled in Richland, early in that century, the family being of German origin. She died 10th-mo. 16, 1827. Their children:

Samuel, 6th-mo. 8, 1789, who married Margaret Roberts, and had two children, David and Abigail. He died at the age of 28 years.

Casper, 3d-mo. 28, 1791, m. Mary Gibson, and had three children, Joseph, Gibson and Milton. He died at the age of 34 years.

David, 6th-mo. 10, 1793, m. Susan Foulke, they having no children. David died at the age of 69 years.

THE ROBERTS MANSION (Germantown)

Spencer Roberts.

Elizabeth, 3d-mo. 7, 1797, m. Samuel Foulke, and had four children: Clayton, Joseph, Abigail, Jesse. Elizabeth died at the age of 81 years.

Joseph, 7th-mo. 14, 1799, died in childhood.

Anthony, 2d-mo. 1, 1802, m. Elizabeth Foulke. They had three children: Ann, Henry, Mary. Anthony died at the age of 90 years.

Mary, 3d-mo. 24, 1805, m. 5th-mo. 4, 1829, Andrew Ambler, born 6th-mo. 12, 1793, d. 3d-mo. 7, 1850. She died 8th-mo. 18, 1868. Her descendants are named below.

Benjamin, 6th-mo. 15, 1808, m. Tacy Stratton. Their children: William, Matilda, Clayton, Eli, Evan. Benjamin died at the age of 41 years.

Of Casper and Mary Gibson Johnson's three children, Joseph, Milton and Gibson, Joseph m. first, Hannah Riner and had four children, Edward, Susan, Amanda, Joseph; by his second wife, Ann Edwards, he had two children, William, Anne. Casper's second child, Milton, m. first, Eveline Edwards, and had two children: Richard, m. Mary Strawn, and Amos, m. Anna Shaw. Milton's second wife, Mary Edwards, had one child, Lewis. Milton's third wife, Ann Shaw, had no children. The third son, Gibson, of Doylestown, m. Sarah Jones, and has several children: Jemima, Fanny, Harry and others.

For further details as to descendants of Benjamin and Abigail (Roberts) Johnson, other than the Amblers, Chapter V, "Records of Richland Meeting," may be consulted. The descendants of their daughter, Mary Johnson Ambler, are:

Joseph Mather Evans Ambler, 7th-mo. 23, 1830, m. 2d-mo. 16, 1854, Hannah Cleaver, of a well-known Gwynedd family. He died 4th-mo. 7, 1895.

Benjamin Johnson Ambler, 10th-mo. 20, 1831, d. 12th-mo. 9, 1858.

Isaac Ellis Ambler, 7th-mo. 1, 1833, m. 5th-mo. 1, 1856, Eliza Moore. Their children were Edwin Moore Ambler, Anna Ambler. Edwin M. Ambler, 4th-mo. 13, 1860, m. 4th-mo. 18, 1883, Annie Foulke Webster. Their children: William W. Ambler, 10th-mo. 3, 1884; Alice Hannah Ambler, 3d-mo. 14, 1889; Eliza Moore Ambler, 9th-mo. 6, 1893.   Edwin M. is deceased.

Edward Henry Ambler, 11th-mo. 9, 1834, d. 11th-mo. 5, 1869.

David Johnson Ambler, 3d-mo. 22, 1837, m. 3d-mo. 6, 1862, Caroline F. Penrose.   She died 9th-mo. 13, 1891.   Their child, Ella Ambler, 3d-mo. 27, 1864, m. 5th-mo. 7, 1884, Daniel M. Leedom.   Their children: David Ambler, 3d-mo. 9, 1885; Caroline Foulke, 1st-mo. 11, 1887; Susan A., 5th-mo. 7, 1891, d. 2d-mo. 8, 1892, Daniel M., 1st-mo. 11, 1894.

Lewis Jones Ambler, 2d-mo. 17, 1839, m. 9th-mo. 25, 1862, Rachel Walton.   They had one child, Benjamin G., born 6th-mo. 9, 1864, d. 8th-mo. 24, 1890.   Rachel W. Ambler d. 5th-mo. 26, 1874.   Lewis m. 3d-mo. 4, 1880, Rebecca Penrose.   They have one child, Aaron Penrose Ambler, 5th-mo. 10, 1882.

Evan Jones Ambler, 1st-mo. 8, 1841, m. 4th-mo. 26, 1877, Mary Jenkins, daughter of William H. and Catharine Jenkins, of Gwynedd.   He died 8th-mo. 16, 1893.

Andrew Ambler,, 11th-mo. 26, 1842, d. 11th-mo. 7, 1870.

Mary J. Ambler, 3d-mo. 17, 1848, d. 4th-mo. 29, 1848.

The Amblers are old residents of the flourishing borough of that name, formerly Wissahickon station, on the North Pennsylvania railroad, and most of them who survive live in that vicinity.   Andrew Ambler, husband of Mary J., descended from Joseph Ambler, who, on May 1, 1723, purchased of William Morgan ninety acres of land in Montgomery township, then in Philadelphia county.   The tract passed to Joseph's son Edward, in 1768, who bequeathed it (1770) to his brother John, grandfather of Andrew.   Andrew was a fuller by trade, and, in 1832, purchased and located on the tract, in Upper Dublin, on which is now a portion of Ambler.   There had been an old fulling mill on the property, once owned by Daniel Morris.   On its site Andrew Ambler erected another, which remained in use many years, until it was destroyed by fire, December 31, 1869.   In the summer of 1856 a very serious accident occurred on the railroad, near Fort Washington, about two miles below the home of the Amblers.   Mary J., widow of Andrew, was soon on the

SPENCER ROBERTS

ground, with such appliances as were available for the relief of the wounded. Many lives were lost on this occasion, due to the collision of an excursion train from Philadelphia with another.

SPENCER ROBERTS.

Spencer Roberts, eldest son of Hugh and Sarah Spencer Roberts, August 10, 1811, d. October 22, 1885, m., March 3, 1835, Elizabeth Yerkes Hagy, February 4, 1813, d. in February, 1842. Their children:

1. Hugh Oscar Roberts, February 2, 1836, m., September 21, 1865, Anna Maria Gemrig, October 22, 1842, daughter of Jacob H. Gemrig. Their children: Alvirda Dunham, July 12, 1868, d. May 13, 1874; Adelaide M., October 25, 1873; Clarence J., February 7, 1878; Anna Gertrude, October 21, 1879. Hugh Oscar Roberts served in the Union army during the War of the Rebellion, and was thrice severely wounded.

2. Susanna Hagy Roberts, August 27, 1837, m. 1866, Lylburn H. Steel, son of Canby and Amelia Steel. Their children: (1) Helen Wriggins, m. Clarence J. Peterson, they having one child, Clarence, Jr.; (2) Canby, (3) Estelle and (4) Lylburn. Susanna has been a widow many years.

3. Charles Rorer Roberts, April 4, 1839, m. April 30, 1873, Janie Shaw Pearson, born March 2, 1850, d. September 26, 1877, daughter of Hamlet and Sarah Elizabeth Pearson. Their children: (1) Hamlet Pearson, March 10, 1874, d. the same day; (2) Charles Hamlet, May 29, 1875; (3) Janie Shaw, September 16, 1877, d. same day. Charles R. Roberts m. (second wife) April 21, 1881, Louisa Jane Gay, April 9, 1855, daughter of John and Deborah A. Gay. Their children: (4) Lulu Evelyn, March 28, 1882, d. August 18, 1882; (5) Thomas S. Gay, August 25, 1883, d. July 7, 1884; (6) James Gay, July 7, 1885; (7) Mary Louisa and (8) Adelaide Gay, twins, February 17, 1888; (9) Spencer Roberts (3d) August 18, 1892.

4. Algernon Sidney Roberts, September 27, 1840, d. March 3, 1870, m. November 22, 1864, Elizabeth Justice Pearson, August 30, 1839, daughter of Isaac and Ruth Pearson. Their

child, Isaac Pearson Roberts, March 26, 1868, m. April 9, 1891, Louisa Pharo Willits, July 4, 1864, daughter of Samuel Cauley and Phebe Pearson Willits; their children: Elizabeth Pearson, April 26, 1892, d. July 30, 1892; Ruth Pearson, October 13, 1892; Samuel Willits, September 29, 1894.

Spencer Roberts m. (second wife) July 21, 1845, Elizabeth Ann Taylor, May 16, 1815, daughter of Maris Taylor. She died January 26, 1886. Their children:

5. John Taylor Roberts, August 14, 1847, m. March 10, 1870, Hannah Maul Matlack. Their children: (1) Sarah Matlack; (2) Spencer, (3) Edith, m. April 17, 1895, Walter Gibson Sibley, son of Edward Abbott and Ellen Gibson Sibley, and have one child, Edward A.; (4) Elizabeth A., d. March 10, 1892, aged sixteen years; (5) John T. Spencer is an architect. The engravings, "Old Roberts Mill," page 116, and "The Roberts Mansion," page 128, are from pen-drawings by him.

6. Enoch Taylor Roberts, January 25, 1849, m. Helen A. Woods, of Pittsburg, February 22, 1851, daughter of George and Caroline Woods. Their children: (1) Elizabeth T., April 15, 1875, and (2) Annie, November 23, 1878.

7. Annie Taylor Roberts, August 19, 1850, m. Ferdinand V. Hoyt. Their child: Albert Maurice.

8. Lizzie Roberts, December 4, 1851, m. William H. Wriggins. Their children: (1) Annie R. m. W. Seymour Runk; (2) Thomas, (3) Charles C., (4) Helen V. Lizzie Roberts Wriggins m. (second husband) B. F. Dewees, December 16th, 1895.

Spencer Roberts, in 1835, bought the mill belonging to his father's estate, and operated it until 1858, when he transferred his business to the Wm. G. Spencer steam mill. He was for many years a School Director in the Twenty-second ward of Philadelphia (Germantown), and long a member of the Philadelphia Board of Education. He was for a number of years prior to his death president of the Mutual Fire Insurance Company of Germantown. He was a man of superior worth and intelligence, and was esteemed by all.

HUGH ROBERTS

HUGH ROBERTS, SECOND.

Hugh Roberts, son of Hugh and Sarah Spencer Roberts, 8th-mo. 5, 1821, was a posthumous child, his father having died several months previously. His mother married again, before he had passed beyond the period of infancy, and he became an object of tender regard and solicitude to his paternal aunt, Mary Roberts, who cared for him as though he had been her own son. At the age of eight years, his lot was cast on the Lower Makefield farm, with his maternal uncle, Thomas P. Spencer. Here he remained until the time came for him to learn a trade, which he did at the old Roberts mill. In 1840, having completed his apprenticeship, he went to Wilmington, Delaware, where he secured employment at Brandywine Mills, then operated by William Lea and the Canbys.

There he was employed during the next twelve years, with the exception of a brief interval, devoted to carrying on business for himself at Harmony Mills, a few miles from Wilmington. In the early forties he met, and in due time married, Alice A. Gallagher, the ceremony being performed by John M. Scott, Mayor of Philadelphia, 8th-mo. 8, 1842. Their children, all born in Wilmington or its vicinity, were:

Charles Henry, 6th-mo. 18, 1843, m. 3d-mo. 23, 1865, Sarah Elizabeth Stradling, daughter of Samuel and Louisa Stradling, the latter long deceased. Their children: Alice Anna, 4th-mo. 16, 1866, at present a teacher in the public schools of Kansas City, Missouri, where the family reside; Hugh, 1st-mo. 8th, 1868, an attorney; Samuel, 8th-mo. 1, 1871, a druggist of Lemars, Iowa; and Louisa, 1886. Charles H. Roberts was in early life a teacher, but is now a leading lawyer of Kansas City.

Edmund, 6th-mo. 30, 1844, d. 5th-mo. 30, 1845.

Ellwood, 1st-mo. 22, 1846, m. 9th-mo. 12, 1878, Mary Long Carter, daughter of Job and Rachel Carter, of Mickleton, New Jersey. Their children: Howard Carter, 7th-mo. 6, 1879; Charles Alfred, 5th-mo. 30, 1881, d. 3d-mo. 14, 1888; Alice Rachel, 6th-mo. 15, 1886; William Hugh, 2d-mo. 12, 1888; Mary Carter, 1st-mo. 31, 1892.

Mary, 10th-mo. 25, 1847, m. 11th-mo. 7, 1877, Samuel Livezey (see Heath-Livezey genealogy, Chapter VI).   Their only child: Thomas Hugh Livezey, 10th-mo. 18, 1879.

William, 12th-mo. 1, 1851, d. 1st-mo. 27, 1855.

Spencer, 8th-mo. 8th, 1854, d. 10th-mo. 11, 1855.

Alfred, 3d-mo. 10, 1857, d. 11th-mo. 20, 1860.

Alice A. Roberts, wife of Hugh Roberts, daughter of John and Margaret Stotsenburg Gallagher, is thus descended from Scotch-Irish and Pennsylvania-German ancestry.   There is a blending of nationalities in the family which is quite unusual, her husband being of Welsh-English origin, as we have seen. The family removed to Bucks county from the vicinity of Wilmington in 1861, and ultimately to Gwynedd, Montgomery county, and thence about twenty years later to Norristown.

Hugh Roberts died 8th-mo. 23, 1894, after an illness of several months, being a few days more than seventy-three years of age.

WILL OF EDWARD ROBERTS.

By way of closing the chapter relating to Edward Roberts, the founder of the family whose various branches are mentioned or fully set forth in it, it may be fitting, perhaps, to give the document wherein he disposed of his worldly effects, as follows:

To all Christian People whom these presents may concern, be it known that I Edward Roberts of Richland Township in the County of Bucks and Province of Pennsylvania Yeoman being in a pretty Good State of Health and Sound Memory Considering my advanced Age Praise be therefore given to the Author of all our Mercies, and Considering the Mortallity Incident to this frail Body, do make and put in Writing this my Last Will and Testament in manner and form following First I will that all my just Debts and Funeral Expences be carefully paid and discharged 2dly. I give and bequeath nuto my Son Nathan All my Tract of Land and Plantation whereon I now dwell Containing Two hundred and fifty acres Together with all ye Improvements and buildings thereunto belonging, to hold to him his Heirs and Assigns forever together also with all my Stock of Creatures and Implements of Husbandry &c. he paying

out of ye same the Legacies hereinafter mentioned and ordered.
3dly. I Give and bequeath unto my well beloved Wife
Mary all my Household Goods and furniture whatsoever to be
entirely at her disposal Excepting two new Cupboards (viz.) the
one in the Parlour ye other in the New Room both which I give
unto my Son Nathan aforesd. I give her also the free use of
the said New Room at the East end of my dwelling House both
below and above Stairs during her Life and I will that my sd.
Son Nathan shall provide for her sufficient fire Wood fit for the
Fire and furnish her with a Suitable Riding Creature whenever
she may require it and he shall also pay unto his sd. Mother
yearly the Sum of Ten Pounds of lawful Money, or the Value
thereof if he shall so chuse in such Necessaries as may be most
agreeable to her during her life as aforesaid And Moreover I
Give unto my said Wife the Sum of Sixty Pounds of lawful
Money of Pennsylvania and our Servant Maid Barbara to be at
her disposal 4ly. I give unto my Son Abel the Sum of Twenty
Pounds lawful Money of sd. Province 5ly. I give unto my Son
John the Sum of Thirteen Pounds which is due from him to me
by virtue of a Penal Bill. 6ly. I give unto my Son David ye
Sum of Thirteen Pounds being part of Thirty-five Pounds due
from him to me by Bond 7thly. I Give unto my Son Everard
ye following books (to wit) Barclay's Apology, Penn's No Cross
No Crown and the first Vol. of George Fox's Journal, he having
already received his Equtable portion of my Estate 8ly. I give
unto my Son in Law Johr Roberts Thirty Pounds of lawful
afores. to be paid unto him at the end of two Years after my decease 9ly. I give unto my Son in Law John Foulke Thirty
Pounds of lawful Money aforesd. to be paid to him at the end
of three years after my decease 10ly. I Give unto my Son in Law
Thomas Foulke ye like Sum of Thirty Pounds to be paid unto
him at the end of one year after my decease 11ly. I Give and
bequeath unto the Monthly Meeting of Frds. at Richland aforesaid the Sum of Twenty Pounds of Lawful Money aforesaid, the Use of it to be by them applied towards a School at ye
said place forever 12ly. If my said Wife should happen to dye
without making a Will, it is my Will that after her funeral Expences are paid, the remainder of her goods and Effects shall
be equally divided among the surviving Children of to wit Martha, Mary and Jane the Wives of my
of my three Daughters, Sons in Law above named Share and
Share alike. 13ly. I give unto my Daughter Martha Roberts
the Book of Francis Howlgil's Works in folio, to my Son John
I Give Edward Bourrough's Works, to my Son David I give
my large Concordance and to my Son Nathan I give Sewels His-

tory; the rest of my Books to be equally divided among all my Children in ye manner which may appear most agreeable to their several Inclinations.

Lastly I do Nominate Constitute and appoint my Son Nathan and my Son in Law Thomas Foulke above named to be my Executors of this my Last Will and Testament hereby revoking all other and former Wills and Testaments and Executors by me before this time made or named Ratifying this and no other to be my last Will and Testament In Witness whereof I have hereunto set my Hand and Seal the twenty-fifth day of ye twelfth Month in the year of our Lord one thousand seven hundred and sixty.

Edward Roberts (SEAL)

Signed Sealed & declared by ye said Edward Roberts to be his Last Will & Testament in the presence of us.
Saml. Foulke Thos. Stafford Job Hughes.

Proved before Benjamin Chew Regr. Gen. at Philadelphia January 10, 1769.

CASPER SOUDER, JR.

(See page 125.)

VIII.
JOHN ROBERTS (EDWARD'S SON).

The descendants of Edward Roberts have been given very fully in all lines except those of his daughters, Mary, who married John Foulke; Jane, who married Thomas Foulke, and Martha, who married John Roberts (son of Thomas and Alice), and his son John, who married Margaret Enochs Gaskill. The descendants of Mary and Jane are given in the Foulke line further on and those of Martha in the Thomas Roberts line. Those of John Roberts, 11th-mo. 22, 1719, d. 8th-mo. 8, 1776, are as follows:

The children of John and Margaret Gaskill (maiden name Enochs) Roberts, married in 5th-mo. 1753, were Hannah, Uriah, Enoch, David, Samuel, Uriah, Margaret, Martha and Abel.

Hannah, 4th-mo. 19, 1754, married an Edwards and removed to Muncy. Her descendants, if any, are unknown.

Uriah, 10th-mo. 28, 1755, d. 8th-mo. 14, 1762.

Enoch, 2d mo. 28, 1757, m. Rachel Blackledge, born 4th-mo. 13, 1760. He d. 1853.

David, 11th-mo. 27, 1758, d. 2d-mo. 7, 1828, m. Elizabeth Chilcott.

Samuel, 1st-mo. 13, 1761, d. 8th-mo. 8, 1762.

Uriah, 11th-mo. 13, 1762, d. young.

Margaret, 8th-mo. 1, 1768, d. young.

Martha, 10th-mo. 25, 1764, d. 8th-mo. 13, 1831, m. 2d-mo. 26, 1789, Benjamin Foulke. (Continued in Foulke genealogy.)

Abel, 9th-mo. 27, 1770, m. Martha Penrose, b. 2d-mo. 25, 1772.

Margaret Enochs came from New Jersey, her first husband's name being Gaskill.

Enoch Roberts, son of John and Margaret, m. Rachel Black-ledge. Their children: Joel, m. Bethulia Deane, b. in 1787 and d. 3d-mo. 27, 1857; they left no children; Hannah m. Philip Sellers. Their children were Rachel, m. Dr. Walters; Lewis, m. Martha ———; Charles unmarried, lived at Nazareth; Daniel, m. Mary Ann Bush; Elizabeth, m. Joseph Albright, of Scranton; Frances, m. ——— ———; Philip, m. Susanna Jacoby; Hannah Amanda, m. Dr. Massey, of Scranton, Pa. Rachel Walters' children were: William, d. young; William 2d, d. young; Eugene, Philip, Lucinda, m. Dr. Sharon; Emma. Lewis Sellers' child; Amanda. Daniel and Mary Ann Sellers' children: Hiram Francis, m. ——— Oakford; Charles, unmarried; Alfonso; Daniel, m. ——— Brunner; Harry. Frances' children: Mary, Lucinda, m. ——— Stover. Philip and Susanna Jacoby's children: Milton, killed in the Rebellion; Lizzie, m. Nathan Houck; Mary, m. ——— Frey; Warren, d. young; Hannah, d. young.

The children of David and Elizabeth (Chilcott) Roberts were (1) Samuel, (2) Margaret, (3) William, (4) Jane, (5) Elizabeth, (6) Mary and (7) Rachel.

1. Samuel Roberts m. (1) Mary Anne Penrose; (2) Jane Walton. Samuel and Mary Anne's child, Mary Ann, d. young Samuel and Jane's children: James m. Susan Anderson and had two children, Jane, m. ——— Bair; Samuel m. ——— Fegley and had one child, Jane; Asenath, m. Lewis Richard and had one child, Clarence; Barton m. Margaret Kinsey, and had one child, Margaret.

2. Margaret Roberts m. (1) Samuel Johnson and had two children: Abigail who m. Ephraim Heller and had three children: Samuel, m. Rebecca Carr, Henry, m. Mary Carr, Margaret, m. Charles Lancaster; and David who m. Hannah Heller. David's children: Edward, m. Annie Strawn Foulke, having four children, Russell, Helen, Emily and Hortense; Samuel, m. Elizabeth Roberts, having two children, Herbert and Emma; Irvin, m. Lydia Eilenberger and had one child Tracy; Henry, m. Camilla ———; Harriet, m. Thomas Frazer, and had one child, Bernard; Meredith. Margaret, by her second marriage with Amos Edwards, had but one child, who d. young.

3. William Roberts, 1788, d. 1862, m. Elizabeth, d. 1825, and had four children, (1) Margaretta, m. A. Moore; (2) David m. Eliza Ann Ball and had three children, Sarah Roberts who m. first James Hoot and had one son James, and m. second, Isaiah Flitcraft; Elizabeth Roberts who m. Samuel Johnson and had two children, Herbert, m. Carrie Ahlum, and Emma; Emma Roberts, who m. Allan J. Flitcraft, they residing in Chicago. where he is prominent in life insurance circles, and have several children. (3) Milton Roberts, 11th-mo. 10, 1821, m. 3d-mo. 23, 1848, Missouri Foulke, born 6th-mo. 14, 1826, d. 3d-mo. 22, 1867, daughter of Joshua Foulke. Their children: Edward, m. Lydia Bartholomew, and had one child Franklin, d. young; Caroline, d. young, Harry, David, m. Alice ———— and have one child Russell; Ellen. (4) Chilcott Roberts m. first, Elizabeth ————, by whom he had one daughter Sarah, m. James Simon. Chilcott m. (second wife) Mary Shoch.

4. Jane, 1st-mo. 12, 1791, d. 8th-mo. 28, 1855, m. 5th-mo. 18, 1817, Samuel Jamison, b. 4th-mo. 7, 1783, d. 12th-mo. 27, 1834. Their children: (1) Margaret Jamison, 11th-mo. 28, 1818, m. 2d-mo. 18, 1846, John T. Penrose and had two children, Stephen, m. Hannah Morgan, and Esther who d. young; Stephen and Hannah Penrose had two children, A. Melvina m. H. Johnson and Martha. (2) Charles R. Jamison, 11th-mo. 29, 1819, m. 1847 Mary Strawn, b. 7th-mo. 6, 1824, d. 9th-mo. 26, 1893. Their children: Jane and Caroline, both d. unmarried; William, residing in Bridgeport, m. Elizabeth Kinsey; their children, Walter, Caroline, Alfred, Helen, Charles, Byron, William and Elizabeth; Allen, m. Ella S. Ball, and has two children, Florence and Mary. (3) John Jamison, 2d-mo. 15, 1823, d. 1st-mo. 12, 1890, m. Deborah Nice; their children: Catharine, d. unmarried, Jane, John, Samuel, William, d. young. (4) David, 8th-mo. 27, 1826, d. 3d-mo. 14, 1889, m. first, 6th-mo. 21, 1853, Cornelia Foulke, b. 7th-mo. 12, 1828, d. 4th-mo. 2, 1857; their children: Lucinda, m. Charles W. Timmons and had three children, Cornelia, David and John; Cornelia, d. young. David Jamison m. 6th-mo. 15, 1858, Matilda G. Foulke, b. 12th-mo. 27, 1830, d. 3d-mo. 6, 1894; their children: Alice and Frank, d. young; Mary Louise, Ida, Fannie, David, d. young. Mary Louise Jamison m. Samuel T. Bleam and had one child Frank, d. young.

The children of Abel Roberts (son of John and Margaret) and Martha Penrose were (1) Abigail, (2) Anna, (3) Sidney, (4) Sarah, (5) John, (6) Enos, (7) Rachel, (8) Benjamin, (9) Sarah, (10) Martha, (11) Martha.

1.   Abigail, 4th-mo. 19, 1796, m. Amos Edwards.   They had two children, Eveline, m. Milton Johnson, and Benjamin, m. Lydia Bartholomew.   Eveline and Milton Johnson's children: (1) Richard, m. Mary Strawn and had five children, Henry m. A. Melvina Penrose, Walter, Milton, Morris, Arthur; (2) Amos, m. Anna Shaw and had one daughter Alice.   Benjamin and Lydia's children: (1) Ella, m. George Hirsh; (2) Eveline, d. young; (3) Henry, m. Mina Brown, and had two children, Hattie, Carrie, d. young; (4) Sarah, m. Milton Bean and had two children, Nellie and Harry; (5) Amos.

2.   Anna, 4th-mo. 19, 1797, d. unmarried.

3.   Sidney, 11th-mo. 22, 1798, d. 11th-mo. 6, 1870, m. 4th-mo. 17, 1823, John Strawn, b. 12th-mo. 13, 1792, d. 9th-mo. 2, 1868.   Their children: 1 Abel, 2d-mo. 2, 1824, d. 4th-mo. 6, 1847, unmarried; (2) Enoch R., 7th-mo. 18, 1825, m. Susan Van Buskirk and had one child Eunice who m. Theodore Stotsel. (3) Myra Ann, 12th-mo. 16, 1826, m. first Joseph Van Buskirk; their children: William, d. unmarried; John, Maria Melvina, m. Allen Harmer and had four children, Harry, Albert, Carrie and Anna; Emma m. ——— ——— and had two children, Bross and Steward Beers; Sidney Jane m. George Englet; George Joseph m. Ellen ———. Myra Ann. m., second, Henry Trumbower and had one child Ida who married ——— Casey.   Myra Ann m., third, Peter Bross and had one child, Abel Sylvester.   (4) Emeline Sidney R., 1st-mo. 19, 1838, m. John G. Jordan; their children: John O. Miles, m. Ella Geisinger; Leo Elmer and Anna Emma.

4.   Sarah, 8th-mo. 12, 1800, d. young.

5.   John, 11th-mo. 4, 1801, d. young.

6.   Enos, 9th-mo. 7, 1803, m. first, Elizabeth Strawn and had one child, Franklin, who m. Susan Ornt and had two children, Rachel, d. young, and Allen m. Emma ———.   Enos m. second, Sarah Edwards; their children: Jackson and Ann, both d. unmarried; Martha, m. George Scypes, and had three child-

ren, Roberts, May, Emma, d. young; Sarah Jane, d. young; Abel, d. young; Nathan, d. young.

7.   Rachel, 11th-mo. 30, 1806, d. unmarried.

8.   Benjamin, 3d-mo. 19, 1808, m. Maria Penrose; their children: Joseph, d. young, Joseph, d. young; Ellen, d. young; Penrose, m. Lydia Carter.

9.   Sarah, 7th-mo. 19, 1810, unmarried.

10.   Martha, 10th mo. 18, 1811, d. young.

11.   Martha, 1st-mo. 22, 1817, m. Frank Rawlings; their children: (1) Thomas, of St. Joseph, Mo., m. Sarah ———— and had three children, Erminna, m. Lewis Sherman; Etta, m. Frederick Johnson, and Eugene. (2) Richard, m. Hannah Kenderdine, and had two children, Elmer and Herbert. (3) Charles, of Lyons, Kansas, married Emma ————. (4) Amos, d. young. (5) Anna, m. William P. Roberts, and had two children, Rachel and Arthur; (6) Emma and (7) Martha, both d. young; (8) Amos of Chicago, m. and had one child; (9) Joseph, of Green Bay, Wisconsin, m.

IX

HUGH FOULKE.

The Foulkes of Richland have been an important element among its Friends since 1713, the probable date of the removal of Hugh Foulke, their ancestor, from Gwynedd to Great Swamp. Hugh was the second son of Edward and Eleanor Foulke, the immigrants. In order to present a history of the family, it is necessary to refer to Edward, the progenitor of all of the name at Gwynedd, Richland and elsewhere, a reunion of whose scattered members it is proposed to hold at Gwynedd in a few weeks in connection with the bicentennial of the township.

Edward Foulke, 5th-mo. 13, 1651, has left an account of himself and his family, dated 11th-month 14, 1702, and his coming from Wales to America. The following Foulke genealogy shows the generations of the family in Great Britain for several centuries, running back through female lines to the Kings of England:

"Edward Foulke from Wales, settled in Gwynedd in 1698, was the son of Foulke ap Thomas, son of Thomas ap Evan, son of Evan ap Thomas, son of Thomas ap Robert, son of Robert Lloyd, son of David Lloyd ap David, son of David ap Ievan Vychan, son of Ievan Vychan of Llanuwchllyn, son of Ievan ap Gruffyd, son of Gruffyd ap Madoc, son of Madog ap Iorwerth, son of Iorwerth of Penllyn, Lord of Penllyn, son of Madog of Rhiwaedog, son of Rhirid Flaidd.

"Robert Lloyd's wife was Mary, daughter of Lowry, daughter of Ellison, of Griffydd, son of Lowry, daughter of Owen Glendower Tudor, son of Eleanor, daughter of Thomas ap Llewellyn, son of Eleanor de Barr, daughter of Eleanor, daughter of Edward I, son of Henry III, son of John, King of England, born December 24, 1166, crowned May 27, 1216."

In Edward Foulke's account of himself he says:

"When arrived at mature age, I married Eleanor, the daughter of Hugh, ap Cadwallader, ap Rhys, of the Parish of Spytu, in Denbighshire; her mother's name was Gwen, the daughter of Ellis, ap William, ap Hugh, ap Thomas, ap David, ap Madoc, ap Evan, ap Cott, ap Evan, ap Griffith, ap Madoc, ap Einion, ap Meredith of Cai-Fadog; and [she] was born in the same parish and shire with her husband.

"I had by my said wife nine children, whose names are as follows: Thomas, Hugh, Cadwallader and Evan; Grace, Gwen, Jane, Catharine and Margaret. We lived at a place called Coed-y-foel, a beautiful farm, belonging to Roger Price, Esq., of Rhiwlas, Merionethshire, aforesaid. But in process of time, I had an inclination to remove with my family to the Province of Pennsylvania; and in order thereto we set out on the 3d day of the 2d-month, A. D. 1698, and came in two days to Liverpool, where with divers others who intended to go the voyage, we took shipping the 17th of the same month, on board the "Robert and Elizabeth," and the next day set sail for Ireland, where we arrived, and stayed until the first of the 3d-month, May, and then sailed again for Pennsylvania, and were about eleven weeks at sea. And the sore distemper of the bloody flux broke out in the vessel, of which died five and forty persons in our passage; the distemper was so mortal that two or three corpses were cast overboard every day while it lasted. But through the favor and mercy of Divine Providence, I, with my wife and nine children, escaped that sore mortality, and arrived safe at Philadelphia, the 17th of the 5th-month, July, where we were kindly received and hospitably entertained by our friends and old acquaintance.

"I soon purchased a fine tract of land of about seven hundred acres, sixteen miles from Philadelphia, on a part of which I settled, and divers others of our company who came over sea with us, settled near me at the same time. This was the beginning of November, 1698, aforesaid, and the township was called Gwynedd or North Wales."

The home of Edward Foulke, whose first purchase of land in Gwynedd was 400 acres, but who patented 712 acres, was on the site at Penllyn station, on the North Pennsylvania railroad, occupied for many years by Jesse Spencer, and owned by D. Clark Wharton. For many additional interesting and valuable details of Edward Foulke and his family, the reader is referred to Howard M. Jenkins' "Historical Collections of Gwynedd."

Of Edward Foulke's children the one who immediately concerns the reader is Hugh, born 1685, d. 1760, his second son. He m., 1713, Ann Williams, b. 11th-mo. 8, 1693, d. 9th-mo. 10, 1773. A memorial of Richland Monthly Meeting concerning him, shows that he was a minister, and that he was a member of the meeting for thirty years or more. Hugh's children were:

1.   Mary, 7th-mo. 24, 1714, d. 2d-mo. 20, 1756, m. James Boone, of Exeter, b. 5th-mo. 7, 1709, d. 9th-mo. 1, 1785. James was a brother of Squire Boone, father of the celebrated Daniel Boone, of frontier fame.

2.   Martha, 5th-mo. 22, 1716, d. 4th-mo. 17, 1781; m. October 4, 1738, William Edwards and (second husband) John Roberts. She was a minister, a memorial concerning her being given in Chapter VI.

The children of William and Martha Foulke Edwards, of Milford, were: (1) Mary, 7th-mo. 14, 1739; d. 12th-mo. 17, 1755; (2) Thomas, 1st-mo. 6, 1742, d. 5th-mo. 13, 1745; (3) Ann, 12th-mo. 26, 1743-4; (4) William, Jr., 5th-mo. 13, 1746; (5) Thomas, 2d-mo. 28, 1749; (6) Martha, 6th-mo. 7, 1751; (7) Hugh, 2d-mo. 13, 1754, d. 8th-mo. 30, 1760; (8) Mary, 6th-mo. 15, 1756, d. 1st-mo. 19, 1770; (9) Hannah, 7th-mo. 10, 1758; (10) Hugh, 3d-mo. 16, 1761, d. 10th-mo. 4, 1764. William (Martha's husband) d. 8th-mo. 13, 1764, in his fifty-second year. John Roberts had no children by his marriage with Martha, they being all by Martha, daughter of Edward Roberts, his first wife.

3.   Samuel, 1718, d. 1797, m. Ann Greasley, their marriage being the first after the establishment of Richland Monthly Meeting.

4.   Ellen, 1st-mo. 19, 1720, m. John Lloyd, of Horsham, 8th-mo. 21, 1742.

5.   John, 1722, d. 1787, m. Mary Roberts, daughter of Edward Roberts.

6. Thomas, 1724, d. 1786, m. Jane Roberts, a sister of Mary.

7. Theophilus, 1726, d. 1785, m. Margaret Thomas.

8. William, 1728, d. 1796, m. Priscilla Lester.

9. Edward, 1729, d. 1747.

10. Ann, 1st-mo. 1, 1732, m. William Thomas.

11. Jane, 1st-mo. 3, 1734, d. 8th-mo. 1771, m. John Greasley.

The children of James and Mary Foulke Boone were twelve in number:

Ann, 2d-mo. 3, 1737, d. 4th-mo. 4, 1807, m. Abraham Lincoln, who was of the same family as the President of the United States of that name.

Mary, 11th-mo. 17, 1738, m. Thomas Lee, of Oley.

Martha, 1742.

James, Jr., 1743.

John, 1745.

Judah, 1746, m. 11th-mo. 15, 1770, Hannah Lee, of Oley.

Dinah, 1748.

Rachel, 1751.

Moses, m., 1779, Sarah Griffith.

Joshua; Hannah, 1752; Nathaniel, 1753, died in infancy.

James Boone, Jr., acquired considerable distinction in his time as a mathematician.

SAMUEL FOULKE.

Samuel Foulke was prominent in Richland Meeting for many years, being thirty-seven years its clerk. He was a member of the Provincial Assembly from 1761 to 1768. Frequent mention has been made of him and of his usefulness to the community in preceding pages. He was familiar with the Welsh tongue as well as the English. The children of Samuel and Ann were:

1. Eleanor, 1744, d. 7th-mo. 6, 1833, m. Randall Iden.

2. Thomas, 4th-mo. 11, 1746, d. 10th-mo. 7, 1784.

3. Amelia, 1753, d. 8th-mo. 7, 1811, m. Joseph Custard.

4. Hannah, 9th-mo. 15, 1756, d. 3d-mo. 1840, m. George Iden.

5. Israel, 1760, d. 1824, m. Elizabeth Roberts. Their descendants have been given in the Edward Roberts line, Chapter VII.

6. Judah, 1763, m Sarah McCarty. A list of their children is given on page 44. They removed to Miami, Ohio, in 1818.

7. Cadwallader, 1768, d. 1830, m. Margaret Foulke.

8. John, 12th-mo. 6, 1767, m. Letitia Roberts. They had eight children, named on page 44, as are those of Randall Iden.

Israel, 1749, and Judah, 1752, d. in childhood.

In a letter to a ministering Friend, dated Richland, 8th-mo. 22, 1790, Samuel Foulke gave the following excellent counsel:

Now, as the use and end of speaking is to be distinctly heard and understood, in order to impress the minds of the hearers with a due sense of the matter or truth intended to be inculcated,—permit me, my dear friend, without offence, to offer the following observations: Though there may be some occasions that would justify the raising of the voice to a high key, yet I think those occasions are rare, and should be judiciously directed; for I have seen many instances, when good words and pertinent matter have been expressed too loud and too fast; so that some of the good sense and savour has been lost in the sound; more especially in the most solemn and awful part of public worship, I mean the addressing of the Almighty Being, by vocal prayer. Yet fervency of spirit is efficacious, and will accompany the arising of divine life in the instrument, who, keeping in the right line, will be duly furnished with energy of expression, and emphasis of diction, without vehemency. Oh! the transcendent loveliness of the true gospel ministry! Its beauty and excellence are indescribable! It is clearly discerned, only by those who are favoured with a true internal sense of the divine evidence attending it, and have a true relish for the bread which comes down from Heaven, and are thirsting to partake of the pure stream which flows from the fountain of life.

The following obituary notice of Samuel Foulke is from "Friends' Miscellany," Vol. 4, page 16:

"The 21st day of the 1st-month, 1797, died Samuel Foulke, of Richland, in the seventy-ninth year of his age. He was a man, who from his youth had his mind impressed with the love of religion and religious meetings. At the first establishment of

Richland monthly meeting, he was appointed clerk thereof, in which service he continued about thirty-seven years; and nearly thirty years served as clerk to the meeting of ministers and elders. In civil life his invariable wishes and endeavours were to cultivate peace and benevolence among men; and though his inclination would have led him to a life of retirement, which he ever deemed the most desirable, yet he yielded to the solicitations of his friends and countrymen to serve them in several public stations. In the decline of life, under the infirmities of old age, he delighted to sit with his Friends in their silent meetings, and to spend much of his time in reading the holy Scriptures, which, in his estimation, contain a divine treasure surpassing all other writings whatsoever."

Cadwallader Foulke, son of Samuel and Ann, born at Richland, 7th-mo. 14, 1765, was a surveyor and a notable man in his day. He married, 1792, his first cousin, Margaret Foulke, 1771-1845, daughter of Theophilus and Margaret (Thomas) Foulke. This being a disownable offense, Cadwallader's case was brought before the meeting, with the result, however, that he was continued in membership. Cadwallader and Margaret removed to Gwynedd about 1805, having purchased the farm at the location now Gwynedd station, owned later by Jacob Craft, Rodolphus Kent, Charles Roth and others.

Cadwallader died 3d-mo. 22, 1830. He had a high reputation as a surveyor and business man. He held the position of Auditor of Gwynedd township for many years, and, during his time, the township records were models of neatness, fullness and accuracy, everything that he undertook being invariably well done. He learned the trade of a weaver with Edward Ambler, of Montgomery (referred to in Chapter VII). Having succeeded him, after many years, in the position of Auditor, and having had an opportunity to examine his work in this line, as well as in that of surveyor and conveyancer, the author can bear testimony to the accuracy and care which were characteristic of the man. The line of Cadwallader and Margaret Foulke is extinct, they having had but one child, Benjamin Franklin Foulke, 5th-mo. 25, 1796, m. Maria Heston Tyson, b. 12th-mo. 29, 1799, d. Feb. 12, 1829, daughter of Levi anl Susanna Heston, her first husband being Jesse Tyson. The only child of B. F. and Maria Foulke, Eleanor, 1828, died in infancy.

John Foulke, 1767-1840, who m. Letitia Roberts, 1767-1854, daughter of Thomas and Letitia, was a minister, especially concerned for the maintenance of the testimonies of the Society against slavery and intemperance, among the most serious evils of his day, as intemperance continues to be of ours. His record in reference to slavery is enlarged upon in a memorial by Richland Monthly Meeting. He lost no opportunity of pleading the cause of the oppressed, often visiting Washington when Congress was in session and urging upon those high in office the injustice of the system. The children of John and Letitia Foulke were:

1. James, 8th-mo. 2, 1790, d. 4th-mo. 8, 1866, m. 10th-mo. 19, 1815, Hannah Shaw, 3d-mo. 7, 1793, d. 5th-mo. 28, 1859, daughter of William and Sarah Shaw.

2. Sidney, 12th-mo. 30, 1791, d. 12th-mo. 9, 1862, m. 11th-mo. 14, 1822, Samuel Shaw, 2d-mo. 26, 1784, son of William and Sarah.

3. Abigail, 1st-mo. 5, 1794, m. 11th-mo. 14, 1833, Thomas Wright. Their children: Thomas, m. Elizabeth Morgan, Jr.; Ann, unmarried. Thomas and Elizabeth Wright's children: Allen, m.; Mary, m.; Elizabeth, d. young.

4. Elizabeth, 10th-mo. 13, 1795, m., 1816, John Kinsey, Jr. Their child, Nathaniel, d. 11th-mo. 28, 1865, m. Elizabeth Morgan. Their children: (1) Ann, 1st-mo. 11, 1845; (2) John F., 9th-mo. 25, 1847, m. Rettie Williams, and have two children, William and John Kinsey; (3) Howard, 7th-mo. 12, 1849, m. Ella Deacon; (4) Letitia, 7th-mo. 9, 1852, m. William P. Roberts (continued in Thomas Roberts' line); (5) Elizabeth, 3d-mo. 15, 1860, m. William Jamison; their children: Walter, Caroline, Alfred, Helen, Charles, Byron, William, Elizabeth.

5. Ann, 11th-mo. 23, 1797, m. 11th-mo. 14, 1822, James R. Green.

6. Hannah, 7th-mo. 4, 1799, m. 12th-mo. 4, 1848, Bartholomew Mather. He d. 2d-mo. 7, 1872, aged 87 years.

7. Kezia, 4th-mo. 4, 1804, d. 12th-mo. 31, 1884, unmarried.

8. Mary, 12th-mo. 5, 1806, m. 10th-mo. 14, 1847, Joseph Paul.

1. James and Hannah Shaw Foulke's children: Abby Ann,

10th-mo. 16, 1816; d. 2d-mo. 24, 1859; Sarah, 4th-mo. 30, 1822, unmarried; John, 10th-mo. 12, 1830, unmarried; Stephen, 1st-mo. 3, 1819, m. 11th-mo. 13, 1845, Matilda Penrose, 6th-mo. 15, 1815, daughter of Enoch and Esther Penrose; their children: Martha, d. young; Penrose, m. Sarah Walton and had three children, Matilda, Florence and Viola; Anne.

2. Samuel and Sidney (Foulke) Shaw's children: (1) James Shaw, 5th-mo. 4, 1824, m. Ann Johnson; no children; (2) Sarah Shaw, 12th-mo. 3, 1826, m. 3d-mo. 21, 1848, William Ball, 7th-mo. 28, 1823; d. 10th-mo. 27, 1859, son of Aaron and Sarah J. Ball; their children: Ellwood, 3d-mo. 24, 1849, m. Sarah Todd; Sidney A., 2d-mo. 16, 1853, m. William Kirkpatrick, and had one child, Herman; Ella, 5th-mo. 30, 1860, m. Allen Jamison, and had two children, Florence and Mary; (3) William Shaw, 10th-mo. 14, 1829, m., 3d-mo. 16, 1854, Hannah Morgan; their children: Morgan, 10th-mo. 15, 1857, m. Alice Johnson; Samuel, 12th-mo. 22, 1859; Anna, 3d-mo. 20, 1862, m. Amos Johnson; Morris, 5th-mo. 31, 1865, m. Jane Johnson; Elizabeth M., 3d-mo. 14, 1867, m. Eli Strawn, no children; (4) Ann, 6th-mo. 6, 1832, m. Milton Johnson, no children; (5) Edward, 9th-mo. 20, 1835, m. Mary Good; their children: Margaret, J. Wilmer, 12th-mo. 29, 1869, Emma.

Descendants of other children of John and Letitia Foulke have been given, or will be noted in other lines.

JOHN FOULKE.

John Foulke, son of Hugh and Ann, who married Mary, daughter of Edward and Mary Roberts, was born 12-mo. 21, 1722, d. 5th-mo. 25, 1787. Their children:

1. Edward, 7th-mo. 16, 1758, d. 11th-mo. 22, 1839, m. 11th-mo. 1, 1781, Elizabeth Roberts, b. 8th-mo. 7, 1759, d. 7th-mo. 25, 1793. Edward m. (second wife) Ann Roberts, b. 11th-mo. 12, 1764, d. 12th-mo. 8, 1830. They were sisters, both being daughters of Thomas and Letitia Roberts. Edward and Elizabeth had six children as follows:

Jane, 8th-mo. 2, 1782, m. William Fussell.

Rowland, 12th-mo. 29, 1783, m. Eliza Maus and removed to Philadelphia.

Agnes, 8th-mo. 27, 1785, d. unmarried.

Mary R., 9th-mo. 29, 1787, d. 1847.

John, 10th-mo. 28, 1789, d. unmarried.

Edward, 5th-mo. 26, 1792, d. 1859, m. Matilda Green, daughter of William and Mary Green, b. 1st-mo. 20, 1809.

The children of Edward and Ann Foulke were:

Joshua, 10th-mo. 12, 1797, d. 9th-mo. 23, 1888, m. 5th-mo. 15, 1825, Caroline Green, daughter of William and Mary Green, b. 2d-mo. 6, 1805, d. 2d-mo. 18, 1888.

Elizabeth, m. Anthony Johnson; their children: Henry, m. Hannah Roberts; Ann, m. James Shaw; Mary m. Manasses Ochs.

Penninah m. James Conway, their children being Edward, m. Sarah Clymer; Henry, Charles, d. young. Edward and Sarah Conway had four children: Annie, Byron, m. Annie Transue; Howard, Irvin.

2. Anne, 10th-mo. 27, 1760.

3. Jane, 8th-mo. 2, 1763, d. 3d-mo. 18, 1780.

4. Aquilla, 3d-mo. 2, 1766. He m. Amelia Roberts, his first cousin, and both were disowned by Richland Monthly Meeting, 1789.

5. Margaret, 10th-mo. 17, 1768, m. Thomas Gibson; their children: Mary, m. Casper Johnson; John, Robert.

6. Evan, 5th-mo. 6, 1771, m. Sarah Nixon. Their children: Olivia, Charles, Asenath, m. Samuel Foulke, son of Judah and Sarah Richards Foulke; Susanna, Samuel, Edward and others. Evan and Sarah removed to Deerfield, Ohio, a certificate being given them from Richland 5th-mo. 3, 1839.

7. Lydia, 10th-mo. 2, 1775, m. Nathan Edwards.

William and Jane (Foulke) Fussell had five children, as follows:

1. Elizabeth, m. Neal Hardie, of Indiana; their children: Mary Jane, m. John Fussell; William, m. Maria Thomas; Solomon, m. Rebecca James; T. Morris, m. Margaret Wilson; Eliza Ann, m. first Martin Knickerbocker and second John Bos-

ton; Emily, m. Albert G. Lewis; Sarah, m. Joseph Kinnard; Margaret, d. young.

2. Edwin, m. Rebecca Lewis, was a physician and the first president of the Woman's Medical College of Philadelphia; he resided in that city many years, but afterwards removed to Me- dia, where he died. Their children: (1) Emma Jane, 6th-mo. 7, 1839, d. 7th-mo. 30, 1862, unmarried; (2) Charles, 10th-mo. 25, 1840, artist, unmarried; (3) Linnæus, 9th-mo. 2, 1842, m. Edith Johnson; (4) Mary Townsend, 10th-mo. 23, 1849, m. Harry Fus- sell; (5) Horace, 1st-mo. 3, 1853, d. 1st-mo. 16, 1853; (6) Edwin Neal, 3d-mo. 17, 1863, m. Sarah Haswell, deceased; they had two children, Edwin Briggs and Paul.

3. Esther Ann, m. Charles Jacobs, of Pendleton, Ind.; their children: Cassius, m. Sarah Vernon; Elmira, d. unmarried.

4. Joseph Fussell, of Germantown, 1820, m. Sarah Emily Roberts, daughter of Lewis and Harriet Roberts; their children were five in number: (1) Florence, 7th-mo. 4, 1850, d. young; (2) William Lewis, 9th-mo. 14, 1851; m. Alice Cook Leedom; (3) Marion, 8th-mo. 18, 1854, d. 2d-mo. 8, 1866; (4) Emily R., 4th- mo. 25, 1859; (5) Harriet Jane, 12th-mo. 21, 1865.

5. Milton Fussell, of Narberth, Pa., m. Tamar Haldeman. They had four children: (1) William Henry, 1st-mo. 18, 1850, m. Laura C. Lewis, and had three children, Helen L., d. young, Howard Lewis and Willis; (2) Anne White, 7th-mo. 16, 1852, m. Edward B. Entwisle; their children: Elizabeth, Mabel, Edward, Robert Morgan; (3) Dr. Howard M., 11th-mo. 24, 1855, m. Sarah Entwisle; their children: Anne Entwisle, George Dock, Milton; (4) Elizabeth H., 6th-mo. 22, 1864, m. John Coffin, now deceased, leaving one child, Lewis.

Rowland and Eliza M. Foulke had five children, as follows:

1. Richard, m. Mary Bellerjeau; their children: (1) Catha- rine, d. 1897, m. Philip Pistor; their children: Josephine, Ella, Louisa; (2) Elizabeth, m. Charles E. Brower; their children: Henry B., Rowland, Richard.

2. Edward, unmarried. 3. Charles, m. 4. Mary Ann, unmarried.

5. Elizabeth, m. Israel Michener; their children: Horace, d. young; Fannie, m. Walter Ludwig.

Agnes, Mary R. and John, children of Edward and Elizabeth Foulke, died unmarried. Edward, 1792, d. 1859, and Martilda Green Foulke had eight children, as follows:

1. Elizabeth, 1st-mo. 31, 1833, m. Jacob B. Edmunds; no children.

2. Joseph W., 10th-mo. 31, 1834, m. Mary Ann Strawn; no children.

3. William G., 1st-mo. 5, 1837, m. Anna C. Jeanes, daughter of Isaac and Caroline Jeanes; their children: Edward, Anna L., Walter L., Marguerite.

4. Martha R., 7th-mo. 4, 1839, d. unmarried. 5. Evan, 5th-mo. 18, 1842. 6. Mary G., 9th-mo. 6, 1844. All d. unmarried.

7. James. 9th-mo. 3, 1847, of Jersey City.

8. Agnes, 3d-mo. 29, 1855, d. unmarried.

Joshua Foulke, 1797-1888, son of Edward and Ann, and Caroline (Green) Foulke, had six children, as follows:

1. Missouri, 6th-mo. 14, 1826, d. 3d-mo. 22, 1867, m. 3d. mo. 23, 1848, Milton Roberts. Their descendants are given in the line of John Roberts (son of Edward). See Chapter VIII.

2. Cornelia, 7th-mo. 12, 1828, d. 4th-mo. 2, 1857, m. David R. Jamison. See Chapter VIII.

3. Matilda, 12th-mo. 27, 1830, d. 3d-mo. 6, 1894, m. David R. Jamison. See Chapter VIII.

4. Jane, 9th-mo. 2, 1837, m. 3d-mo. 27, 1860, Lewis Ellwood Roberts. See Thomas Roberts line.

5. Edward, and 6, Alice, d. in infancy.

The lines of Elizabeth and Penninah, sisters of Joshua, have been traced above.

Of the descendants of John and Mary Roberts Foulke, all have been enumerated, as far as possible, except those of their youngest child, Lydia, who married Nathan Edwards. They had four children: John, m. Mary Ball; Sarah, m. Enos Roberts; Tacy and Martha, unmarried.

John and Mary Edwards had one child, Anna A., m. William Emley, of Philadelphia. Their children: Frank, Joseph, Warren, Helen.

Enos and Sarah Roberts' children: Jackson, Ann, Sarah Jane, Abel, Nathan, all unmarried; Martha, m. George Scypes. See John Roberts' (son of Edward) line, Chapter VIII.

JOSHUA FOULKE

THOMAS FOULKE.

Thomas Foulke, 1st-mo. 14, 1724, d. 3d-mo. 31, 1786, son of Hugh and Ann, m. 10th-mo. 10, 1754, Jane Roberts, 11th-mo. 3, 1732, d. 7th-mo. 25, 1822. She was a daughter of Edward and Mary Roberts. Their children:

1. Everard, 9th-mo. 8, 1755, d. 9th-mo. 5, 1827, m. 9th-mo. 29, 1778, Ann DeHaven. He was one of the United States Assessors who were forced to abandon their duties in Lower Milford and Quakertown by John Fries and his followers in 1798. He was for many years a Justice of the Peace, and was prominent in the settlement of estates and the transaction of business generally.

2. Edward, 1756, d. in infancy.

3. Samuel, 1761, d. in infancy.

4. Abigail, 10th-mo. 4, 1763.

5. Susanna, 11th-mo. 19, 1767.

6. Samuel, 11th-mo. 19, 1767.

The children of Everard and Ann were:

1. Abigail, 5th-mo. 18, 1779, m. 5th-mo. 2, 1805, Abel Penrose. (See Penrose line.)

2. Eleanor, 7th-mo. 18, 1781, d. 4th-mo. 28, 1815.

3. Caleb, 8th-mo. 29, 1783, d. 2d-mo. 22, 1852, m. 11th-mo. 26, 1807, Jane Green, 2d-mo. 8, 1785, d. 3d-mo. 3, 1835, daughter of Benjamin and Jane Green.

4. Samuel, 3d-mo. 28, 1786, m. Elizabeth Johnson and had three children: Joseph J., Abigail, Jesse D.

5. Thomas, 4th-mo. 13, 1789, d. in Kentucky, leaving two daughters.

6. Susanna, 9th-mo. 18, 1791, d. 4th-mo. 19, 1883, m. David Johnson.

7. Anna, 5th-mo. 3, 1794, d. 9th-mo. 16, 1820.

8. Margaret, 12th-mo. 24, 1796, m. 5th-mo. 25, 1820, Peter Lester, 7th-mo. 17, 1797, son of Thomas and Mary Lester. Their children: Anna, m. Aaron B. Ivins; Mary, d. unmarried. Aaron and Anna had one daughter, Emma, m. Albert Dingee. The latter have two children, Lester and Blanche.

9. Everard, 7th-mo. 21, 1800, m. Frances Watson, d. 2d-mo. 11, 1868, aged 71, daughter of John Watson, of Bucking-

ham, and removed to Illinois. Their children: (1) Watson, 1826; (2) William D., 6th-mo. 5, 1828, m. Alice G. Thomas, daughter of Jervis and Jane Thomas, and had four children, Susan J., 2d-mo. 20, 1855, d. unmarried; Mary Ella, 9th-mo. 20, 1856, m. and died without children; Jane T., 2d-mo. 20, 1858; Alice Lulu, 1st-mo. 26, 1864, d. unmarried; (3) Jonathan Ingham, 1830; (4) Thomas D., m. Maria Whiteman; (5) Lester E.

Watson Foulke, son of Everard, Jr., and Frances, 9th-mo. 10, 1826, m. 11th-mo. 29, 1860, Ollive Sayles. They live in Kansas. Their children: (1)Fannie M., 11-mo. 1, 1861, m. 10th-mo. 4, 1880, Charles B. Haskins; they have three children. (2) Asa M., 1863, d. in infancy. (3) Everard L., 10th-mo. 25, 1868, a lawyer at Hutchinson, Kansas. (4) Myron S., 2d-mo. 21, 1872, m. 1894, Nora Combs. (5) Amy Bell, 1876. (6) Grace P., 1881.

Thomas DeHaven Foulke, son of Everard, Jr., and Frances, m. Maria E. Whiteman. Their children: (1) Fannie W., 1869, m. 1891, Frank M. Ross. (2) Charles Whiteman, 1871. (3) Edith Penrose, 1875. (4) Thomas Everard, 1878.

Lester E. Foulke, son of Everard Jr., and Frances, m. 1882, Lenora M. Duncan, resides in Kansas. Their children: William E., 1883; Ollie B., 1884, d. 1886; Lenora Grace, 1886, d. 1889; Ingham T., 1887, d. 1889; Lilian E., 1889; Lester D., 1891; Edward, 1893.

Caleb Foulke is mentioned above as having married Jane Green. The couple had six children, as follows:

1. Caroline, d. in infancy.

2. Caroline, 2d-mo. 25, 1810, d. 12th-mo. 17, 1838.

3. Maryetta, 7th-mo. 30, 1811, d. 4th-mo. 26, 1851, m. Aaron Penrose. Their children, Benjamin F. Penrose, of Cheltenham, m. Alice Thomson (con. in Penrose line); Caroline, m. David J. Ambler; Rebecca, m. Lewis J. Ambler. (See Amblers, Chapter VII, for last two.)

4. Benjamin G. Foulke, 7th-mo. 28, 1813, d. 8th-mo. 14, 1888, m. Jane Mather, daughter of Charles and Jane Mather, b. 3d-mo. 24, 1817, of Whitpain, at Gwynedd, on 3d-mo. 6, 1838.

5. Eleanor, 3d-mo. 12, 1816, d. 8th-mo. 13, 1842, m. 3d-mo. 4, 1841, Samuel J. Levick, and had one child, Jane, m. Edwin A. Jackson.

Benjamin G. and Jane Mather Foulke, mentioned above, had the following children:

1. Caleb, 12th-mo. 3, 1839, d. 10th-mo. 20, 1865.

2. Charles M., 7th-mo. 25, 1841, m. 12th-mo. 10, 1872, at Paris, France, Sarah A., daughter of Horace C. and Harriet C. Cushing, of New York City; their children: Horace C., 7th-mo. 6, 1876; Helen S., 7th-mo. 12, 1878; Gladys, 4th-mo. 29, 1881; Gwendolyn, 12th-mo. 31, 1883.

3. Job Roberts, 2d-mo. 23, 1843, trust officer of Provident Life and Trust Company, of Philadelphia, m. 5th-mo. 25, 1869, Emma Bullock, daughter of Samuel and Jemima R., of Mount Holly, N. J. They have two children: Roland R., 5th-mo. 10, 1874; Rebecca Mulford, 7th-mo. 18, 1875.

4. Anna, 1846.

5. Jane, 1848, d. 1853.

6. Eleanor, 1850.

THEOPHILUS FOULKE.

Theophilus and Margaret (Thomas) Foulke had a large family of children, as follows:

1. Hugh, 8th-mo. 29, 1758, d. 9th-mo. 1846, m. 1st, 4th-mo. 8, 1785, Sarah Roberts, 2d, 12th-mo. 27, 1798, Sarah Lester, 3d, 1st-mo. 17, 1804, Catharine Johnson. By the first marriage there were no children; by the second, Joseph, Martha, Joseph; by the third, Deborah, Sarah, Hugh, Theophilus, Casper, Benjamin.

2. Jane, 8th-mo. 22, 1759, d. 3d-mo. 16, 1816.

3. Theophilus, 8th-mo. 26, 1761, d. 7th-mo. 28, 1798, m. 5th-mo. 31, 1792, Hannah Lester. He was accidentally killed by falling from a tree which he had ascended to release a fishing line. He had been a member of the Pennsylvania Legislature, 1794-7, and a Justice of the Peace. The children of Theophilus, Jr., and Hannah Lester Foulke were: (1) Antrim, a well-known physician of Gwynedd, 3d-mo. 21, 1793, d. 9th-mo. 6, 1861, m. Letitia Lancaster, 12th-mo. 18, 1799, d. 1st-mo. 6, 1877, daughter of Thomas and Ann Lancaster, of Whitemarsh; (2) Sarah Foulke, 1st-mo. 10, 1797, d. 10th-mo. 25, 1852, m. 1819, Richard

Moore, 4th-mo. 20, 1794, d. 4th-mo. 30, 1875, son of Henry and Priscilla, of Montgomery Square.

4.   Benjamin, 1763; d. in infancy.

5.   Sarah, 1764, d. 1828, m. Edward Jenkins, of Gwynedd, 7th-mo. 12, 1758, d. 1829, and had six children.

6.   Benjamin, 11th-mo. 19, 1766, d. 2d-mo. 28, 1821, m. Martha Roberts (1764-1831) daughter of John and Margaret Roberts. (See Chapter VIII.)   Their children: (1) Hannah, 12th-mo. 25, 1789, m. George Custard and had two children, Martha F., 2d-mo. 3, 1817; Joseph, 4th-mo. 12, 1819; (2) Jane, 1st-mo. 25, 1793, m. Thomas Strawn; (3) Charles, 10th-mo. 14, 1796, d. 1857, unmarried; (4) Rachel, 1st-mo. 16, 1800; (5) Rachel, 2d, 3d-mo. 14, 1803.   Benjamin was an Assemblyman from Bucks county, 1816.   He died at Harrisburg while attending to his duties.

7.   Margaret, m. her first cousin Cadwallader, son of Samuel and Ann Foulke.   Their descendants have been given in Samuel's line above.

8 and 9.   Rachel and Charles (twins), 1773, died in infancy.

10.   Rachel, 3d-mo. 17, 1775, d. 3d-mo. 3, 1830, m. Dr. Joseph Meredith, of Gwynedd.   They lived at Gwynedd.   He died 8th-mo. 7, 1820.   Their children: (1) Hannah Hough, d. March 6, 1870; (2) Dr. Charles F. Meredith, 6th-mo. 1808, of Quakertown, d. 3d-mo. 1, 1896, m. Olivia Weisel, their children being Bella, Rachel, Sallie (d. 3d-mo. 15, 1876), Dr. William Henry m. and Flora, m. Johnson Strawn and has children; (3) Margaret, deceased; (4) Edward J., 12th-mo. 20, 1811, d. 4th-mo. 5, 1865, at Gwynedd.

Edward and Sarah Jenkins' children:

1.   Charles F. Jenkins m. Mary Lancaster.   They had seven children, of whom five d. young.   Algernon S., d. 1890, m. Anna Maria Thomas, daughter of Spencer and Hephziba Thomas (see Spencer genealogy Chapter VII), and had one child: Howard Malcolm.   Algernon's second wife was Alice A. Davis. Their child: George Herbert, a member of the Philadelphia Bar. Howard M. Jenkins m. Mary Anna, daughter of Thomas A. and Hannah Atkinson, of Upper Dublin.   Their children:

(1).   Charles F., associated with Wilmer Atkinson in the publication of the "Farm Journal," a successful monthly devoted to agriculture. Charles m. Marie Cope; they have two children, Algernon S. and Isabella.

(2). Anna, m. Daniel Webster and reside at Mankato, Minnesota. They have two daughters, the older Dorothea.

(3). Thomas A., m. Marion Magill, daughter of ex-President Edward H. Magill, of Swarthmore College. They have two children: Beatrice and Edward.

(4). Edward A., m. M. Ellen Atkinson. They have one child, Howard Malcolm. They reside in Chicago.

(5). Florence.

(6). Arthur Hugh.

George Herbert Jenkins m. Jessie Stockton Allen, a niece of the famous novelist, Frank R. Stockton. She died about two years ago, leaving one child, Dudley Allen Jenkins.

It may be added that the store and residence of Walter H. Jenkins occupies the site of a building, part of which is still in existence, which was a hotel during the Revolutionary War. It was bought from John Martin by Edward Jenkins in 1794, who built the store end and kept it until his death in 1829. The post-office, established in Edward's time, has always been in the family, Walter having succeeded his father as Postmaster.

William H. Jenkins, d. 1896, brother of Algernon S., m. Catharine Hallowell, recently deceased, leaving two children: Mary J., widow of Evan Ambler (see Amblers, Chapter VII), Walter H., m. Esther Lukens, and have five children: Sarah S., Horace, William, Esther, Evan A. Horace, another son of William H. and Catharine Jenkins, d. young. William H. Jenkins was for many years Postmaster at Gwynedd. Algernon S. was an exceedingly careful and correct business man, his conveyances of property and other papers being invariably prepared with the most scrupulous exactness. He was Justice of the Peace for many years, and his good judgment caused his counsel to be sought by many.

Howard M. Jenkins is a journalist and author of note, most of his time being devoted to editing the "Friends' Intelligencer and Journal." He has published many historical papers, largely on topics connected with Friends. His most important work, "Historical Collections of Gwynedd," published in 1884, a new edition being issued in 1897, stands very high among works of this character. He takes an active interest in Society matters generally, and is a very useful member.

2. Ann Jenkins, daughter of Edward and Sarah, d. unmarried.

3. Jesse Jenkins, m. Mary R. Ambler, and, in 1840, removed to Peoria, Illinois, dying there at a very advanced age. Jesse and Mary have several children, of whom three survive, John A., 1st-mo. 20, 1831, Albanus, 7th-mo. 24, 1833, and Lydia, 2d-mo. 15, 1845. Albanus is married and has several children. The other children of Jesse and Mary, all deceased, were: Edward, 8th-mo. 10, 1829; Mary Ann, 1st-mo. 31, 1836; Thomas, 12th-mo. 10, 1837; Letitia, 5th-mo. 30, 1839; Charles Edward, 5th-mo. 10, 1842.

4. Margaret Jenkins, 3d-mo. 6, 1800, m. Peter C. Evans, son of Caleb and Catharine Evans. Their children: Catharine, 10th-mo. 21, 1832, m. Chalkley Ambler; Sarah, 9th-mo. 7, 1836, d. unmarried; Charles Edward, 8th-mo. 9, 1838, m. Arabella Green. C. Edward and Arabella Evans have three children: Edward Jr., William S. and Henry. Edward, the father, has long been blind, the result of an accident. Catharine and Chalkley Ambler's children are: Jennie, a teacher at Friends' Central School, Philadelphia; Anna M., a teacher at Abington Friends' School; and Melville, residing in Philadelphia.

5. Rachel Jenkins, youngest daughter of Edward and Sarah, 10th-mo. 7, 1802, m. Meredith Conard, 3d-mo. 15, 1801, eldest son of Streeper and Sarah Conard. Their children: Henry, 1st-mo. 20, 1830 (died at birth); Henry Streeper, 2d-mo. 27, 1831, d. 7th-mo. 11, same year; Edward Jenkins, 10th-mo. 4, 1833, d. 3d-mo. 28, same year; Eleanor, 1st-mo. 14, 1836, m. William H. Shoemaker; Sarah Ann, 3d-mo. 20, 1838, d. 9th-mo. 10, same year; Mary Margaretta, 11th-mo. 7th, 1840, m. Aaron Ambler.

6. Caleb, d. at the age of 11 years, 6 months.

Eleanor Conard and William H., son of Joseph and Phebe Shoemaker, were m. 1st-mo. 14, 1857. William d. 3d-mo. 8, 1871. Their children:

1. Estelle, 2d-mo. 23, 1858, m. 10th-mo. 20, 1881, Charles Major, son of John and Margaret Major. Their children are Charles Percy, 4th-mo. 25, 1883, Eleanor S.

2.   Edward Conard, 4th-mo. 11, 1861.

3.   Joseph, 1st-mo. 15, 1869.

Mary Margaretta Conard and D. Aaron Ambler, son of David and Margaret Ambler, were m. 1st-mo. 17, 1866.   Their children : Ellen and Isabel, the last-named deceased.

WILLIAM FOULKE.

William Foulke, 12th-mo. 10, 1728, d. 4th-mo. 11, 1796, son of Hugh and Ann, m. Priscilla Lester, 1st-mo. 18, 1736, d. 3d-mo. 17, 1795, daughter of John Lester.   Their children :

1.   Asher, 2d-mo. 15, 1758, m. 11th-mo. 11, 1779, Alice Roberts, and had five children : Phebe, Anthony, William, Anne, Elizabeth.

2.   Isaachar, 1st-mo. 31, 1760, and his wife Jane had the following children : Priscilla, 8th-mo. 11, 1793 ; Bathsheba, 11th-mo. 15, 1794 ; Mary, 8th-mo. 3, 1797 ; Sarah, 10th-mo. 3, 1799 ; Rebecca, 5th-mo. 30, 1801 ; Jane, 12th-mo. 1, 1802 ; Aaron, 10th-mo. 26, 1804 ; Mercy, 9th-mo. 25, 1806, d. 11th-mo. 5, 1806 ; and Barton.   They removed to the West, but do not appear to have been granted a certificate.

3.   Jesse, 4th-mo. 28, 1762, and Sarah his wife (d. 9th-mo. 21 1791) had four children : Ellen, Hannah, Rachel and William.

4.   John, 10th-mo. 18, 1764 ; d. 12th-mo. 28, 1765.

5.   Mary, 10th-mo. 24, 1766.

6.   Phebe, 10th-mo., 1769 ; d. 11th-mo. 13, 1773.

ANTRIM FOULKE.

Antrim Foulke, of Gwynedd, son of Theophilus and Hannah, of Richland, m. Letitia Lancaster.   They had six children :

1.   John L., 2d-mo. 14, 1822, d. in Philadelphia, 10th-mo. 30, 1870.   He studied medicine with his father, and practised with much success at Gwynedd and Philadelphia, entering the United States service during the war and continuing as a hospital surgeon until its end.   He m., 1857, Anzonette Poulson (d. 1863).   Their only child, Charles Antrim, d. in 1865, in his third year.

2. Ann L., 4th-mo. 26, 1824, d. 2d-mo. 17, 1845, unmarried.

3. Henry, 1825, d. 1864, m. 1852, Maria L. Banks. Their children: (1) William W., m. Elizabeth C. Kent; (2) Letitia L., m. Ellis C. Kent and had four children, Ellis C., 1881; Henry Antrim Foulke, 1884; Edward Lyon, 1886; Lester F., 1894; (3) May, 1856, m. Charles O. Beaumont, and had two children: Mason F., 1887; Gwen Elizabeth, 1890; (4) Hannah, 1860, d. 1876.

4. Jane, 1827, d. 1833.

5. Hannah, 1829, d. 1884, m. 1851, Thomas W. Baily, d. 1893.

6. William, 1831, d. 1855.

CHARLES AND CATHERINE FOULKE.

Mention has been made, page 150, of Evan and Sarah Foulke, the husband being a son of John and Mary (Roberts) Foulke. Among their children was Charles, m. Catharine P. Edkin.

Children of Charles and Catharine Foulke, of Stroudsburg:

1. Frances A., 1832, d. 1889.

2. Sarah Jane, 1834, d. in her 15th year.

3. Susan L., 1836.

4. Joseph F., 1838, m. Caroline McCully. Their children: Maria, Charles M., Helen.

5. Hannah M., 1840, m. Sydenham Rhoads. Their children: Joseph F., m. Matilda Snyder; Anna, m. William Hager; Arthur, m. Estelle Hager; Edna, m. William Latham.

6. Samuel L., 1842, m. Mary Wolf; their children: Benjamin T., Elizabeth, Marguerite.

7 and 8. Tacy, Keziah, twins, 1844, d. in infancy.

9. Martha E., 1845, m. J. P. B. Primrose; their children: Theodore, Elizabeth W., Walter, Joseph, William.

10 and 11. Mary (d. in infancy), Elizabeth, 1848, twins. Elizabeth m. Theodore G. Wolf. They have one son, William S.

No acknowledged minister of her time was better known than Catharine Foulke. Her labors in this direction gave great satisfaction, and accomplished much good.

X.

PETER LESTER.

Peter Lester, mentioned as a pioneer of the early immigration to Great Swamp, he being spoken of as "our ancient Friend" in the account of the settlement of Richland Meeting, in connection with the statement that meetings for worship were held at his house for several years, came to Pennsylvania in 1682. At Chester Monthly Meeting, Fourth-month 6, 1685, of that year he and Mary Duncalf (or Duncof) declared their intention of marriage with each other. The following month the declaration was repeated, according to the discipline of the Society, and the couple were married, there is no doubt, a few days later. At Abington Monthly Meeting, Sixth-month 25, 1710, John Ball and Catharine Lester "passed meeting," as it is called. Previously, Seventh-month 27, 1708, Abraham Griffith and Peter's daughter Hannah had declared their intentions of marriage at the same place. Eighth-month 29, 1716, Peter, his wife and daughter Elizabeth received a certificate to Gwynedd, they having already removed to the Great Swamp.

The following account, undoubtedly correct in the main, was obtained from a member of the family:

Peter Lester came to this country with William Penn in 1682, who gave him a square of ground on Market street, Philadelphia, which he afterward sold for thirty pounds.

He settled near Quakertown, where he purchased several hundred acres of land.

He had several children, among whom were John, William, Catherine and Priscilla.

William went to Maryland or Virginia, where he married

and had four children—Thomas, Shipley, Jane and Priscilla. The last-named married a Dickerson.

John 3d married Jane Antrim, who had six children, among them Thomas, who first married Mary Stokes, and had one son Peter, who married Margaret Foulke. They had two daughters.

Thomas Lester's second wife was Hannah Green, and they had three children—Evan, Mary and Sarah Ann. Evan married Cynthia E. Jones, of Gwynedd, and had one son, Evan Jones Lester, who married Elizabeth G. Green, and have three sons—Barton G., Joseph G. and Evan J. Barton married Elizabeth C. Lothrop, and is living in Denver, Col. Evan J. married Helen G. Satterthwaite. They have three children—Helen May, Gertrude and Evan.

Mary [daughter of Thomas Lester] married Watson Comly [of Byberry]. They had four children—Lester, Mary, Rachel and Cynthia. Lester married Mary Bowman. [He died several years ago.] They had two children—Alice and Rowland. Rachel [now deceased] married Thomas Shallcross, and had five children—Watson, Thomas, Mary, Bessie and Wilmer. Cynthia married Joseph Bosler. They have four children—Mary, Caroline, Charles and Lester. Mary [daughter of Watson Comly] married J. Howard Ervien. They have one child, Horace. Sarah [daughter of Thomas Lester] married Arthur DeCernea, M. D. They have one son, Edward, living in New York.

Shipley Lester married and had several children—among them Albert. His children: Maria, Hannah, Jane and Sallie.

The Lester place at Quakertown has been occupied by five generations of the name. It was called Leicestershire.

The Lesters are mentioned in connection with many of the families whose genealogies are given in this volume, they having intermarried with several of the older families of Richland.

The following is a paper in the possession of Elizabeth G. Lester. It was written by her father, Joseph Green, about 1855:

"This is my genealogy as far back as I have been able to trace it.

"My Great Grandfather took up a large tract of land on Saucon Creek in Bucks County, at that time right amongst the Indians, he settled on it, and married a Widow Large a daughter of Ellis Lewis, they had three sons whose names were Francis, James and Joseph, Joseph is my Grandfather.

"Francis and James emigrated to the northern part of Virginia, took a tract of land and settled amongst the Indians. My Great Grandfather and Great Grandmother remained with their son Joseph in Bucks County until his death, when Francis and James came on for their aged parents on horseback, for there were no roads then, but Indian paths, and the old couple returned with their sons riding on horseback, having to swim the rivers, and they were then each of them over eighty years, they stood the journey well, and spent the remainder of their days with their two sons Francis and James. Further tradition sayeth not."

"Joseph Green, of the third generation, now in his sixty-fifth year, is the only survivor of the eleven children of Benjamin and Jane Green.

"My mother was a daughter of John and Martha Roberts, [he] one of the early settlers in Richland. He died at the age of eighty-five years. Edward Roberts, his eldest son, died at the age of eighty years, four months. John, the second son, died at the age of 89 years, 7 months. William, the third son, died at the age of 85 years, 7 months, 20 days. Jane Green, my mother, died at the age of 88 years, 1 month, 2 days. Aunt Ann Penrose, another sister, died at the age of 96 years, 2 months, 12 days. Aunt Mary, Aunt Sarah and Aunt Martha lived to a like good old age. The average age of the six of this Roberts family was nearly ninety years, being an unusual instance of longevity in one family. Benjamin Green, my father, was born April 27, 1750, and lived to the age of 78 years."

THE STRAWNS.

Jacob Strawn or Strawhen, the pioneer of the Strawn family in Richland, was born in Middletown township, Bucks county, Pa., in 1717, where his father, Launcelot Strawhen, died a year later. His mother, Mary Strawhen, was the second daughter of William Buckman, of the parish of Billinghurst, County of Sussex, England, who arrived in the Delaware river in the "Welcome," in 1682, with wife, Sarah, and daughters Sarah and Mary. The latter was born November 23, 1680, and married in 1703, Henry Cooper, a blacksmith, of Newtown, who died in 1710, leaving three sons, William, Henry and John, and two daughters. The eldest daughter, Sarah, married Thomas Strickland, in 1727, and after his death in 1737, Jonathan Abbott. Ruth Cooper m. Dennis Pursell, who removed to Bethlehem township, Hunterdon county, New Jersey. The widow, Mary Cooper, married Launcelot Strawhen prior to the date of her father's will, in 1716, and was disowned by Friends therefor, Launcelot not being a member.

After the death of her second husband it is presumed that Mary Strawn made her home with her daughter Ruth, in New Jersey, as her will, dated 1738, proved 1740, was dated there, though proved in Pennsylvania.

Jacob Strawn married Christiana Pursell (mentioned upon the Friends' Records at Richland as "Staunchy," which seems to have been a nickname applied to her on account of her stocky build), in 1741, and removed to Richland, where he became a large landholder and a useful and prominent citizen. He had twelve children, nine sons and three daughters: Thomas, 1742; John, 1744; Jacob, 1747; William, 1749; Daniel, 1752; Hannah,

1756, m. John White; Isaiah, 1758; Job, 1760; Jerusha, 1762, m. Jeremiah Reed; Abel, 1765; Enoch, 1768; and Mary, 1754.

Thomas m. Mary Heacock and removed to Redstone, and from there to Richmond, Kentucky, where he left numerous descendants.

John m. Kezia Dennis, and settled at Turkeyfoot in 1799, but later removed to Kentucky; had 19 children.

Jacob m. Susanna VanBuskirk and removed to Redstone, Fayette county.

William m. 1st Ann VanHorn, 2d, Mary Raudenbush, and remained in Richland, as did Daniel, the grandfather of Eli Strawn, now living in Quakertown.

Daniel's first wife was Ann Lloyd, 2d Margaret Pursell, 3d Sarah (Shaw) Moore.

Isaiah removed from Richland to Redstone and thence to Ohio.

Job m. Mary Cooper and removed to Fayette county, and thence to Indiana.

Mary m. a Van Buskirk; Jerusha m. Jeremiah Reed; Abel m. Elizabeth Raudenbush; Enoch m. Rebecca Raudenbush.

All raised large families of children, many of whom have become prominent and useful citizens in various parts of the union. The Strawns were noted for their size and strength.

Daniel and Ann had four children: William L. and John and two daughters, who died in infancy. Ann dying, Daniel m. (second wife) Margaret Pursell. They had fourteen children: Ann, Christiana, Isaiah, Jacob, Mary, Hannah, Margaret, Thomas, Daniel, Jane, Elizabeth, Jesse, Abel and Ellen. Daniel married a third time but had no children by that marriage.

Johnson Strawn, 4th-mo. 4, 1811, d. 8th-mo. 28, 1858, was a son of Thomas. He m. 10th-mo. 10, 1833, Jane Penrose, 2d-mo. 27, 1808, d. 12th-mo. 10, 1853. Their children: Joseph P., 8th-mo. 16, 1836, d. 8th-mo. 8, 1858; Thomas, 4th-mo. 9, 1838; Mary Ann, 4th-mo. 18, 1841, m. Joseph W. Foulke; Johnson, 10th-mo. 15, 1849, m. Florence Meredith, daughter of Charles F. and Olivia.

Eli W. Strawn, of Quakertown, b. 1st-mo. 25, 1822, is a son of William L. and Jane. He m. 12th-mo. 12, 1844, Margaret Penrose, 9th-mo. 11, 1821. Their children: Henry P., 10th-mo.

30, 1845; Mary P., 9th-mo. 26, 1847; Rebecca Jane, 7th-mo. 20, 1851, d. 7th-mo. 13, 1854; William L., 7th-mo. 1, 1855; Eli, 2d-mo. 6, 1858. Jane, mother of Eli W., d. 2d-mo. 1859.

Thomas Strawn, father of Postmaster Charles F. Strawn, married Mary Johnson. She died in 1827, and in 1829 he married Jane, daughter of Benjamin Foulke. Charles Foulke Strawn married a daughter of Charles F. and Margaret Warwick. Their children are Harry W., Fred. P. and Mary F.

Isaiah Strawn was born 10th-mo. 28, 1758, at the farm homestead, in Haycock, near Quakertown, Bucks county, Pennsylvania. His parents were Jacob and Christiana.

To them were born nine sons and three daughters. They all lived to ripe old age and raised families of sons and daughters. In point of size, activity and physical endurance, this family of twelve children was remarkable. Isaiah was the eighth child. He was scarcely sick in his life and died at the age of 84 without the twitching of a muscle. If there was any one thing about which he delighted to talk it was what he remembered about the Revolutionary War and Washington. Too young for a soldier when that war began, and his parents being Friends, and therefore opposed to the shedding of blood, young Strawn was kept at home until the fall of 1777, when he obtained his parents' consent to enter the service as a teamster, and on the 4th of October, in that most disastrous battle between General Washington (with a loss of 1200 men) and the British under Gen. Gray and Col. Musgrove (with a loss of 600 men), at Germantown, Isaiah, then in his 19th year, left his team and went to the front. One of his neighbor's sons fell, mortally wounded, when the impetuous youth seized the musket of his fallen friend, resolved to avenge his death. He soon, however, received a charge of large-sized buckshot in his left leg, and was carried from the field. One shot lodged and became incrusted in the hollow of his foot. This he would not permit to be taken out. He prized this piece of British lead above everything and carried it there for over 64 years, and was buried with it still in his foot.

He learned the blacksmith trade and followed that as a means of support until the year 1812, and then turned his entire attention to farming and stock-raising, in which he was for the time quite successful.

On the 12th of August, 1781, he married Rachel, daughter of John Reed, and located in Turkeyfoot township, Somerset county, Pennsylvania, carrying on his trade until the spring of 1817, when he sold out his shop and tools and moved overland to a farm he had previously purchased in Knox county, Ohio, near where Martinsburg now stands. Here he remained happy and prosperous until the year 1837. In the meantime, five of his six children had married and gone to the then new state of Illinois. John and Jeremiah had gone there in 1829, Jacob and Elsie in 1831, and Joel in 1834, leaving but one child in Ohio, and she thirty miles off. This induced the old folks to sell their fine farm and comfortable home in Ohio and move to Illinois. This they did that spring, although they were both nearly octogenarians.

He purchased a finely improved farm adjoining that of his son Jeremiah, in Florid township, Putnam county, Illinois. His wife died in her chair on the evening of April 2, 1843, without a moment's warning and apparently without pain, and just four months later her husband followed her. They were buried side by side in the beautiful cemetery at the village near their home. On the slabs, in plain raised letters, are the following inscriptions: "Rachel Strawn, born July 1, 1763, died April 2, 1843." "Isaiah Strawn, born October 28, 1758, died August 2, 1843."

Their union was blessed by four sons and two daughters— Joel, 7th-mo. 13, 1782; Mary, 3d-mo. 19, 1785; Elsie, 11th-mo. 24, 1789; John, 11th-mo. 26, 1791; Jeremiah, 8th-mo. 4, 1795; and Jacob, 5th-mo. 31, 1800, all of whom survived their parents and lived to ripe old age. Isaiah Strawn and wife united with the Methodist Episcopal Church soon after their marriage, and from thence on they were active members of that denomination.

Having acquired the reputation of being the swiftest runner in the army of Washington, he concluded that he could outrun anybody and continued in that belief until he had passed three-score and ten.

Joel Strawn, 7th-mo. 13, 1782, the oldest son of Isaiah and Rachel, married Sarah Tannyhill, 9th-mo. 26, 1805, and moved to a tract of wild land in Perry county, Ohio.

His wife, Sarah, died 1822. He married, 11th-mo. 25, 1824, Lydia M. Chalfant.

He held the position of Associate Judge for many years and served in the War of 1812.

In 1834 he sold his farm in Ohio and purchased a tract of unimproved land near Ottawa, Illinois, and moved to it, where he improved and cultivated his new farm and continued to occupy and enjoy it up to the time of his death, 8th-mo. 24, 1864.

By the first marriage there were four children: Isaiah, 10thmo. 7, 1808; Jemima, 2d-mo. 20, 1810; James, 2d-mo. 15, 1813; Sarah Ann, 1st-mo. 6, 1819; and by the second marriage, Robert Chalfant, 9th-mo. 1, 1825; Abner, 7th-mo. 4, 1830; Rachel, 3d-mo. 22, 1829.

Mary Strawn, second child, was born in Somerset county, Pa., 3d-mo. 19, 1785, m. Mordecai Chalfant, 1st-mo. 14, 1802. In 1813 they moved to Coshocton county, Ohio, where they had purchased a farm. Here they remained during life. They raised a family of five children—James, Margaret, John, William and Rachel. For many years he held the office of Associate Judge and also represented Coshocton county in the State Legislature. He died about the year 1842. Mary, his wife, died at the homestead, April 24, 1864, at the age of 82 years.

Elsie Strawn, 3d child, 11th-mo. 24, 1789, married Joseph Armstrong, 5th-mo. 19, 1808, in Somerset county, Pa., and settled on a farm in that county. In 1811 her father purchased for her a fine tract of wild land in McCain township, Licking county, Ohio, to which they moved, and lived in a small log cabin for several years while they were improving it.

Her husband conducted a distillery and in time acquired a taste for liquor. He became intemperate and abused his family and this his high-spirited wife could not endure. She took her sons, left him, going to her father's home, in Knox county, Ohio, and filed a bill for divorce. Litigation ensued, but a compromise was effected by which she retained the household goods, the four horses, wagon and harness with which she left home, and $700, with the custody of her eight sons.

Her brother, Jacob Strawn, had been West and bought a large farm near Jacksonville. The two families, Jacob, his wife and three sons, and Elsie S. Armstrong, with her seven sons started together and traveled in company to Vincennes, where they separated, Jacob going to Jacksonville, and Elsie to Marshall county, Illinois.

She was a woman of great energy and courage, small of stature but hardy and talented. Though the mother of nine sons: John S., 5th-mo. 29, 1810; George W., 12th-mo. 11, 1812; William E., 10th-mo. 25, 1814; Joel W., 1st-mo. 6, 1817; James H., 6th-mo. 27, 1819; Jeremiah R., 7th-mo. 5, 1821; Perry A., 4th-mo. 15, 1823; Clifford I., 4th-mo. 27, 1825, and Isaiah J., 7th-mo. 4, 1828, she was well preserved and full of energy.

Elsie S. Armstrong died at her residence in Morris, Ill., May 29, 1871, aged nearly 83 years.

John Strawn, 11th-mo. 26, 1791, d. July 4, 1872. He married Mary McClish, 1st-mo. 1, 1813. To them were born nine children: William, 10th-mo. 16, 1814; Rachel, 2d-mo. 18, 1818; Mrs. Mary Ann Thompson, 2d-mo. 28, 1820; Enoch, 2d-mo. 18, 1822; Caroline, 6th-mo. 5, 1823; Emily, 10th-mo. 4, 1824; Salome, 6th-mo. 26, 1826; Susan M., 4th-mo. 6, 1828; Savicy H., 2d-mo. 16, 1833. John's wife, Mary, d. September 4th, 1858. In 1861 he married Mary Haskins, to whom was born John M., 6th-mo. 9, 1862. She dying in 1863, he married 7th-mo. 9, 1864, Ellen Calvert, to whom were born two daughters, Mary R., 5th-mo. 26, 1865; Ellen C., 7th-mo. 25, 1868.

Jeremiah Strawn, 5th child, 8th-mo. 7, 1795, m. 5th-mo. 23, 1815, Hannah Bauscher and moved to Perry county, Ohio, where he purchased and improved a fine farm. In 1829 he sold out in Ohio and moved overland to Putnam county, Ill., where he purchased and finely improved a large farm.

He died November, 1883, at Ottawa. Hannah, his wife, died in 1874. To Jeremiah and Hannah Strawn were born ten children: Eli, 3d-mo. 24, 1814; David, 10th-mo. 18, 1818; Isaiah, 2d-mo. 20, 1820; Louisa, 4th-mo. 10, 1822; Matilda, 11th-mo. 6, 1823; Phebe, 10th-mo. 15, 1826; Henry C., 12th-mo. 4, 1828; Mary, 2d-mo. 29, 1830; Zilpha, 2d-mo. 16, 1833; Susan, 2d-mo. 19, 1835.

Jacob Strawn, 6th child, 5th-mo. 31, 1800. Born in Fayette county, Pennsylvania, and moved to Knox county, Ohio, with his parents in 1811. In 10th-mo., 1819, he married Matilda Green, daughter of John Green, of Knox county, Ohio.

His father, Isaiah, having given him a hundred and sixty acres of timber, and adjoining his land, Jacob erected a cabin on his wild land and commenced with vigor to make his fortune.

As the price of land in that locality became high he determined, in 1830, to go West.   In that year himself and wife, mounted each upon a good horse, visited the state of Illinois, and purchased a farm of several thousand acres in Morgan county, some four miles west of Jacksonville, and in the spring of 1831 they moved overland thereto with their three sons: William, 1823; James, 1824, and Isaiah, 1827.   Jacob Strawn became the most extensive cattle dealer in the West.   He introduced the practice of stall-feeding in the novel plan of cutting and shocking his corn and feeding it by the wagon load to cattle in a dry or elevated lot, having three lots for use at the same time and changing lots daily.   Thus the fodder, with the corn on, would be given to the cattle he desired for market the first day, in one of these lots; the day following stock cattle would be placed in this lot and the beef cattle in another lot and fed as the day previous, and the third day a change was again made and his hogs were put in the lot first occupied by the beef cattle to pick up and utilize the offal, thus alternating daily.   This system proved to be a success, and has been very generally adopted by cattle dealers all over the state.

His wife, Matilda, dying soon after coming to Illinois, he, at the age of thirty-two, married Phebe Gates, daughter of Samuel Gates, Esq., of Green county, Ill., aged 16 years.   By the second marriage six children were born: Daniel, Julius E., Jacob, Samuel G., David and Martha.   Jacob Strawn died 8th-mo. 25, 1865, leaving an immense fortune.   His widow Phebe erected an Italian villa in Jacksonville, where she lived in splendor.

XII.

RICHARD MOORE.

The Moores of Richland were descended from Mordecai Moore, a physician, by his first wife, his second wife being a daughter of Thomas Lloyd, well known in the early history of Pennsylvania. The son Richard m. 5th-mo. 27, 1709, Margaret Preston, b. 1689, daughter of Samuel Preston, who was born in Pantuxent, Md., in 1665, and became Mayor of Philadelphia in 1711. Margaret Preston's mother was Rachel, daughter of the same Thomas Lloyd, mentioned above. Richard Moore was a physician and merchant, and resided most of his life in Maryland. Richard had five children.

Mordecai Moore, son of Richard, m. Elizabeth Coleman, and had eight children: Margaret, Mary, Richard, Samuel Preston, Rachel, Deborah, Henry and Hannah. Mary m. Jonathan Dickinson, and Hannah became the second wife of Charles Willson Peale, the famous artist. Henry, 5th-mo. 29, 1753, m. Priscilla Hill Jackson. His father, Mordecai, died at Montgomery Square, Pa., 7th-mo. 31, 1800.

Henry Moore, son of Mordecai and Elizabeth, resided in Montgomery county, and afterwards in Lancaster county. They had seven children, Mordecai, Mary, Samuel Preston, Elizabeth, Milcah Martha, Richard and Charles. Henry d. in 1829; his wife in 1821.

Richard Moore, of Richland, was prominent in the Society of Friends, as was his son, John Jackson Moore. He was active in the Anti-Slavery movement, sheltering and feeding many fugitives from bondage. He m. 1st-mo. 7, 1819, Sarah Foulke, daughter of Theophilus and Hannah Foulke, as we have seen. Their children: (1) John Jackson, 11th-mo. 17, 1819, m. Jane daughter of Isaac and Elizabeth Warner, they having three children, Alfred, Ellen, Arthur; (2) Hannah, 7th-mo. 27, 1821, m. 10th-mo. 5, 1843, William M. Levick, of the Philadelphia bar, a brother of Samuel J. Levick.   William d. 6th-mo. 10, 1874. Their children: Anna F., Elizabeth J.

Edward H. Magill, ex-President of Swarthmore College, in a paper read at a recent meeting of the Bucks County Historical Society at Doylestown, says:

"The home of our friend Richard Moore, in Quakertown, was the last important station of the underground railroad in our county, and the point where the northern Chester county line and most of the Bucks county lines converged.   His home soon became known to the Friends further south as a place where all fugitives forwarded would receive kindly care and needed assistance in their continued flight.   Thence they soon began to come directed to this home in very considerable numbers.   Although slaveholders rarely proceeded so far as this in pursuit of their slaves, they occasionally did so, and more than once the master has presented himself at the front door of Richard Moore a few moments after the object of his search, being forewarned of his approach, had escaped by a back door to a place of concealment in the rear.   Many of the fugitives, on reaching Quakertown, feeling comparatively safe, were willing to hire out there, and Richard Moore was ever ready to give them work himself, or find them employment among his friends and neighbors.   Still there were many slaves whose fear was so great that they were anxious to be passed on as soon as possible to a land of real freedom in Canada.   These were, of course, sent on at once, and generally with letters to Friends in Montrose or Friendsville.

"One of the slaves who reached this safe station at Quakertown about the year 1850, just at the time of the passage of the Fugitive Slave law, seemed especially brave, being destitute of fear even in that trying time.   He was a slave of Abraham Shriner, of Pipe Creek, Maryland, and was known as Bill Budd at home, but on running away from bondage, assumed the name of Henry Franklin, it being naturally a very common practice with runaway slaves to take an assumed name.   This man did not care to be sent to Canada, and was employed as a carter by Richard Moore for several years.   During this time he was much engaged in carting coal from the Lehigh river, there being then no railroad to Quakertown. There were often slaves to be sent northward, and he would load his wagon with them in the evening, cover them well with straw, and take them up during the night, giving them so much of a start on the lonely road towards Friendsville, and return with a load of coal the next day. Alfred Moore is quite confident that one of the slaves thus carried north by Henry Franklin was Parker, the principal actor in the tragedy of the "Christiana riots," in Lancaster county. Franklin afterwards came to Philadelphia, where he was for a number of years janitor in the Academy of Fine Arts, and lived in Philadelphia until his death.

"Richard Moore had sent on fugitives for several years, and when the number became quite large he began to keep a regular record, and after that time, until the war made escape from slavery unnecessary, he recorded the names of about 600."

Richard Moore started the first boarding-school in Quakertown and taught until 1825, when he gave up the profession on account of his health.

XIII

THOMAS ROBERTS.

Thomas and Alice Roberts, with several children, came from Wales about 1725, and with them came Letitia Rhea, from Ireland, who afterwards married their son, Thomas Roberts, Jr. Purchasing a horse and cart and other necessaries in Philadelphia, they commenced their journey into the wilderness, finally locating on a tract of land in Milford township, along the banks of "Butter Creek," where they soon built a log house, in which they continued to live until 1740 or 1742, when they built a substantial stone house, which was standing but a few years ago. This tradition was received from the late Joshua Foulke, of Quakertown, who in turn had received it from his mother, Ann, and from his Aunt Letitia Foulke, they being daughters of Thomas, Jr., and Letitia Roberts, and granddaughters of the original settlers, Thomas and Alice Roberts.

The draft of Richland township, made in 1734, when it was formed, shows that Thomas Roberts owned a tract of 250 acres adjoining lands of John Edwards and others, and, according to the inventory of his estate, made by Samuel Foulke and Joseph Rawlings, on the 18th day of June, 1767, he died possessed of what at that time was a considerable estate.

To distinguish the descendants of Thomas Roberts from those of Edward Roberts, both being early settlers in the locality, and, so far as is now known, not related to each other, one family was known in earlier times as "Pot Robertses" and the other as "Kettle Robertses," but which was "Pot" and which was "Kettle" cannot now be determined.

These designations appear to have vanished a century or more ago, as the two families became more and more connected by intermarriages with each other. They are said to have originated from the names applied to the sub-district of Merioneth-shire, Wales, from which the two settlers respectively came.

Of the numerous descendants of Thomas and Alice Roberts there are comparatively few now residing in Quakertown or its vicinity, and but one family having Roberts for its surname, the heads of various branches removing years ago to Chester county, Cheltenham and Muncy, Pennsylvania, and many of them now being found in Philadelphia and its vicinity.

The author is indebted to Clarence V. Roberts, of Philadelphia, for the greater part of the information contained in this chapter and in several succeeding ones, he being also a descendant of Edward Roberts, and connected by the ties of consanguinity, as is the author, with the majority of the families whose descent is traced in this volume.

The children of Thomas and Alice Roberts were:

1.   John, 6th-mo., 1716, d. 2d-mo. 2, 1797, m. 1st, in 1742, Martha Roberts, daughter of Edward and Mary, b. 8th-mo. 16, 1715, d. 1st-mo. 26, 1768; he m. second, 11th-mo. 1, 1770, Martha Edwards; and third, Mary ————, who survived him.

2.   Ann, 6th-mo., 1718, d. 3d-mo., 1807, m. William Heacock.

3.   Thomas, 2d-mo. 1720, d. 5th-mo. 30, 1786, m. 9th-mo. 14, 1750, Letitia Rhea.

4.   Richard, 12th-mo., 1722, m. Elizabeth Tyson.

5.   Alice, 2d-mo., 1724, d. 8th-mo. 6, 1767, m. 10th-mo., 1749. Edward Thomas.

6.   Rachel, 2d-mo., 1727, d. 8th-mo., 1767, m. ———— Jones.

7.   Abraham, 1st-mo. 14, 1730, m. first, 12th-mo. 9, 1756, Catharine Lester, and second 10th-mo. 7, 1779, Pennina Thomas.

8.   William, d. 8th-mo. 13, 1731.

A deed from Jesse Roberts, a descendant of Thomas Roberts, of Marlborough township, county of Montgomery, storekeeper, to Andrew Reed, of Rockhill, dated April 10th, 1811, and recorded at Doylestown in Deed Book No. 39, page 464, conveys eighty acres and fifty perches in Rockhill, "part of 115 acres granted to Thomas Roberts by patent from John, Thomas and Richard Penn, Proprietaries of Pennsylvania, dated January 20, 1738, 'Then said to be situated in Milford Twp' and which said land Thos. Roberts by deed dated April 2, 1750, granted to his son Richard Roberts, who by will dated January 22, 1789, devised the same to his son Jesse Roberts, party hereto."

JOHN ROBERTS.

John Roberts resided in Milford. His first wife, as noted, was Martha Roberts, and his second, Martha Edwards, 5th-mo. 22, 1716, d. 4th-mo. 17, 1781, widow of William Edwards and daughter of Hugh and Ann Foulke. His children, all by the first marriage, were:

1. Edward, 7th-mo. 3, 1743, d. 11th-mo. 3, 1823, unmarried.

2. Ann, 2d-mo. 16, 1745, d. 4th-mo. 28, 1841, m. 11th-mo. 8, 1764, John Penrose. (See Penrose line.)

3. John, 10th-mo. 28, 1746, d. 6th-mo. 22, 1836, unmarried.

4. Mary, 9th-mo. 30, 1748, d. 11th-mo. 30, 1843, m. 11th-mo. 8, 1770, William Penrose. (See Penrose line.)

5. Jane, 12th-mo. 28, 1751, d. 1753.

6. Jane, 4th-mo. 16, 1753, d. 5th-mo. 18, 1841, m. 11th-mo. 9, 1775, Benjamin Green. (See Green line.)

7. William, 8th-mo. 18, 1755, d. 4th-mo. 8, 1841, m. Rebecca Pennington.

8. Martha, 1st-mo. 23, 1758, m. Josiah Worrough (Worrell).

9. Sarah, 1st-mo. 23, 1761, m. 4th-mo. 28, 1785, Hugh Foulke, and had three children, Joseph, Martha and Joseph. (See Theophilus Foulke's line, Chapter IX.)

The Worrells have been referred to on page 96, the two daughters, Jane, 1st-mo. 31, 1792, and Abigail, 12th-mo. 24, 1793, having been placed with Robert Morris and his son-in-law, Jonathan Roberts, by their kinsman and guardian, Amos Roberts, in 1810. Nothing has been ascertained as to whom they married, if at all. They were probably the only children of the couple, as no others are mentioned.

William Roberts, who resided near Corner Store, Chester

county, was a son of John and Martha, of Milford, Bucks county. He was born 8th-mo. 18, 1755, d. 4th-mo. 8, 1841, m. Rebecca Pennington. Their children:

1. Joseph, 8th-mo. 7, 1785, m. Mary Walker.
2. Sarah, 12th-mo. 18, 1787, m. 6th-mo. 20, 1806, Daniel Conard.
3. Maria, 7th-mo. 22, 1789, m. 11th-mo. 24, 1808, Joseph Conard, Jr.
4. Martha, 4th-mo. 2, 1791, m. Thomas Matlack.
5. John, 12th-mo. 25, 1796, m.
6. Rebecca, 12th-mo. 25, 1796.
7. Nathan, 2d-mo. 26, 1800, d. 10th-mo. 21, 1805.

1. The children of Joseph and Mary Walker Roberts: (1) Sarah, m. John Williams; (2) Rebecca, unmarried; (3) William, m. Susan Havard; (4) Lewis, m. Sarah Jane Maris; (5) Mary, m. Caleb Hoopes, of Baltimore; (6) Stephen, m. Cordelia ———.

(1) The children of John and Sarah Roberts Willams: J. Roberts, m. Jane Kunkle, children being Sarah, Caroline and Mary; Mary Jane, m. William Johns, their children being Preston, Harvey, Davis, Venning, Frank and Lillian; Davis, m. Sarah Pennypacker, their children being Emma and Millie; I. Walker, m. Susan Stephens, their children being John and Leila; Sarah Ann, m. Everett W. Andrews, their child being Mary S.; Dr. William K., m. Wright, their child being May; Henrietta, m. John Kinsey, their children being William and John (see John Roberts line, Chapter VIII); B. Frank, m. Josephine Stephens, their child being Howard.

(3) The children of William and Susan Havard Roberts: Benjamin, d. 1st-mo. 29, 1862, at Camp Pierpont, Va.; Isaac W., m. Anna F. Daniel, their children being Alan and Dr. Burton; Mary Emily, m. Isaac Walker, Jr., their child being Benjamin R.; David H., m. Margaret Rodney, their child being Dr. Norman; William H., m. Kate Errett, their children being Emily May, Anne, Havard; George W., m. Janet McInnes, daughter of Hugh and Rebecca McInnes, of Norristown, their child being Rebecca; Dr. Charles J., m. Mary Rickabaugh, their children being Charles and Harold; Clarence B., unmarried; Sue R., m.

Elliot J. Thomas, their children being Pauline, Clarence, William, Herbert, Frank.

(4)   The children of Lewis and Sarah Jane (Maris) Roberts; Cornelia, m. Uriah Ullman, their children being Lewis, Clayton, Joseph, Harry and Howard; Rachel, m. Preston Rhoads, their children being Frank, Kate and Albert; David, m. Martha ——, their children being George and Mary E.; Kate, m. Amos Schillich; Lewis, unmarried; Joseph, unmarried.

(6)   The children of Stephen and Cordelia Roberts: Isaac W., Albert, John.

2.   The children of Daniel and Sarah (Roberts) Conard (of Tredyffrin township, Chester county, Pa.): Nathan, m. —————— Albertson; Maria.

3.   The children of Joseph and Maria (Roberts) Conard, of Tredyffrin; Charles, Lewis, Paul, John, David, m. Lucretia Wilson; William, Sarah.

4.   The children of Thomas and Martha (Roberts) Matlack: Joseph, William, Nathan, John, Jesse, Albert, m. Eliza Fudge; Lewis, Mary, Deborah, m. John Shaw.

THOMAS ROBERTS, JR.

Thomas, Jr., third child of Thomas and Alice Roberts, as we have seen, m. Letitia Rhea, b. in Ireland, who accompanied the family to this country.   Their children:

1.   Abigail, 7th-mo. 28, 1751, d. 7th-mo. 15, 1843, m. 3d-mo. 25, 1773, John Thomson.   (See Thomson line.)

2.   Martha, 3d-mo. 9, 1753, m. 11th-mo. 3, 1774, John Hallowell.   (See Hallowell line.)

3.   Alice, 4th-mo. 3, 1755, m. 11th-mo. 11, 1779, Asher Foulke, son of William and Priscilla.   (See Chapter IX.)

4.   Israel, 1st-mo. 14, 1757, d. 9th-mo., 1824, m. 6th-mo. 6, 1782, Ann Foulke, daughter of John and Mary.

5.   Elizabeth, 8th-mo. 7, 1859, d. 7th-mo. 25, 1793, m. 11th-mo. 1, 1781, Edward Foulke, son of John and Mary.   (See Chapter IX.)

6.   Isaac, 1st-mo. 25, 1762, m. Mary Green and had one

child, Alice, who m. —— Warner and had two children, Spencer and Ann. The latter m. —— Myers.

7. Ann, 11th-mo. 12, 1764, d. 12th-mo. 8, 1830, m. Edward Foulke, son of John and Mary (his second wife). (See Chapter IX.)

8. Letitia, 9th-mo. 10, 1767, d. 10th-mo. 18, 1854, m. 10th-mo. 29, 1789, John Foulke, son of Samuel and Ann. (See Chapter IX.)

9. Richard, 9th-mo. 27, 1777, d. 3d-mo. 7, 1836, m. first, Tacy Shoemaker; second, Rebecca Jones.

Of the children of Thomas and Letitia, the descendants of Abigail and Martha Roberts, first and second daughters of Thomas and Letitia, who m. respectively John Thomson and John Hallowell, are given under the Thomson and Hallowell lines in subsequent chapters. Those of Elizabeth and Ann have been previously given, as well as those of Letitia, who became the wife of John Foulke.

3. The children of Asher and Alice Foulke: Phebe, 10th-mo. 27, 1781; Anthony, 6th-mo. 19, 1784; William, 5th-mo. 15, 1786, d. 9th-mo. 20, 1787; Ann, 6th-mo. 6, 1788; Elizabeth, 6th-mo. 23, 1790, d. 10th-mo. 4, 1791.

4. Israel Roberts, son of Thomas, Jr., and Letitia, was born in Milford (1757), m. Ann Foulke, b. 10th-mo. 27, 1760, daughter of John and Mary (Roberts) Foulke. In 1808, they removed to Schuylkill township, Chester county, Pa., near Corner Store, where he resided the remainder of his life and was buried in Schuylkill Friends' ground. Their children: (1) Lydia, 4th-mo. 14, 1783, d. 1st-mo. 5, 1866, m. William Edwards; (2) Jane, 3d-mo. 10, 1785, d. unmarried; (3) Thomas, 7th-mo. 16, 1787, m. Rachel Phillips; (4) Letitia, 8th-mo. 21, 1789, d. unmarried; (5) Lewis, 12th-mo. 21, 1791, d. 10th-mo. 21, 1861, m. 5th-mo. 24, 1821, Harriet Brooke; (6) Mary, unmarried; (7) Joseph, unmarried; (8) Seth, m. Eliza Todd; (9) Tacy, d. in infancy.

(1) The children of William and Lydia (Roberts) Edwards: Ann R., 10th-mo. 4, 1817, m. Joseph Johnson, their children being William, m. —— Carr, and Anne, d. unmarried; Algernon, 6th-mo. 6, 1822, m. Mary Roberts; Mary H., 3d-mo. 29, 1827,

d. 2d-mo. 26, 1867, m. Milton Johnson, having one child, Lewis, who d. unmarried.

(3) The children of Thomas and Rachel (Phillips) Roberts: Albanus Logan, m. Mary ——— and had no children; Jones Dixon, unmarried; Ellis Lewis, m. and had children; Thomson, m. and had children; John Phillips, m. ——— Millison, and had one child; Anne F., unmarried.

(5) Lewis Roberts, son of Israel and Anne (Foulke) Roberts, lived and died near Corner Store, Chester county, Pa., and was for many years engaged in business as a wheelwright and plow-manufacturer, for which latter he had an extensive reputation. His wife, Harriet (Brooke) Roberts, was the daughter of Nathan and Susanna Brooke. Their children:

Clementina Brooke Roberts, m. Samuel Lee, their children being (1) Lewis, d. young; (2) Howard, d. in his twenty-first year.

Anne Foulke Roberts, m. Evan Vanderslice. Their children: (1) Lewis Ellwood, (2) Ella. Ella m. first, Edward McCarty, of West Virginia, and had two children, Ethel Gertrude, d. in infancy, and Thalia Beatrice, and m. second, Thomas Peart.

Sarah Emily Roberts, m. Joseph Fussell. (See Chapter IX, under the head of John Foulke.)

Charles B. Roberts, of Perry county, Pa., m. Rebecca Rossiter. Their children: (1) Sarah E., m. John Bell; (2) Anne, m. Linnæus Moore; (3) Charles, (4) William, m. Sarah White; (5) David Brooke, (6) Harriet, (7) Ellwood, all three d. young; (8) Joseph Howard, (9) Clementine Lee.

Mary J. Roberts, m. Charles Fish and had one child, Lewis.

Lewis Ellwood Roberts, 2d-mo. 26, 1835, m. 3d-mo. 27, 1860, Jane, daughter of Joshua and Caroline Foulke. Their children: (1) Lewis E., 12th-mo., 1860, d. in infancy. (2) Clarence V., 8th-mo. 25, 1862, m. 4th-mo. 2, 1895, Frances A. Walton, daughter of Barclay and Jane Walton, of Philadelphia. They have one child, Jane L.

Joseph Jones Roberts, d. in the Rebellion, unmarried.

David Brooke Roberts, killed in Rebellion, unmarried.

William P. Roberts, of Quakertown, m. first, Anne Rawlings;

second, Letitia Kinsey. His children by the first marriage: Rachel Estelle, William Arthur, Warren, d. in infancy; by the second marriage: Linford Brooke, Joseph Nathaniel, Marion Elizabeth.

The children of Seth (son of Israel and Ann Roberts) and Eliza Todd Roberts, of Trappe: Mary, m. first, Algernon Edwards; second, —— Wilder; Matilda, m. James Allison; John Marshall, m. Mary Rapp; Henry Clay, Joanna m. Jacob Snyder; Joseph, Jane, m. Frank Thomas; Lewis, Winfield Scott.

Richard Roberts, the youngest child of Thomas, Jr., and Letitia Roberts, who m. first, Tacy Shoemaker, daughter of George and Martha Shoemaker, of Cheltenham, and, she dying, m. 9th-mo. 10, 1804, Rebecca Jones, b. 6th-mo. 18, 1777, d. 8th-mo. 19, 1825, left a very numerous line of descendants, mostly residing in the lower end of Montgomery county. His children by the first marriage:

1.   George S., 12th-mo. 4, 1797, d. 3d-mo. 24, 1850, m. Tacy Shoemaker, of Abington. Their child: Eleanor, 1828, m. Richardson L. Wright, they having five children, Richardson, Mary, George, Robert, Eleanor.

2.   Charles, 1st-mo. 14, 1799, d. 7th-mo. 26, 1825.

3.   Jonathan, d. in infancy.

The children by the second marriage:

4.   Jehu J., 11th-mo. 4, 1805, d. 9th-mo. 13, 1881, m. Letitia Foulke (see Chapter VII), daughter of Israel and Elizabeth Foulke. Letitia was b. 6th-mo. 6, 1818, d. 4th-mo. 6, 1896, their children being (1) Thomas F., m. Rebecca Walton; (2) Annie L., m. Robert R. Croasdale (deceased), no children; (3) Caroline, unmarried; (4) Sarah F., m. John Walton; (5) Tacy, m. Charles R. Knight. Thomas F. and Rebecca (Walton) Roberts' children: William M., m. and has two children; Sarah F., m. Harry Dungan, no children; George W., Louisa. Sarah F. and John Walton's children: Letitia, m. William Negus, their children being Edith, Mary, William and Catherine; Mary. Tacy and Charles Rees Knight's children: Mary A., Carrie R., m. Harry Lukens and have one child, Madeline; Roberts, m. Rachel Eckfeldt and have two children, Margaret and Henry; Annie C., m. Harry J. Lott; Katharine and Edna.

5. Tacy, 2d-mo. 27, 1807, deceased, m. first, William Thomas; second, William Gyger. The children by the first marriage: Herbert, Rebecca, m. Charles Elliott and had two children, John, d. young, and Mary. By the second marriage there was one child, George Gyger, m. and has a son living in Ohio.

6. Catharine J., 12th-mo. 7, 1808, d. 11th-mo. 29, 1874, m. Charles Sloan. Their children: (1) George, m.; (2) Albanus, m. Tacy Wetherill, and have three children, Barton Green, Charles and May, m. Edward Zoll, their children being Howard, May and Tacy E.; (3) Annie, m. Martin Jamison, and have a daughter, Lena J., also m.; (4) Ann, (5) Thomas and (6) Howard, all unmarried; (7) Mary, m. John Perry, their children being John, Mary and Eva.

7. Joseph W., 7th-mo. 16, 1810, deceased, m. Julia Vandegrift. Their children: William, m. Frances Brown; Joseph, m.; Bessie, d. young.

8. Richard, 4th-mo. 19, 1812, d. 12th-mo. 27, 1891, m. Catherine Thomson. Their children: (1) Charles, m. Hannah Chandler and have one daughter, Eva. (2) J. Thomson, m. Georgeanna Hallowell, their children being five: George Franklin, Catherine, m. Joseph Shoemaker, and have two children, Millie and Leslie; Susan, m. Charles Obricht, and have one child, Franklin; Abel and William. (3) Rebecca, m. Jacob L. Hallowell, and have two children, Richard and William. (4) Jane, m. Abel Hallowell, and have one child, Theodore. (5) Franklin, d. young.

9. Thomas, 3d-mo. 11, 1814, d. young.

10. Isaac, 3d-mo. 2, 1816, drowned in New Zealand in 1839.

11. Albanus L., 4th-mo. 26, 1817, m. Margaret Seipler. Their children: (1) Franklin, m. in California, had five children, and was lost in a blizzard about 1896; (2) George S., and (3) Charles, both m. and residing in Dakota; (4) Edward, m. Emily Armitage, and had two children, Russell (deceased) and Raymond; (5) Sarah R., m. John Neiman, of Philadelphia, and have five children, Norwood, Walter, Laura, Maggie, Annie.

12. Margaret, 5th-mo. 11, 1820, d. 11th-mo. 11, 1839.

13. William Montgomery, 10th-mo. 7, 1822, d. 5th-mo. 15, 1891.

RICHARD ROBERTS (OF ROCKHILL).

Richard Roberts, son of Thomas and Alice, 12th-mo, 1722, m. Elizabeth Tyson, of Upper Dublin. Their children:

1. Mary, 4th-mo. 2, 1785, d. 11th-mo. 15, 1843, m. William Green. (See Green line.)

2. Jesse, 2d-mo. 9, 1786, m. Martha Green.

3. Alice, 2d-mo. 11, 1787, m. Dr. Benjamin Green. (See Green line.)

4. Elizabeth, 6th-mo. 14, 1788, d. unmarried.

5. Grace, 5th-mo. 11, 1790, d. 6th-mo. 19, 1819, m. 2d-mo. 5, 1818, Dr. James R. Green.

This family is somewhat remarkable from the fact that all who married at all married Greens. After the death of Richard Roberts, his wife Elizabeth m. William Edwards and had two children, Meribah, who m. Joseph Green, and Samuel.

2. Jesse, son of Richard and Elizabeth, m. Martha Green, daughter of Benjamin and Jane Green. Their children: (1) Hersilla, m. Amos Edwards, no children; (2) Richard, m. Julia Fries. Their children: Harry, of Merchantville, N. J., m. first, Emma E. Van Buskirk and had three children, Stella, A. Edwards and Julia L. Harry m. second, Annie E. Scott and had one child, Elsie E. Howard, of Philadelphia, m. Carrie Armstrong; their children: Howard, Fannie; Anna, m. Joseph Galley; their children: Roberts, Mabel. Julia, m. Benjamin Tate; their children: Elsie, Sarah. (3) Clementine, unmarried. (4) Hannah, m. Henry F. Johnson, their children being Jesse, d. young; Elizabeth, m. William Strawn; Alice m. Morgan Shaw, their children being Caroline, Jesse and Elizabeth; Jane m. Maurice Shaw and have two children, Harry and William. (5) Benjamin, unmarried. (6) Jesse, of Chestnut Hill, m. Elizabeth Houston, and have one son, Jesse. (7) Isabella, d. 1883, m. Thomas Morris; their children: Alfred W., m. Annie E. Doebler, their children being Emily and Mary; Robert, m. 1897, Rovilla L. Siner; Hercilla E., Walter, d. at eighteen years of age; Annie, Ella, Thomas, d. in infancy; Clementine, d. in infancy; Jesse R. Thomas Morris was a Justice of the Peace at Quakertown.

ALICE AND EDWARD THOMAS.

Alice Roberts, daughter of Thomas and Alice, m. 10th-mo., 1749, Edward Thomas, 1723, d. 4th-mo. 4, 1782. Their children:

1. Margaret, 9th-mo. 2, 1751, m. 11th-mo. 30, 1775, Amos Roberts. (See Chapter VII.)
2. Miriam, 9th-mo. 2, 1753, m. 9th-mo. 16, 1773, William Heacock.
3. Mary, 10th-mo. 2, 1755, d. 12th-mo. 19, 1831. See "An Old Letter," page 95.
4. Martha, 1st-mo. 22, 1758.
5. Samuel, 7th-mo. 15, 1760, d. 5th-mo. 17, 1847, m. Elizabeth ———.
6. Andrew, 1st-mo. 20, 1764, d. 5th-mo. 15, 1765.
7. Elizabeth, 9th-mo. 17, 1776.

The children of Samuel and Elizabeth: (1) Amanda, 7th-mo. 3, 1807; (2) Jervis, 9th-mo. 9, 1808, m. 5th-mo. 20, 1830, Jane R. Green (see Green line); (3) Louisa, 6th-mo. 2, 1810; (4) Thomas, 10th-mo. 29, 1811; (5) Edward, 3d-mo. 27, 1813, m. Anne, daughter of Thomas and Sarah Foulke. He is deceased; for their children see pages 106 and 107; (6) Hannah, 1st-mo. 6, 1815; (7) Benjamin, 3d-mo. 27, 1817.

ABRAHAM ROBERTS.

Abraham Roberts, 1730, son of Thomas and Alice, m. first, 12th-mo. 9, 1756, Katharine Lester; Abraham m. second, 10th-mo., 1779, Peninah Thomas.

Levi, 10th-mo. 21, 1759, d. 1st-mo. 4, 1846, m. Phebe McCarty, b. 8th-mo. 2, 1766, daughter of Thomas and Elizabeth. If the above dates of marriage are correct, as is probable, Levi was the son of Katharine. Their children:

1. Elizabeth, 2d-mo. 11, 1803, d. 5th-mo. 12, 1858, m. Hugh Foulke. (See page 107.) Their children: Amos R., 5th-mo. 26, 1822, d. 4th-mo. 21, 1853; Barton L., 11th-mo. 18, 1823, d. 8th-mo. 18, 1856; Phebe R., 1st-mo. 27, 1825, d. 12th-mo. 22, 1832; Jordan, 10th-mo. 9, 1826, d. 6th-mo. 21, 1836; Elizabeth,

3d- mo. 13, 1828, m. 11th-mo. 13, 1862, Penrose Hicks; Sarah
E., 6th-mo. 1, 1831, d. 4th-mo. 19, 1844; Franklin, 5th-mo. 5,
1833, d. 6th-mo. 24, 1835; Abigail Jane, 7th-mo. 1, 1835, d. 3d-
mo. 10, 1845; Franklin, 7th-mo. 24, 1838, d. 3d-mo. 18, 1860;
Jane R., 6th-mo. 9, 1842, d. 1st-mo. 24, 1860; Susan J., 6th-mo.
7, 1844.

2. Abigail, 4th-mo. 16, 1808, m. 10th-mo. 16, 1842, Joel
Heacock, 3d-mo. 26, 1794, d. 3d-mo. 17, 1853. Their child: Joel
Levi, 10th-mo. 2, 1843.

The Heacock family came from the north of England, and
settled in what is now Delaware county about the year 1711.
The emigrants were Jonathan and Ann Heacock. Their descendant, William, settled in what is now Rockhill in 1740.
The house which he built is still standing and bears the date,
1748. He married Ann Roberts, of Milford. One of their
sons was Jesse, who married Tacy Thompson. They had elev-
en children, of whom Joel, born 3d-mo. 26, 1794, married 10th-
mo. 16, 1842, Abigail Roberts, of Milford, and had one child,
Joel Levi. The father died at Germantown 3d-mo. 17, 1753,
while on his way to market. His widow died 3d-mo. 21, 1882,
at Quakertown, where she resided with her son.

WILL OF THOMAS ROBERTS.

The will of Thomas Roberts, of Lower Milford, may
appropriately end the chapter devoted to his descendants. His
wife being deceased at the time he made his will, the document
is considerably shortened by the absence of the customary elab-
orate provision for the widow which characterizes most of the
wills of that day. No real estate is mentioned in his will, it having been previously transferred, as already noted. The will follows:

To all Christian People whom these presents may Concern
be it known that I Thomas Roberts of Lower Milford in the
County of Bucks Yeoman being in good Health & my Advanced
Age Considered of pretty Sound Memory for which favour and
all other Blessings I have Received I return Thanks and Praise

to God the Author of all good Gifts and Calling to mind the uncertainty of this Life do make and put in Writing this my Last Will and Testament in manner and form following, First I will that all my Just Debts and funeral Expences be Carefully paid and Discharged, Item I give and Bequeath unto my Son in Law William Heacock the Sum of Five Pounds Lawful Money of Pennsylvania which Lyes in his Hands due to me by Note, Also I give and bequeath unto my Son in Law Edward Thomas the Sum of Ten Pounds of like Lawful Money Also I give unto my Grand-Daughter Abigail the Eldest daughter of my Son Thomas the Sum of Fifteen Pounds of Lawful Money aforesd., Also I give unto my Grand-Daughter Martha another Daughter of my said Son Thomas the like Sum of Fifteen Pounds Pounds of Lawful Money aforsd. Also I give unto my Grand-Daughter Alice another Daughter of my said Son Thomas the like Sum of Fifteen Pounds of Lawful Money aforsd. but in Case that either of my sd. Grand Daughters shall or do proceed in Marriage Contrary to the Will of their said Father I will that her portion so offending shall be at the Disposal of my said Son Thomas, Also I give unto my Grand Daughter Abigail above Named my Feather Bed & all ye furniture thereunto belonging and unto my Grand-Daughter Martha above named I give my chest, Also I give unto my Son John the Sum of Five Shillings and to my Son Richard I give the Sum of five Shillings and unto my Son Abraham I give the Sum of Fifteen Pounds of Lawful Money aforsd. Also I give unto my Daughter Rachel Five Shillings and all the Rest and Residue of my Estate Goods and Chattels I give unto my Son Thomas before named Lastly I do nominate Constitute & Appoint my said Son Thomas and my Son in Law William Heacock before named to be my Executors of this my Last Will and Testament hereby Revoking and Disanulling all other & former Will or Wills and Testaments by me before this time made Ratifying and Confirming this and no other to be my last Will and Testament In Witness whereof I have hereunto Set my Hand and Seal the Twenty fourth day of the Fourth Month in the year of our Lord One Thousand Seven Hundred and Sixty one 1761

his
THOMAS X ROBERTS　[Seal]
mark

Sealed Signed and Declared by the said Thomas Roberts to be his Last Will and Testament in the presence of us
William Edwerds Saml Foulke Ann Edwerds.

When the will was proved at Philadelphia, August 3, 1767, two of the above witnesses, Samuel Foulke and Ann Edwards (then the wife of William Burr), were present, and affirmed to the usual facts that they saw and heard testator sign, seal, publish and declare the instrument to be his last will and testament.

On the same day letters testamentary were granted to Thomas Roberts and William Heacock, executors, Benjamin Chew being Regr. Genl.

XIV.

JOHN THOMSON.

John Thomson, 12th-mo. 22, 1750, d. 9th-mo. 28, 1838, of Cheltenham, m., in 1773, Abigail Roberts, 7th-mo. 28, 1751, d. 7th-mo. 15, 1843, daughter of Thomas and Letitia Roberts, of Milford, Bucks county. Their children:

1. Hannah, 12th-mo. 15, 1773, d. 8th-mo. 6, 1827, m. Thomas Shoemaker; one child, Mary, d. unmarried.

2. Thomas, 9th-mo. 30, 1775, d. 12th-mo. 26, 1825, m. Jane Jarrett.

3. Sarah, 3d-mo. 25, 1780, d. 6th-mo. 2, 1852, m. Samuel Rowland.

4. Catharine, 7th-mo. 25, 1782, d. 2d-mo. 2, 1795.

The children of Thomas and Jane (Jarrett) Thomson, of Cheltenham:

1. Ann, m. Jacob Jarrett. Their children: (1) John, (2) William, (3) Joseph, m.; (4) Jane, m. Newton Smith, their children being Walter, Anna, Caroline, Susan; (5) George, m. Jane Kerbaugh, their children being Anna, Benjamin, Mary, Arthur; (6) Susan, became the second wife of Newton Smith, whose first wife was her sister Jane, their children being Elizabeth and Sarah.

2. Hannah, m. John Roberts. Their children: (1) Abigail, m. Nathan Tyson, their children being Emma, m. Benjamin Walton, they having four children; John R., m. Laura Twining and have four children, Warren R., Edward, Fannie A., Edith L.; George W., m. (2) Thomas, m. Elizabeth W. Holt, their children being John, d., and William. (3) Ann, m. Wilmer Ridge, their children being Albert, m. Rebecca Harper, and Edward.

(4) Mary, unmarried. (5) William, d. (6) Jane, m. John Kirkbride.

3. Catherine, m. Richard Roberts, son of Richard and Rebecca. (See Chapter XIII.)

4. Sarah, m. first, Anthony Williams, they having children, Edward, Joseph and Anthony, all m. and a daughter Jane; second, Jesse Shoemaker; third, Cyrus Betts. Sarah was an acknowledged minister for many years. A daughter by her second marriage, Sarah Shoemaker, m. Alvin Haines, an acknowledged minister residing at Abington. She is deceased, leaving two daughters, Sarah, Lydia. Alvin m. (second wife) Mary, daughter of the late Matthias Shoemaker.

5. John, m. Caroline Jones. Their children: (1) Charles, d. young; (2) Alice, m. Benjamin F. Penrose, no children; (3) Thomas, m. Mary Eyre, their children being Elizabeth, m. Herbert Taylor; John, Alice, George, the latter deceased; (4) Samuel, m. Fannie Twining, they having one child, Caroline; (5) Jane; (6) Margaret, m. Henry W. Hallowell, they having two children, Jane and Israel; (7) John and (8) William, both d. unmarried; (9) J. Dawson, m. Annie Knight, they having one child, Florence.

6. Abigail, m. John Wildman, of Langhorne; their child, Jane, m. Joseph J. Watson. Joseph J. and Jane Watson's children: (1) Franklin; (2) Abigail, m. Joseph Taylor, they having one child, Jane. Jane Watson is deceased, and Joseph m. second, Anna, widow of Hector Wildman.

7. Elizabeth, d. unmarried.

The children of Samuel and Sarah (Thomson) Rowland (she being the daughter of John and Abigail Roberts Thomson):

1. Ann, unmarried.

2. William, m. Margaret Gillingham, their children being: (1) Samuel, d. unmarried; (2) Hannah, m. Joseph Richardson and had four children, Margaret, who m. Newton Comly, their children being Rowland, Bessie, Edith, Byron, Mary; Mary, Samuel and Joshua.

3. Thomas, m. Tacie Rowland, and have one child, William.

XV.

JOHN HALLOWELL.

John Hallowell, of Cheltenham, Montgomery county, Pa., m. 11th-mo. 3, 1774, Martha Roberts, 3d-mo. 9, 1753, daughter of Thomas, Jr., and Letitia Roberts, of Milford, Bucks county. After the marriage of the couple they resided in Abington, where he died in 1793, of yellow fever. The progenitor of the Abington Hallowells was also John, who came from Nottinghamshire, England, with William Penn, in 1682, and settled in Abington, where in 1696 he purchased 630 acres of land. The children of John and Martha (Roberts) Hallowell:

1. Isaac, m. Mary Fletcher.
2. Israel, m. Mary Jarrett.
3. Ann, m. Joseph Williams.
4. John R., m. Ann Jarrett.

The children of Isaac and Mary (Fletcher) Hallowell:

1. Yarnall, m. Mary Ashbridge, their children being: (1) Pemberton, m. Rachel Jarrett, whose children were Susan, m. Howard Jarrett, they having two children, Alice and Rachel; Mary, m. Dr. John Sibbald, and had one child, Agnes. (2) Elizabeth. (3) Susan, m. Hallowell Smith, having one child, Fannie, who m. William Gillingham. (4) Frank. (5) Tacie. (6) George, m. Mary Vandegrift.
2. Edward.
3. Sarah Ann.
4. Charles.
5. Hannah, m. Caleb Clothier. Their children: (1) Elizabeth, m. Jacob Bunting; (2) Louisa; (3) Isaac H., m. Mary Jackson; (4) Annie; (5) William; (6) T. Clarkson, m.; (7) Sarah.

6. Elizabeth, m. John Grant. Their children: (1) Mary, (2) Sarah, m. Thomas Saunders; (3) William.

ISRAEL HALLOWELL.

Israel Hallowell, b. 1776, was a miller and also the owner of valuable farms in Abington. His wife, Mary Jarrett, was a daughter of William Jarrett, of Horsham. Israel d. in 1853. In this connection it may be mentioned that John Hallowell, father of Israel, owned and operated a grist mill on Pennypack creek, prior to the Revolutionary War. His death, due to yellow fever, contracted while engaged in business in Philadelphia, has been mentioned. The children of Israel and Mary (Jarrett) Hallowell:

1. Ann, m. Isaac Mather. Their children: (1) Martha, (2) Israel, m. Sarah Lloyd and had two children, Howard who m. Caroline Yerkes, their children being Sarah, Frank S., Emley; and Annie, m. Charles Jarrett, their children being Samuel, Martha, Caroline, Charles, Mary; (3) Isaac.

2. Martha, m. Samuel Parry. Their children: (1) Priscilla, m. Henry Lippincott and had four children, Caroline, George, Mary, Martha; (2) Mary Elizabeth, m. Joshua Lippincott, and had one son, Samuel; (3) Israel, (4) Samuel.

3. John J. Hallowell, b. 6th-mo. 25, 1811, m. Rachel Williams. Their children: (1) Thomas W., m. Sarah Tyson, and had one daughter Willietta; (2) Elizabeth, (3) Franklin W., m. Sarah Fenton, and have two children, Caroline and Helen.

4. Tacie, m. David Eastburn. No children.

5. W. Jarrett, m. Lydia Ann Lloyd. Their children: (1) John, m. Laura Phillips, and have two children, Walter and Alfred; (2) Ellie, (3) Mary, m. Morris Williams, they having one child, Mary; (4) Tacie.

6. Israel, Jr., m. Rebecca Williams. Their children: (1) Mary Anna, (2) Henry W., m. Margaret Thomson; their children being Jane and Israel. (See Thomson line.)

7. Mary, m. George Ely. Their children: (1) William, (2) Israel, m. Elizabeth W. Hallowell.

8. Jonas, m. Esther L. Fenton. Their children: (1) Israel, m. Ruth Anna Branin, they having two children, George and Alice; (2) James, m. Emma Lloyd, they having one child, Marion; (3) John J.

Ann Hallowell, daughter of John and Martha (Roberts) Hallowell, m. Joseph Williams. Their children:

1. Anthony Williams, m. Sarah Thomson, daughter of Thomas and Jane Thomson. Their children: (1) Charles, of Buckingham, m. Esther Ann Eastburn, they having three children, Elizabeth, married George Brown and had one child; Sarah, m. George Brown; Edith. (2) Edward, of Buckingham, m. Emma Cottman, they having three children, Helen, m. Edward Wallestine, and has one child, Edward; Sarah, m. Comly Smith and has one child, Agnes; Arthur, m. (3) Joseph, of Easton, m. Margaret J. Buckman, they having four children, Emma, Sarah, Frank, Charles. (4) Anthony, m. Mary A. Roberts, they having two children, Phebe and Mary. (5) Jane, d. unmarried.

Sarah Thomson m. (second husband) Jesse Shoemaker, and had one daughter, Sarah, deceased. (See Thomson line.) Sarah Thomson m. (third husband) Cyrus Betts. Both are deceased, leaving no children.

2. Alice Williams m. Mahlon R. Ambler, of Norristown. Their child: Martha, m. J. Schrack Shearer (both deceased). Their children: (1) Mahlon A., 1st-mo. 17, 1861, m. Hannah Smith; their children are Frank R. Shearer, Naomi Shearer (deceased), Norris W. Shearer, Edith Shearer (deceased), Alice W. Shearer. (2) Augustus W. Shearer, 10th-mo. 31, 1864, m. Maggie Barkdoll; no children. (3) Alice W. Shearer, 5th-mo. 1, 1862. (4) Eunice N. Shearer, 11th-mo. 2, 1863; both unmarried. (5) Charles Watson Shearer, 12th-mo. 26, 1869, m. Maggie Tyson, daughter of Matthias and Annie Tyson. They have one child: Annie T. Shearer.

Mahlon R. Ambler m. (second wife) Martha Jeanes, of Whitemarsh. Both are deceased, leaving no children.

3. Charles Williams m. Hannah Stokes. Their children: (1) Joseph, m. Anna Satterthwaite, daughter of Edwin and Martha Satterthwaite, they having six children, Charles, Edwin, m.

Bertha Kratz; Morris, Albert, Clarence, Lillie; (2) Annie, m. John Lloyd, they having three children, Emma, m. James Hallowell and have one child, Marion; Charles, Joseph; (3) Tacie, m. John Mather, their children being Annie, m. Samuel Shoemaker; Hannah, m. Dr. Longaker; Alice; (4) Martha, m. Amos Haines, their children being Ellie, Hannah, m. Morris Michener; (5) Alice, m. Isaac Michener, their children being Charles and Annie; (6) Morris, m. first, Mary Hallowell; second, Lottie Helmbold. He has one child, Mary, by the first marriage; (7) John J., m. Alice Roberts, their children being Helen and Edith.

John R. Hallowell, son of John and Martha Roberts Hallowell, m. Ann Jarrett. Their children:

1. William J. Hallowell, m. Tacie Ann Paul, their children being: (1) Annie, m. Ellwood Lukens and had one daughter, Annie; (2) Hannah, m. William Satterthwaite, they having four children, John, E. Burton, m. Lizzie Green; William, Paul; (3) William, m. Anna Thomas, their children being Howard, Elizabeth and Eleanor; (4) Elizabeth, m. Israel H. Ely; (5) Mary, m. Dr. C. B. Hough, their children being William, Pauline, Tacie, Israel.

2. Lydia Hallowell, m. Morris Paul. Their child, Hannah, m. William Penrose, they having four children, Howard, Walter, William, Lydia.

3. Martha Hallowell, m. Edwin Satterthwaite. Their children: (1) Anna, m. Joseph Williams. Their children are named under Charles Williams, who m. Hannah Stokes. (2) James, m. Anna Sill, their children being Edwin, George, Howard, Mary, Oliver. (3) Lydia, m. Oliver Parry, their children being Edwin and Mary.

4. Joseph W. Hallowell, m. Hannah Lloyd. Their children: (1) Emma, (2) Edwin, m. Mary Linton, and have five children, Hannah L., Mary L., Emma, Francis, Rebecca L.; (3) Fannie, (4) Annie.

5. Penrose Hallowell, m. Elizabeth Warner. Their children: (1) Rachel, (2) H. Warner, m. Anna Davis, their children being Edith, Elizabeth, Margaret, Charles K.; (3) Morris, m. Catherine Mann, their children being Lottie May and Joseph; (4) Alfred, (5) Penrose, (6) Martha.

XVI.

THE GREEN FAMILY.

The traditions in reference to this family have been repeated in the paper (p. 162) written in 1855 by Joseph Green, of Philadelphia. Joseph Green does not give the name of his great-grandfather, who, according to his version, was the first settler, although he says he married a widow Large, daughter of Ellis Lewis. In 1743 among other residents in Springfield township was James Green, who may have been the first settler of this family in that locality.

In the "Registry of Arrivals in Bucks and Philadelphia Counties," 1676 to 1693, it is recorded that the ship Delaware arrived 5th-mo. 11, 1686, and among others on board were Thomas Greene and Margaret, his wife, Thomas and John, his sons. This family frequently appears in records of the lower end of Bucks county and in court records. William Penn, in 1684, transferred to John Greene 200 acres of land adjoining the Delaware river and land of William Dungan. In 1693 "John Green and Thomas Green his son and Katherine Green wife of John and mother of Thomas" transferred the same tract to Joseph Large.

That there is a connection between the two admits of little doubt, though it does not seem to have been precisely ascertained.

A remarkable coincidence of brothers marrying sisters is shown in the marriage of William, Benjamin, James and Joseph Green, sons of Benjamin and Jane Green, and Jesse Roberts.

William, Benjamin and James married respectively, Mary, Alice and Grace Roberts, daughters of Richard and Elizabeth Roberts. Joseph married Meribah Edwards, a half sister, she being a daughter of William and Elizabeth Edwards, Elizabeth Roberts having married William Edwards after the death of her first husband, Richard Roberts. Jesse Roberts, a brother of Mary, Alice, Grace Roberts, and a half-brother of Meribah, married Martha Green, a sister of William, Benjamin and James Green.

Assuming that James Green married Widow Large, daughter of Ellis Lewis, their children were: Francis, removed to Virginia; James, removed to Virginia; Joseph, b. about 1718, d. 5th-mo. 26, 1757, m. 3d-mo. 10, 1744, Catherine Thomas.

After Joseph's death Francis and James removed their aged parents, then over 80 years of age, to Virginia, where they were living.

Joseph Green, of Springfield, 1718, d. 5th-mo. 26, 1757, m. 3d-mo. 10, 1744, Catherine Thomas, d. 7th-mo. 12, 1770. Their children:

1. Margaret, 11th-mo. 28, 1744, m. 11th-mo. 4, 1766, David Walton.

2. Joseph, 12th-mo. 23, 1745.

3. Samuel, 10th-mo. 21, 1748, m. Rachel ———.

4. Jane, 2d-mo. 27, 1749, d. 2d-mo. 2, 1767.

5. Benjamin, 4th-mo. 27, 1750, d. 5th-mo. 22, 1828, m. 11th-mo. 9, 1775, Jane Roberts.

6. Ezekiel, 5th-mo. 14, 1752. Removed to Hopewell.

7. James, 3d-mo. 22, 1754, d. 8th-mo. 10, 1788 (Meeting Record adds "much lamented"), m. Martha Foulke.

8. Thomas, 7th-mo. 27, 1756.

3. Samuel Green and Rachel, his wife, removed to Exeter, a certificate being granted to them 7th-mo. 18, 1793, by Richland Monthly Meeting. Their children:

(1) Catharine, 3d-mo. 11, 1770; (2) Mary, 8th-mo. 28, 1771; (3) Jane, 2d-mo. 5, 1773; (4) Green, 8th-mo. 17, 1774; (5) Rachel, 6th-mo. 18, 1776; (6) Thomas, 1st-mo. 22, 1778; (7) Alice, 8th-mo. 7, 1781; (8) Samuel, 8th-mo. 3, 1783.

Benjamin Green, 1750, d. 1828, m. 11th-mo. 9, 1775, Jane Roberts, 4th-mo. 16, 1753, d. 5th-mo. 18, 1841, daughter of John and Martha Roberts, of Milford. Benjamin, for a number of years, was engaged in making hats in a log house on the old homestead in Springfield, which is still standing. About 1790 he moved into Quakertown and bought and afterwards built an addition to the old frame house that formerly stood where Charles Dolls' buildings are now located, on Main street. Their children:

1. William, 11th-mo. 10, 1776, d. 9th-mo. 24, 1851, m. 4th-mo. 17, 1804, Mary Roberts.

2. Hannah, 9th-mo. 29, 1778, d. 4th mo. 12, 1826, m. (second wife) Thomas Lester.

3. Evan, 11th-mo. 10, 1780, m. first Isabella Slaymaker, second Cynthia E. Lester, daughter of Evan Jones.

4. Benjamin, 12th-mo. 10, 1782, m. Alice Roberts.

5. Jane, 2d-mo. 8, 1785, d. 3d-mo. 3, 1835, m. Caleb Foulke. (See Foulke line, Chapter IX, page 153.)

6. James R., 3d-mo. 4, 1787, d. 7th-mo. 27, 1832, m. first Grace Roberts, second, Ann Foulke.

7. Lydia, 12th-mo. 20, 1789, d. 10th-mo. 26, 1850, unmarried.

8. Joseph, 2d-mo. 14, 1791, d. 6th-mo. 30, 1867, m. Meribah Edwards.

9. Martha, 2d-mo. 14, 1793, m. Jesse Roberts. (See Thomas Roberts.)

10. John, 3d-mo. 24, 1795, d. in infancy.

11. Abigail, 3d-mo. 18, 1797, d. 8th-mo. 21, 1854, m. Dr. Samuel Carey.

WILLIAM GREEN.

William Green, 1776, d. 1851, m. Mary Roberts, 4th-mo. 21, 1785, d. 11th-mo. 15, 1843, daughter of Richard and Elizabeth Roberts, of Rockhill, and opened the first store in Quakertown about 1800, in an old frame house built by Moses Shaw, located on Main street, where the present residence of Dr. W. H. Meredith stands. That house was destroyed by fire about 1862. Being a shoemaker by trade it was his custom to make shoes when not engaged in waiting on customers, which were few and far between. When a stock of shoes collected he would start out with them in a bundle and travel many miles until they were all sold. In 1803 he was made the first postmaster and held this position as long as he was engaged in the store business. In 1805 he built the brick store and dwelling still standing at the corner of Main and Broad streets, Quakertown, and continued to keep store with but a few years interruption until succeeded by his son Richard R., about 1847. Their children:

1. Caroline, 2d-mo. 6, 1805, d. 2d-mò, 18, 1888, m. 5th-mo. 15, 1825, Joshua Foulke. (See Foulke line, Chapter IX, page 152.)

2. Elizabeth, 12th-mo. 9, 1806, m. John McCray, a druggist and physician of Philadelphia.

3. Matilda, 1st-mo. 20, 1809, m. 12th-mo. 15, 1831, Edward Foulke. (See Foulke line, page 150.)

4. Jane R., 7th-mo. 23, 1811, m. Jervis Thomas.

5. Grace, 2d-mo. 27, 1815, m. 11th-mo. 12, 1835, Eleazer Shaw, of Plumstead.

6. Mary 7th-mo. 13, 1817, d. 11th-mo. 6, 1869, m. 3d-mo. 12, 1856, Dr. Samuel Carey, whose first wife was Abigail Green; no children.

7. Alice, 4th-mo. 14, 1820, m. 8th-mo. 23, 1848, Dr. Davis D. Walton, of Stroudsburg; no children.

8. Richard R., 8th-mo. 24, 1825, d. 7th-mo. 22, 1892, m. 3d-mo. 15, 1848, Sarah Jackson.

Grace, 1st-mo. 13, 1814, d. in infancy.

2. Dr. John and Elizabeth (Green) McCray had one child, Mary, m. Franklin Diehl. Their children: (1) Harper, m. Mary Rodgers, they having one child, Frank; (2) Stella, m. John Hillpot; no children.

4. Jervis and Jane (Green) Thomas' children: (1) Alice, m. William Foulke; (2) Samuel, m. ——— Ogden; (3) William, m. Rachel Sterner, their children being William Richard, m. Ella Ochs, and Jane, m. Charles Bartholomew, they having three children, Miles, William, George, the last-named dying in infancy; (4) Mary, m. Dr. R. J. Linderman, their children being Dr. Herbert and Bertha, d. unmarried.

5. Eleazer and Grace (Green) Shaw's children: (1) Caroline, m. Jenks Watson, their two children being: Alice, m. C. Al-

len Knight, they having three children, Marion, Helen and
Florence; Elizabeth, m. Edward Woodman, they having also
three children, Watson, Margaret and Allen; (2) Mary Alice, unmarried; (3) Hannah, m. Augustus Pickering, of Carversville,
having one child, Arthur; (4) Henrietta, m. Allen Holcomb, and
had one child, William, d. in infancy.

8.   Richard R. Green, 1825, d. 1892, m. Sarah Jackson,
daughter of James and Mary Ann Jackson, formerly of Philadelphia.   Mary Ann, who died but a few years ago, enjoyed the re-
spect and esteem of all, including the descendants of the early
German settlers as well as Friends.   Many have cause to remember her kindness and benevolence.   Richard R. Green was born
in the house built by his father in 1805, at the cross-roads, Main
and Broad streets, where he continued the general store founded
by his father until his death.   Their children: Mary Emma, unmarried; William, died in early manhood.

THOMAS AND HANNAH LESTER.

The children of Thomas and Hannah (Green) Lester:

1.   Dr. Evan G., 9th-mo. 29, 1806, m. 2d-mo., 1832, Cynthia E. Jones.

2.   Sarah Ann, 10th-mo. 30, 1810, m. Dr. Arthur DeCernea.

3.   Mary, 5th-mo. 17, 1812, m. Watson Comly.

4.   Benjamin, d. unmarried.

1.   Dr. Evan and Cynthia E. Lester, b. 8th-mo. 25, 1805, d.
8th-mo. 17, 1871, had one child, Evan Jones Lester, 9th-mo. 28,
1835, m. 5th-mo. 29, 1862, Elizabeth Green.   Their children: (1)
Barton G., 8th-mo. 14, 1863, m. 11th-mo. 28, 1894, Elizabeth
Culver Lothrop.   They live in Denver, Col.   (2) Joseph G., 7th-
mo. 6, 1865, unmarried.   (3) Evan J., 5th-mo. 18, 1867, m. 5th-
mo. 21, 1889, Helen G. Satterthwaite, daughter of Edward and
Elizabeth G. Satterthwaite.   Their children: Helen May, 5th-
mo. 5, 1890; Frank, d. in infancy; Gertrude A., 9th-mo. 19,
1894; Evan J., Jr., 10th-mo. 18, 1896. (4) Frank, d. in infancy.

2.   Dr. Arthur (1806, of Buckingham) and Sarah Ann
(Green) De Cernea's children: Thomas, d. unmarried; Edward,

.m. Martha Phillips. Edward and Martha (Phillips) De Cernea had but one son, Albert, twice m. By the first marriage there were no children. By the second marriage, with Ethel Stokes, there is one child living. After the death of his first wife, Sarah Ann, Dr. De Cernea m. Sarah Taylor, daughter of William Taylor.

3. Watson Comly, of Byberry, m. Mary Lester; their children: (1) Lester (deceased), m. Mary Bowman, their children being Rowland, m. 10th-mo. 13, 1897, Helen, daughter of Cyrus and Mary P. Chambers, of Overbrook, and Alice, unmarried; (2) Rachel (deceased), m. Thomas Shallcross, of Byberry, their children being Watson C., Mary G., d. 1st-mo. 5, 1888, in her eighteenth year; Thomas, Jr., Elizabeth, Charles Wilmer, m.; (3) Cynthia, m. Joseph Bosler, of Ogontz; their children: Mary W., m. Walter Comly, of Port Chester, N. Y., having two children, Charles B., d. aged four years, and Samuel N.; Caroline C., Charles, Lester; (4) Mary Comly, 1851, d. 9th-mo. 17, 1885, m. 10th-mo. 21, 1880, J. Howard Ervien, of Ogontz, who m. (second wife) Fannie Martin. Howard and Mary (Comly) Ervien had one child, Horace.

EVAN GREEN.

Evan Green, 11th-mo. 10, 1780, d. of cholera at Columbia, Pa.; m. first Isabella Slaymaker, of Lancaster county, and second Cynthia E. Lester, widow of Evan Lester and daughter of Evan Jones, of Gwynedd.

Evan's three brothers, William, Benjamin and James, having married their cousins, Mary, Alice and Grace Roberts, he expressed the opinion that his removal to Columbia would at least prevent his marrying a relative, but after the death of his first wife he returned and married Cynthia E. Lester, the widow of his nephew, Evan G. Lester. The children by the first marriage:

1. Benjamin, died young.
2. Slaymaker, d. unmarried.
3. Henry, m. Margaret Gould, having one child, d. young.
4. Jasper, m. Elizabeth Bond.
5. Cornelia, m. Dr. William Spence, of Virginia.

Evan Green by his second wife, Cynthia E. Lester, had no children.

4. Jasper and Elizabeth (Bond) Green had three children: Elizabeth Shippen, Catharine, d., Leslie, d. young.

5. Dr. William and Cornelia (Green) Spence, now residing in Florida, had four children: Edward, William, Isabel, Mary. Dr. Spence resided in Virginia during the war and entered the Confederate army as surgeon in A. P. Fish's division. His sons, Edward and William, both d. unmarried, served also in the Confederate army, William being badly wounded at Antietam.

BENJAMIN GREEN.

Benjamin Green, 1782, who m. Alice Roberts, daughter of Richard and Elizabeth Roberts, 2d-mo. 11, 1787, d. 11th-mo. 5, 1870, built the large brick house in Quakertown, occupied by the late Samuel Kinsey. Benjamin Green was a doctor.

The portrait of Alice Green is said to have been sent to England at one time when that of a typical American Friend was required for some purpose. Her features were portrayed by her son-in-law, Joseph John, the well-known artist, in a number of his paintings and were greatly admired on account of her kindly and benevolent expression. Her picture, from a daguerreotype, appears on the opposite page.

The children of Benjamin and Alice Green:

1. Dr. Milton, 3d-mo. 1, 1811, d. 1890, m. 1856, Margaret Hazlet, of Zanesville, Ohio. The couple had no children. Dr. J. Milton Green lived for many years at Decorah, Iowa, and died there.

2. Clementine, 1813, d. 1885, m., first, Peter Ruby, and second, Joseph John, mentioned above. There were no children by either marriage.

ALICE GREEN

JAMES R. GREEN.

James R. Green, 1787, d. 1832, m. first, 12th-mo. 5, 1818, Grace Roberts, 5th-mo. 11, 1790, daughter of Richard and Elizabeth Roberts, of Rockhill, and second, 11th-mo. 14, 1822, Ann Foulke, 11th-mo. 23, 1797, d. 1st-mo. 21, 1878, daughter of John and Letitia Foulke. (See page 148.) He built the stone house in Quakertown recently occupied by Hannah Mather, where his widow continued to live until her death in 1878. He was a physician and practised his profession until his death.

The child by the first marriage:

1. Barton R., 5th-mo. 22, 1819, d. 11th-mo. 16, 1825.

By the second marriage with Ann Foulke his children were:

2. Chapman, 6th-mo. 17, 1824, d. 5th-mo. 19, 1836.

3. Hannah, 1st-mo. 19, 1827, d. 9th-mo. 21, 1829.

4. Caroline, 2d-mo 1, 1829, m. 9th-mo. 12, 1848, Israel L. Stokes of Rancocas, N. J.

5. James B., 11th-mo. 10, 1831, m. 6th-mo. 1, 1854, Anna Emley.

4. The children of James B. and Anna (Emley) Green: (1) Franklin E., d. unmarried; (2) William Chapman, m., the couple having one child, Richard C., residing in Colorado. (3) James Walter, m. Ida Wiley. They reside in St. Louis, Mo.

5. The children of Israel L. and Caroline (Green) Stokes: (1) James G., m. Catherine Clothier. They have two children, Lewis and Harry. (2) Elizabeth, m. Henry Troth, they having three children, Lillian, unmarried; Harry, unmarried; William, d. They live at McCook, Nebraska. (3) Annie, m. Tyler Engle; their children: Caroline, m. and has one child; Howard, Tyler, Emily and Helen, all unmarried.

JOSEPH GREEN.

Joseph Green, 1791, 1867, m. 10th-mo. 15, 1822, Meribah Edwards, 12th-mo. 17, 1798, d. 5th-mo. 5, 1871. Meribah was the daughter of William and Elizabeth Edwards, of Quakertown.

After residing at Washington, York county, and Leesport, both in Pennsylvania, they removed to Philadelphia where they resided until their death. Their children: (1) William P., d. in infancy; (2) Evan, 1st-mo. 1 1826, d. 1st-mo. 28, 1871, m.; (3) Barton, 2d-mo 12, 1828, d. 1st-mo. 2, 1866, unmarried; (4) Benjamin, 2d-mo. 12, 1828, m. 3d-mo. 10, 1859, Cynthia Shoemaker and had one child; (5) Elizabeth, 12th-mo. 14, 1829, m. 5th-mo. 29, 1862, Evan Jones Lester.

SAMUEL AND ABIGAIL CAREY.

Abigail Green, 3d-mo. 18, 1797, d. 8th-mo. 21, 1854, m. 9th-mo. 9, 1824, Dr. Samuel Carey, d. 8th-mo. 19, 1864. Their children:

1. Jane, 1st-mo. 24, 1827, m. Samuel Kinsey; no children.
2. Hannah, 8th-mo. 22, 1828, d. 9th-mo. 10, 1828.

Samuel Kinsey came to America from England prior to the Revolution and settled in Buckingham. He was great-grandfather of Samuel Kinsey (Jane's husband). One of his sons, John Kinsey, married Margaret Kitchen, of Solebury. They had several children, one of whom, John, was born 10th-mo. 18, 1794, and married Margaret, daughter of Samuel and Ann (Swayne) Woodward, of Londongrove. In 1811, John Kinsey, Sr., removed to Delaware, and his son John studied medicine under Dr. Baker, of Wilmington, graduating in 1828 or 1829 from the Pennsylvania Medical College.

He removed later to Chester county, and continued in practice for years, dying 1st-mo. 24, 1864. Samuel, his son, was born in Newcastle county, Delaware, 2d-mo. 24, 1822, removing with his parents to Chester county, and to Quakertown in 1839. He learned the trade of potter with Richard Moore, and continued in this business until 1852, when he engaged in farming and stock dealing. He married Martha F., daughter of George and Hannah (Foulke) Custard. Their daughter, Emma I. Kinsey, married Dr. W. H. Meredith. Samuel's second wife was Jane, daughter of Dr. Samuel and Abigail (Green) Carey, now his widow.

JAMES GREEN.

James Green, 1754, d. 1788, m. 5th-mo. 6, 1779, Martha Foulke. Their children:

    1. Ann, 1st-mo. 10, 1780, m. Joel Edwards. Their child: Jane, m. Dubree Knight, of Westtown School; no children.

    2. Elizabeth, 11th-mo. 1, 1781, m. Thomas Paxson; no children.

    3. Thomas, 9th-mo. 7, 1783, removed to Muncy Creek, Pa.

    4. Margaret, 10th-mo. 5, 1785.

After James Green's death Martha m., 10th-mo. 2, 1788, Daniel Walton, and had three children: (1) Jane, m. Samuel Roberts (see the line of John Roberts, son of Edward); (2) David, (3) Lydia, d. young.

CHARLES GREEN.

Charles Green, 1788, son of Thomas Green, m. Margaret Thomas. Their children:

    1. Lydia, m. ——— De Coursey. Their children: (1) Matilda, m. James Campbell, of Philadelphia, they having two daughters, Helen who m. ——— Trust and had one child, Irene, m. Dr. William Hassler, and Clara, m. and has children; (2) Thomas, m. and has children.

    2. Charles, m. Elizabeth Stewart, daughter of Charles and Martha (Poland) Stewart, and became founder of a somewhat numerous family.

Charles Green, just mentioned, left Quakertown, entering upon the occupation of teacher, residing most of his life in Montgomery county, Pa., near Montgomery Square. The grandparents of his wife, Elizabeth (Stewart) Green, name Poland, lost much at the time of the Revolutionary War by the depreciation of Continental money. The wife of County Superintendent R. F. Hoffecker, of Norristown, is a descendant of the same family, her maiden name having been Stewart.

Charles and Elizabeth Green resided for a time in the old building at Montgomery Square, a part of it being used for school purposes, in which the parents of General Winfield Scott Hancock also lived when his father, B. F. Hancock, taught the same school, and in which the infant was born who was many years afterwards to become so distinguished in military affairs.

The children of Charles and Elizabeth Green were three:

1. Beulah Green, d. unmarried.

2. Martha Green, d. 1896, m. first, William Seitzinger, and second, William Davis. William and Martha Seitzinger's child, Edward, m. and has one child, Bella. By the second marriage, with William Davis, there were no children.

3. Charles E. Green, of Norristown, m. Mary Jones, sister of Mark Jones, of Plymouth Meeting.

Charles and Mary (Jones) Green had five children, as follows:

1. William Green, m. first, Mary Kasely, of West Chester, having one child, Mary, d. in infancy; and second, Laura Batten, they having three children, Embury, m. May Detwiler, Metura and Beulah. They live at Malvern.

2. Beulah Green, m. Rev. D. Wesley Gordon, a well-known clergyman of the Methodist Episcopal Church, at one time a Norristown pastor, now of Columbia, Pa. Their children: (1) Embury, d. in infancy; (2) Bernice, m. John Justice, of Frankford, Philadelphia; (3) Elsie, m. Horace Greenwood, residing also at Frankford. Horace and Elsie Greenwood have two children, Wesley Gordon and Horace.

3. Martha Green, m. Rev. D. M. Gordon, another well-known Methodist minister, now of West Chester. They have one child, Mabel, one, Gertrude, having died in infancy.

4. C. Edward Green, of Norristown, a contractor and builder, m. Emeretta Todd. Their children: Bessie and Wallace. C. Edward Green m. (second wife) Mrs. Laura Large, widow of Horace Large (maiden name Barndt). They have three children, Edward Warren, Charles Robert and Mary Elva. Their third child, Gyrlie, d. in infancy.

5. Flora May Green, m. Benjamin Whitehead, of Norristown. They have no children.

XVII.

ROBERT PENROSE.

The Penroses are of English origin. Robert, son of Robert and Jane Penrose, born in Yorkshire, removed to Ireland and in 1669 married Anna Russel. They had three children. His son Robert, born in Blackane, in 1670, married Mary Clayton in 1695, and had thirteen children. With part of his family, he came to Pennsylvania in 1717. A son Robert, born in 1697, followed the others of the family to America. In 1731 he married Mary Heacock.

The children of Robert and Mary Penrose:

1. Jonathan, 1st-mo. 1, 1735-6, m.
2. Joseph, 6th-mo. 10, 1737, m. Eleanor ———; their children: Israel, 12th-mo. 31, 1768; Jane, 1st-mo. 7, 1771; Benjamin, 1st-mo. 3, 1773, d. 9th-mo. 1777; Joseph, 1st-mo. 27, 1777.
3. John, 11th-mo 19, 1739-40, m. 11th-mo. 8, 1764, Ann Roberts, 2d-mo. 16, 1745, d. 4th-mo. 28, 1841, daughter of John and Martha Roberts. (See John Roberts, page 176.)
4. William, 2d-mo. 15, 1742, m. 11th-mo. 8, 1770, Mary Roberts, 9th-mo. 30, 1748, d. 11th-mo. 30, 1843, daughter of John and Martha Roberts. (See John Roberts, page 176.)
5. Robert, Jr., 3d-mo. 6, 1744.
6. Samuel, 6th-mo. 21, 1748, m. 10th-mo. 9, 1777, Sarah Roberts, 6th-mo., 1758, daughter of Abel and Gainor Roberts.
7. Benjamin, 10th-mo. 30, 1749-50.
8. Mary, 6th-mo. 5, 1753.
9. Jesse, 5th-mo. 2, 1755. Removed to Exeter.

JOHN PENROSE.

The children of John and Ann (Roberts) Penrose:

1. Martha, 10th-mo. 13, 1765, m. 4th-mo. 30, 1795, Amos Richardson.

2. Enoch, 8th-mo. 1, 1767, m. 11th-mo. 26, 1801, first, Martha Edwards; second, Esther Tomlinson.

3. Nathan, 4th-mo. 1, 1769.

4. Rachel, 2d-mo. 7, 1771, m. 11th-mo. 26, 1795, George Shaw. Rachel Shaw d. 3d-mo. 9, 1797.

5. Jane, 11th-mo. 3, 1773, unmarried.

6. Thomas, m. 3d-mo. 31, 1796, Rachel Hillman. Their children: Hannah, m. John Ball, and had five children: Gilbert, Thomas, Lewis, Mary and Caroline; John, 3d-mo. 24, 1804, unmarried; Lydia, 3d-mo. 5, 1797, unmarried; Ann, 7th-mo. 6, 1801, unmarried; Elizabeth, 7th-mo. 27, 1806, m. Peter Lear and had children; Clementine, d. 10th-mo. 30, 1810, m. Henry Schneurman, and had children, Rachel, Emelinda, Henry.

7. John J., 2d-mo. 7, 1777, m. Paulina, daughter of Evan and Abigail Roberts. (See William Penrose.)

8. Ann, 6th-mo. 22, 1779.

9. Evan, 4th-mo. 2, 1782, m. 4th-mo. 23, 1807, Rebecca Ball.

10. Mary, 5th-mo. 9, 1785, unmarried.

1. The children of Amos and Martha (Penrose) Richardson: (1) Jane, (2) Sarah, (3) Amy, (4) Rebecca, all d. unmarried.

2. Enoch and Martha (Edwards) Penrose (first wife) had but one child, Meribah, who d. unmarried. Enoch and Esther Tomlinson Penrose had four children: (1) Martha, 8th-mo. 6, 1813, d. 3d-mo. 7, 1848, unmarried; (2) Matilda, m. Stephen Foulke, their children being Martha, d. young, Anne, unmarried, Penrose, m. Sarah Walton, the children of Penrose and Sarah Foulke being Matilda, Florence, Viola; (3) Anne R., 11th-mo. 1, 1816, d. 8th-mo. 6, 1852, m. Samuel Shaw; (4) John T., 1st-mo. 7, 1820, m. Margaret Jamison, they having two children, Esther, d. young, Stephen, m. Hannah Morgan, Stephen and Hannah's children being Alice Melvina and Martha.

8. George and Ann (Penrose) Hicks' children: (1) Penrose, 5th-mo. 9, 1802, m. (first wife) Meribah Edwards, they hav-

ing no children; Penrose m. (second wife) Eliza Foulke; no children. (2) Anne, m. Evan Penrose, their children being William, m. Jane Trumbower and have one child, John Evan; Charles, d. unmarried; Jane, m. William McDevitt. (3) Speakman, m. first, ——· —— ——, their children being Annie, m. Charles P. Whitecar, John, m. —— ——, Esther, m. —— Grove. Speakman m. 3d-mo. 11, 1869 (second wife), Alice L. Strawn, they having no children. (4) Nathan, m. Anne Wilson. (5) Evan, m. Margaret ——, their children being Henry, John, George and Rachel. (6) Rachel, m. Jesse Jones. (7) Martha, d. unmarried. (8) Hannah, m. —— Mann.

9. Evan and Rebecca (Ball) Penrose's children: (1) Aaron, m. 3d-mo. 22, 1838, Maryetta Foulke, having three children, Benjamin F., m. Alice Thomson, Caroline, m. David J. Ambler (see Amblers, page 130), Rebecca, m. Lewis Ambler. (2) Jane, m. Johnson Strawn, having three children, Thomas, unmarried, Annie and Johnson, Jr. Annie Strawn m. first, Joseph Foulke (no children), and second, Edward Johnson, their children being Russell, Helen, Emily, Hortense. Johnson Strawn m. Florence Meredith, their children being Olivia, Thomas, Charles and Harry. (3) Evan, m. Anne Hicks, their children being Charles, William and Jane (see No. 8 above). (4) Margaret, m. Eli W. Strawn (see Strawns, Chapter XI), their children being Henry, deceased; Mary, m. Richard Johnson and have five children, Harry, Milton, Walter, Maurice, Arthur.

WILLIAM PENROSE.

William Penrose, son of Robert and Mary Penrose, m. Mary Roberts, daughter of John and Martha, b. 9th-mo. 30, 1748, d. 11th-mo. 30, 1843. They had two children:

1. Abigail, m. Evan Roberts. Their children, Hannah, Maria, William, all d. unmarried; Paulina, m. John J. Penrose, they having one child, Evan R., m. Kate Birnbaum. They had one child, Harry, d. in infancy. (See John Penrose, above.)

2. Sarah, m. 4th-mo. 4, 1811, Caleb Edwards. Their children: Margaret, first wife of Joseph Foulke, they having no children; Amos, m. Hercillia Edwards; no children.

SAMUEL PENROSE.

Samuel and Sarah (Roberts) Penrose had ten children, as follows:

1. Abel, 8th-mo. 7, 1778, m. 4th-mo. 1, 1802, Kezia Speakman, d. 11th-mo. 11, 1803, and (second wife) 5th-mo. 2, 1805, Abel m. Abigail Foulke.
2. Gainor, 3d-mo. 14, 1780.
3. William, 3d-mo. 14, 1782.
4. Everard, 10th-mo. 7, 1784.
5. Mary, 5th-mo. 11, 1787.
6. Benjamin, 9th-mo. 16, 1791.
7. Susanna, 8th-mo. 21, 1793.
8. Samuel, 8th-mo. 10, 1796.
9. Margaret, 9th-mo. 20, 1798.
10. Morris, 6th-mo. 15, 1801.

They removed to Horsham, Montgomery county, Pa., and 2d-mo. 19, 1801, a certificate was granted by Richland Monthly Meeting to Samuel and Sarah, with their children, William, Everard, Benjamin and Margaret, to that of Horsham. He purchased what is still known as the Græme Park property, and removed to it in that year. Later he bought a farm in Warminster, Bucks county, to which his son Benjamin removed. On the marriage of his son William, he sold the Græme Park farm to him and removed to the Warminster farm.

Of the children of Samuel and Sarah Penrose, William m. Hannah, daughter of William and Ann Jarrett, of Horsham. He bought the Park farm, as already mentioned, of his father, and resided on it until a few years before his death, when he purchased an adjoining property, and spent the remainder of his days thereon.

William and Hannah (Jarrett) Penrose had seven children: (1) Ann J., 9th-mo. 25, 1811; (2) Samuel, 4th-mo. 18, 1813; (3) Jarrett, 4th-mo. 1, 1815; (4) Abel, 5th-mo. 3, 1817, (5) Hannah, 2d-mo. 28, 1820; (6) William, 3d-mo. 26, 1822; (7) Tacy S., 10th-mo. 14, 1823.

Ann J. m. Abraham Iredell, of Horsham.

Samuel d. unmarried, aged thirty-five years.

Jarrett m. Tacy A. Kirk, of Abington.

Abel m. Sarah Beisel, of Allentown.

Hannah m. Isaac W. Hicks (died 3d-mo. 28, 1898, aged 89 years, 2 months, 8 days), son of Edward Hicks, of Newtown, the well-known minister.

William d. in infancy.

Tacy S. m. Morris Davis, of Warminster.

Jarrett and Tacy Penrose's children: Ellen S., 1st-mo. 14, 1843; Elizabeth H., 1st-mo. 4, 1845; William, 7th-mo. 31, 1847; Alfred, 5th-mo. 14, 1849, d. in infancy; Samuel, 5th-mo. 5, 1852.

Ellen S. Penrose m. Edward T. Betts, they residing at Buffalo, N. Y.; their children: C. Walter, m. Lidie P. Haslam; Willam P., Edward T., Jr., and Elizabeth P.

Elizabeth H. Penrose m. Alfred Moore, of Horsham, and resides on the homestead. Their children are Ellie B. and Bertha A.

William Penrose m. Hannah Paul, of Warrington. They reside there, the children being J. Howard, Morris P., William and Lydia.

Samuel Penrose m. Mary C. Farren, of Doylestown. They have children.

Abel Penrose, brother of Jarrett Penrose, and son of William and Hannah, m. 12th-mo. 25, 1856, Sarah C., 4th-mo. 3, 1836, daughter of Daniel and Mary M. Beisel, of Allentown, as has been stated. Their children: (1) Hannah J., 1858, m. 11th-mo. 16, 1882, Dr. A. D. Markley, of Hatboro (now deceased). They had two children, Penrose and Anna Markley. (2) Morris B. Penrose, 1860; (3) William, 1870; (4) Mary M., 1877.

XVIII

WILLIAM JAMISON.

William Jamison, the ancestor of the family of that name, emigrated from Ireland to Pennsylvania, having previously removed from Scotland to Ulster, in Ireland. It is not known positively when he came to this country, but he was here previous to 1730. He took up a tract of two hundred and fifty acres on Swamp creek. He had but one child, a son named John, who married ——— Edwards.

The children of John Jamison and ——— Edwards were (A) Joseph, (B) William, (C) John, (D) Jane, (E) Mary and (F) Margaret.

A. Joseph m. ——— Bean. Their children:

1. Isaias, or Esaias, d. 9th-mo. 27, 1826, m. 4th-mo. 26, 1798, Margaret Hicks Ball, d. 4th-mo. 28, 1840. Their children were: (1) Joseph, 5th-mo. 22, 1799, d. 6th-mo. 13, 1829, m. Elizabeth Wilson. (2) Margaret, 9th-mo. 1, 1800, d. 3d-mo. 10. 1831, unmarried. (3) Mary Ann, 11th-mo. 15, 1802, m. 4th-mo. 4, 1822, Thomas Stradling. (4) Eli, d. young.

2. Hannah, d. 2d-mo. 27, 1826, m. John Martin, d. 8th-mo. 28, 1827. Their children: (5) Mary, unmarried. (6) Kate, unmarried. (7) Esaias, m. (8) John, unmarried. (9) Eli, d. young. (10) Sarah, d. young.

3. Jane, m. Samuel Miller. Their children: (11) William, m. Margaret Wilson. (12) Mary, m. 4th-mo. 6, 1820, Jonathan Shaw. (13) Sarah, d. unmarried.

B. William, son of John, emigrated to Virginia, and his descendants, if any, are unknown.

C. John, 1757, d. 1st-mo. 4, 1834, m. 9th-mo. 10, 1778, Jane Crosley, 2d-mo. 28, 1759, d. 7th-mo. 24, 1839. Their children:

1. Margaret, 6th-mo. 11, 1779, d. 10th-mo. 23, 1811, m. Joseph Penrose. Their children: (14) Ellen, m. Clayton Foulke; no heirs. (15) John, m. Paulina Roberts, daughter of Evan and Abigail. (16) Maria, m. Benjamin Roberts. (17) Samuel, d. young.

2. Mary, 2d-mo. 17, 1781, d. 1st-mo. 6, 1782.

3. Samuel, 4th-mo. 7, 1783, d. 12th-mo. 27, 1834, m. 5th-mo. 15, 1817, Jane Roberts, 1st-mo. 12, 1791, d. 8th-mo. 28, 1855. Their children: (18) Margaret, 11th-mo. 28, 1818, m. John T. Penrose. (19) Charles R., 11th-mo. 25, 1819, m. Mary Strawn. (20) John, 2d-mo. 15, 1823, d. 1st-mo. 12, 1890, m. Deborah Nice. (21) David R., 8th-mo. 27, 1826, d. 3d-mo. 14, 1889, m. 6th-mo. 21, 1853, Cornelia Foulke, 7th-mo. 12, 1828, d. 4th-mo. 2, 1857. David m. (second wife) 6th-mo. 15, 1858, Matilda G. Foulke, 12th-mo. 27, 1830, d. 3d-mo. 6, 1894. David's wives were sisters, both being daughters of Joshua and Caroline G. Foulke.

D. Jane, m. John Edwards. Their children :(22) Aaron, unmarried. (23) Jane, unmarried.

E. Mary, m. John Pennington. No heirs.

F. Margaret, unmarried.

(1). The children of Joseph and Elizabeth (Wilson) Jamison were four in number, as follows:

1. Mary Ann, m. Thomas Smith, their children being Mary Elizabeth, m. John H. Bishop, and Annie, d. young. John H. and Mary Elizabeth (Smith) Bishop's children: Annie, m. William Bartleman, having two children, Bertha May and Paul; May, Walter, Pancoast, Kate.

2. Esaias, m. Ellen Kirk, their children being Jane Elizabeth, who m. Alfred Wilson and had two children, Thomas who m. Hannah Winner, and Ella who m. Albert Worthington; Emma, m. ―――― Radcliffe; Kirk, m. ―――― Shordey; Josephine, m. ―――― Craven (?); Frank, Ella and William, all three d. young.

3. Eli, d. young.

4. Margaret, m. Newton Thomas. Their children: Eli, m. Elizabeth Reynolds, and had one child, Newton, d. young; Jesse, m. Emma Williams, and had two children, Ida, d. young, and

Lillian; Howard, d. young; Ida, m. Oscar Doan, and had one child, Newton Raymond.

(3). The children of Thomas and Mary Ann (Jamison) Stradling: Wilson, d. young; Annie, m. Charles Smith and left no heirs; Mary J., d. young.

(11). The children of William and Margaret (Wilson) Miller: Frank, d. young; Samuel, m. Mary Carver, they having three children, Frank, Caroline and Ellwood, the last-named d. young.

(12). The child of Jonathan and Mary (Miller) Shaw: Samuel, m. (first wife) Annie Penrose, and had no heirs; and (second wife) Sarah Carver, having two children, William and Allen. William's first wife was Alice Steinhauer, who had one child, Lottie. William's second wife, Mary Kline. Allen m. Emma Dill.

(15). John and Paulina (Roberts) Penrose's child: Evan R., m. Kate Birnbaum, and had one child, Harry, d. young.

(16). The children of Benjamin and Maria (Penrose) Roberts: Joseph, Joseph and Ellen, all d. young; Penrose, m. Lydia Carter.

(18). The children of John T. and Margaret (Jamison) Penrose: Stephen F., d. 5th-mo. 6, 1886, m. Hannah Morgan and had two children, Alice Melvina, m. Henry Johnson, and Martha; Esther, d. young.

(19). The children of Charles R. and Mary (Strawn) Jamison; Jane, d. unmarried; Caroline, d. unmarried; William, m. Elizabeth Kinsey and had eight children, Walter, Caroline, Alfred, Helen, Charles, Byron, William, d. in infancy, and Elizabeth; Allen S. m. Ella S. Ball and have two children, Florence and May.

(20). The children of John and Deborah (Nice) Jamison: Catherine, d. unmarried; Jane, John, Samuel, William, d. young.

(21). The children of David R. and Cornelia (Foulke) Jamison: Lucinda, m. Charles W. Timmons, and had three children, Cornelia J., David J. and John S.; Cornelia, d. young.

The children of David R. and Matilda (Foulke) Jamison: Alice and Frank, both d. young; Mary Louise, m. Samuel T. Bleam and had one child, Frank, d. young; Ida, Fannie, David, d. young.

SAMUEL J. LEVICK

XIX.

SAMUEL J. LEVICK.

Although not descended from any of the old Richland families, Samuel J. Levick was closely identified with Quakertown for many years. Coming from a long line of Quaker ancestry, he was by education and conviction a Friend.

The family came originally from France, where the spelling was Leveque, but it became naturalized, as it were, in Derbyshire, England, centuries, perhaps, before it was transplanted to America by the coming of Richard Levick to Kent county, Delaware, in 1680. Richard and Mary Levick had a son William, and he and his wife Sarah had a son of the same name who married Susanna Manlove, a member of a well-known Delaware family. The latter were the parents of Ebenezer Levick, who married Elizabeth Wetherill Jones, of Philadelphia. Ebenezer was born at Little Creek, Delaware, 7th-mo. 16, 1791, and Elizabeth in Philadelphia 6th-mo. 5, 1789. They were married 5th-mo. 1, 1816.

Samuel Jones Levick was the second of six children, all born in Philadelphia, the others being William M., James J., Mary J., Elizabeth R. and Anna, the only survivor being Elizabeth R. William studied law and became a wise counselor in all matters relating to titles. James was a well-known physician, Welsh historian and genealogist. Ebenezer Levick, the father, was a prominent merchant and business man of Philadelphia. He died 10th-mo. 11, 1849, his widow surviving till 11th-mo. 21, 1886, when she died at the age of 97 years, 6 months and 16 days.

Samuel J. Levick was born 8th-mo. 30, 1819. He was at Westtown Boarding School three years, entered his father's counting-house, but, though early plunged into the whirlpool of business life, he was susceptible to those religious impressions which ultimately made of him a highly gifted and valuable minister. From his twentieth to his twenty-fifth year he was engaged much in the work of moral reform characteristic of the Society of Friends, including the anti-slavery movement, the Peace Society, efforts to educate and otherwise benefit the colored race, and labor in general among the class in a large city who present a field for missionary effort.

Samuel J. Levick and Ellen Foulke, daughter of Caleb and Jane Foulke, of Richland, were married 4th-mo. 3, 1841. He bought a farm of eighty-five acres in Richland, which he called "Spring Lawn," and it became their home. At this time he was active in the work of the ministry. In his diary, under the date 9th-mo. 10, 1841, he speaks as follows of a sermon he delivered at Salem on that day:

"After a brief communication from my companion [Dr. Henry T. Child, of Philadelphia], I was, under deep exercise, led to ask the people, What is the Gospel? and to answer the query by endeavoring to show them that the true gospel is the power of God unto salvation, that it is preached to every rational creature under Heaven, from the least to the greatest, and that it cannot be learned in the schools of men—for none know it save those to whom the Father reveals it by the operation of the Holy Spirit in their hearts. But He does not reveal this Gospel in the heart that has not first undergone the purification alluded to by John the Baptist, 'I, indeed, baptize you with water unto repentance; but he that cometh after me is mightier than I, whose shoes I am not worthy to bear. He shall baptize you with the Holy Ghost and with fire; whose fan is in His hand, and He will thoroughly purge His floor, and gather His wheat into the garner; but He will burn the chaff with unquenchable fire.' Here we see the preparation that is necessary before we can become acquainted with this blessed Gospel, and the mission of the Apostles, eighteen hundred years ago, was to call the attention of the people to this preparation, as a means to the great end of receiving a knowledge of the Gospel."

This extract is given because the sentiments therein so clearly and vigorously expressed were characteristic of Samuel J. Levick's preaching, as hundreds who have heard him, from time to time, under the influence of spiritual fervor declare these and many other truths, can testify, with the writer of these lines.

Ellen, his wife, died 8th-mo. 13, 1842, leaving one child Jane F., who became, on reaching womanhood, the wife of Edwin A. Jackson, of New York.

In the autumn of 1844, 11th-mo. 17, he was married to Susanna Morris Mather, a member of Gwynedd Monthly Meeting. Her parents were Charles and Jane (Roberts) Mather, and she was a descendant of Susanna Morris, an eminent minister, for whom she was named. The wife of Benjamin G. Foulke, of Quakertown (now his widow), is her sister. In 1848, Samuel and his family left Richland and went to Philadelphia, where he joined in business with his brother William. After various removals, he returned to Quakertown in 1857, where they continued to live until 1874.

The youngest son, James J. Levick, Jr., died at the age of six years. Another affliction was the death of his son Samuel, at Quakertown, in 1880, he leaving a widow and three children. The other sons were Lewis, Jr., Charles M., Samuel J., Jr., and William.

Of the closing years of Samuel J. Levick's life it may be said that they were usefully spent, as were those of his early manhood and middle age. His death came rather suddenly, 4th-mo. 19, 1885, in his sixty-sixth year. He was interred at Merion Friends' burying ground on the 22d, many who had known him being in attendance, and several testimonies being borne to his worth and usefulness.

Of Samuel J. Levick's power as a speaker, enough, perhaps, has already been said. A man of quick perceptions, strong will and fine physique, he rose at times to a high pitch of eloquence. He became a recorded minister in 1842, before he was twenty-three years old. His last minute was dated 5th-mo. 21, 1884, for himself and wife to visit New York Yearly Meeting, and to appoint meetings there, as way might open.

XX

BIOGRAPHICAL MENTION.

In the preceding pages some attention has been given to biographical facts in connection with various persons of whom mention was made. In the cases of Richard Moore and Samuel J. Levick, separate chapters were prepared, they having been in their day among the most prominent and widely known residents of Richland. There are others whose usefulness and value to the community entitle them to a more extended notice than has been given. In some instances, the introduction of such particulars would have made an undesirable break in the narrative. It is proposed to supply in this chapter such deficiencies of this character as are most noticeable.

There is a notable lack of such information in connection with the pioneers in the settlement of Richland.

What has been already given in reference to the earlier settlers, including Thomas Roberts, Peter Lester, Edward Roberts, Abraham Griffith, Thomas Lancaster, Thomas Nixon, John Edwards, Morris Morris, Hugh Foulke, William Jamison, John Ball, Samuel Thomas and others, embraces practically all that is known of them. It is a matter of regret that there is no other source from which additional particulars can be gleaned. The records of Friends. while they contain much of value in the way of statistical information, are almost destitute of personal details, which must be obtained from tradition, from wills, from family letters, from memorials prepared by the Monthly Meeting, and elsewhere. These have been drawn upon largely in the preparation of this volume, as the reader has probably discovered.

The above remarks apply to the first and second generations of old Richland families. When we pass on to a later period, that succeeding the Revolutionary War, there are more details to be gathered, whose collection and permanent preservation should be a matter of interest to their descendants. The wills and other recorded documents which are elsewhere given, have some bearing as matters of biographical interest in the absence of information from other sources.

Of Hugh Foulke, a memorial by Richland Monthly Meeting says:

"He was a member of our meeting for about thirty years, the latter part of his life. He had a good gift in the ministry, which we believe he endeavored faithfully to discharge. His last illness, which was very sharp, he endured with much patience and resignation." He died 5th-mo. 21, 1760, in his seventy-fifth year, and in the fortieth year of his ministry. His posterity became very numerous. Of eleven children of Hugh and Ann (Williams) Foulke, ten lived to manhood or womanhood and married and raised families, many of their descendants being given in Chapter V by families and in Chapter IX. It is noted by Howard M. Jenkins, a descendant of Hugh and Ann Foulke, that "in seventy years after their marriage (in 1783) the number of their posterity was 343, and in 1810 it was estimated at upward of 500, of whom 115 bore the name Foulke."

Several of the sons of Hugh Foulke were men of note in their day. Samuel's prominence has been mentioned (see pages 145-147), his usefulness in the community being testified to very fully by his contemporaries and others. Portions of his journal kept during the time he was a member of the Provincial Assembly, are to be found in the "Pennsylvania Magazine of History and Biography." His disownment in 1781, along with his brothers, John, Thomas and Theophilus, his nephew Everard and others (see page 23), because of their attachment to the cause of American independence, has been mentioned. This proceeding is not now to be regarded in any other light than of regret that such action should have been taken at all. Samuel was familiar with the Welsh tongue, and rendered good service to posterity by translations of important documents and records from that language into English.

BENJAMIN G. FOULKE.

Referring the reader to previous pages for other particulars as to the Foulke family, the writer desires to place on record a brief account of Benjamin G. Foulke, to whose care in the preservation of family papers and traditions he is indebted for many facts contained in this volume.

Benjamin G. Foulke was a son of Caleb and Jane (Green) Foulke, and was born 7th-mo. 28, 1813, living seventy-five years. The date of his death was 8th-mo. 14, 1888. He was a farmer, surveyor and conveyancer, giving much attention to the settlement of estates and other business of a legal nature, for which his general intelligence and business ability peculiarly fitted him. He married Jane, daughter of Charles and Jane (Roberts) Mather, of Whitpain, at Gwynedd, 3d-mo. 6th, 1838. A list of their descendants appears on page 155.

Benjamin Foulke was for many years a valued elder of Richland Monthly Meeting. In addition to service in various capacities therein, he was for a long time Clerk of Abington Quarterly Meeting and later of Philadelphia Yearly Meeting. In all these stations, his quick discernment, sound judgment, and thorough understanding of the principles and discipline of the Society, made him particularly serviceable.

He was greatly interested in educational matters. He was employed for several years in the capacity of surveyor by the North Pennsylvania Railroad Company.

His widow and two daughters, Eleanor and Anna, reside in the homestead, close to Friends' meeting-house at Quakertown. One of his sons, Charles M. Foulke, resides in Washington. The other, Job Roberts Foulke, who lives in Philadelphia, is an officer of the Provident Life and Trust Company of that city.

DEATHS SINCE 1870.

A glance at the list of dead since 1870 (pages 58 and 59) shows how large the number who have passed away in twenty-eight years. A word or two as to some of them, personally

BENJAMIN G. FOULKE

known to the writer, may be of interest to survivors who appreciate their worth, and serve in some measure, to "keep their memory green."

A remarkable fact is the large proportion of very old persons, affording additional evidence to that given elsewhere as to the longevity of Richland Friends.

Paxson Blakey was one of a well-known family in Middletown (Bucks county). His ancestors on both sides were early settlers in that section.

The oldest of the number was Hannah Foulke, who reached the age of ninety-four years.

Several, including Susan P. Brown, Phebe, Esther, Zachariah and John A. Flagler, and Charles and Catharine Foulke, the Palmers, Phillipses, Waltons and others, were of Stroudsburg.

John Jackson Moore was a worthy son of an honored sire. His earnestness and zeal in behalf of the Society's principles are well entitled to remembrance and emulation.

Dr. Charles F. Meredith lived to an advanced age, being the last of his family. Though not a member, he was in sympathy with Friends. The memory of his kindliness and other excellent qualities will long linger in the minds of those who knew him.

Others who have passed away at an advanced age are Anthony Johnson, Edward Thomas, Penrose Hicks, Antrim Morgan and wife, and many more of whom it may be said in the language of scripture, "The memory of the just is blessed."

XXI

NOTES.

The Phillips Family, page 21, line 18.

Geo. Phillips, Sr., of Richland, had sons Edmund and John; Edmund m. Elizabeth Davies in 1729, John m. Deborah Britton in 1729.

The Quakertown Post Office, page 35.

At the session of Congress of 1805 post-routes were established from Bristol to Quakertown via Newtown and Doylestown, and from New Hope via Doylestown to Lancaster, there and back once a week. These routes appear to have been arranged to facilitate the distribution of Asher Miner's paper "now the Bucks County Intelligencer, established in 1804," and the mails were carried for several years by the late John McIntosh, of Doylestown.

The stamp (see the fac-simile above) used by Joseph A. Lancaster was found in 1791 by A. Jackson Croman in the old log-house, shown on page 35, before it was torn down. It is crude and was probably made by the incumbent himself.

A. J. Croman, who is quite an antiquarian, says:

"In 1847 the first postage stamps were issued. They were in denominations of 5 and 10 cents. In 1851 it was reduced to 3 cents for each half-ounce, if paid in advance, and if paid by the receiver, 5 cents. I well remember the first stamps and the commotion produced at the neighboring post office, the latter part of 1851.

"A teacher coming from a distance, brought a letter to the post office with one of the little red labels pasted on the corner. In response to the inquiring look of the Postmaster, for his 3 cents to pay for the postage, the teacher replied that by looking on the envelope he would see that all the postal regulations had been complied with. The Postmaster was evidently not familiar with the new law, and insisted on having his 3 cents. The teacher left and the Postmaster declared he would make the receiver pay 5 cents for it."

The following is a list of Quakertown Postmasters with the dates of their appointment:

Wm. Green,	March 19, 1803.
John F. Walker,	July 28, 1829.
Jacob L. Duden,	May 20, 1830.
John J. Horn,	March 17, 1832.
Peter Shantz,	April 1, 1833.
Benjamin Shroyer,	March 4, 1834.
Joseph R. Lancaster,	April 22, 1836.
Jacob Slifer,	December 21, 1838.
Benjamin Griffith,	May 5, 1840.
Joseph R. Lancaster,	Jan. 4, 1844.
James L. Gold,	Feb. 11, 1846.
Richard R. Green,	July 6, 1849.
Levi Ochs,	April 29, 1853.
Peter Smith,	October 31, 1854.
John H. Kaull,	January 17, 1855.
Manasses Ochs,	November 7, 1857.
Mary J. Ochs,	September 8, 1860.
Ephraim L. Cope,	October 2, 1867.
Mary J. Ochs,	November 7, 1867.
Joseph Hill,	January 10, 1880.
George H. Kline,	June 10, 1885.
Edward T. Ochs,	June 15, 1889.
Joseph Thomas,	Nov. 19, 1891.

By the year 1867 the population and business at the railroad station had grown to such an extent that the citizens of that vicinity demanded a post-office. The Quakertown post-office was accordingly removed to Shive's store building, at the corner of Front and Broad streets, Ephraim L. Cope being appointed postmaster.

The indignation of the citizens around the Cross-roads was aroused. They framed a petition, signed by a large number, and sent it to Washington. The post-office was restored, after five weeks' absence, to the west end, Mary J. Ochs being reappointed postmistress. At the same time, November 7, 1867, Ephraim L. Cope was appointed postmaster of a new office granted to the east end, bearing the name Richland Centre. It was kept in Tobias Shive's store.

Under Postmaster Kline postage was reduced by a law of Congress to two cents for each ounce.

Josiah Worrell, page 96.

In "The Worrells," cousin "John" Worrell, in the address of Amos Roberts' letter, should be "Josiah" as the context shows.

Dr. George W. Logan, page 111.

Dr. George W. Logan, son of William Logan 2d, and grandson of James Logan, was born at Stenton in 1755. He improved the farm and was a member of several agricultural societies, and of the Philosophical Society, where he was a colleague of Dr. Benjamin Franklin. He was United States Senator, 1801-1807. He went to France in 1798 at his own expense and met Talleyrand, Merlin and others, his object being to assist in preventing war between this country and France. War was happily averted, rather, perhaps, by a combination of circumstances. Dr. Logan was a peacemaker, and knew Romilly, Wilberforce, Clarkson and other eminent Englishmen. In Amos Roberts' day, Stenton, though the estate had been divided years before, stretched from the Germantown pike to the Old York Road. His wife was Deborah Logan, "Debbie Norris," of Sallie Wister's journal. After Dr. George Logan's death, Albanus C. Logan resided at Stenton with his mother, Deborah Logan. The Norris estate was at Fair Hill. Deborah Logan survived her husband eighteen years, dying in February, 1839.

Deborah Logan witnessed the lease, page 111.

Mrs. Logan was the granddaughter of Isaac Norris, a special friend of William Penn. He was Chief Justice of Pennsylvania, at the time of his death, which occurred in Germantown Friends' meeting-house. The warm body was removed to Stenton, where efforts at resuscitation proved vain. Mrs. Logan was a pupil of Anthony Benezet.

Hugh and Sarah Roberts, page 116.

The first child of Hugh and Sarah Roberts, Lydia, b. 4th-mo. 4, 1808, d. 8th-mo. 21, 1809.

The Spencer Genealogy, pages 120-123.

The following additions to the old Spencer genealogy are of interest to persons who are connected by descent with the family:

Elizabeth (144) married Joseph Lukens. Their children: 202 Joseph, 203 Dr. Samuel, 204 Hannah, 205 Gainor [also Eliza and others].

Mary (146) married Jonathan Roberts. Their children: 206 George, 207 Levi, Joseph, Rachel. [Levi, 1777, married Lydia Sharpless; Rachel, 1779, married Matthew Conrad; George, 1781, married Alice Fell; Joseph, 1784, married Bathsheba French; Joseph, died in infancy.]

Margaret (97) married William Worthington. Their child: 208 Spencer.

Sarah (96) married Isaac Walton. Their child: 209 Sarah.

Elizabeth (119) married Thomas Bowers. Their children: 210 Samuel, 211 Sophia.

Ann (120) married Joshua Walton. Their children: 212 Jonathan, 213 Sarah.

Sarah (40) m. David Atkinson. Their children: 214 Rachel, 215 Sarah.

Hannah (154) married Arnold Boon. Their child: 216 Mary.

Charles' (151) child: 217 Ruth.

Some additions may be made at this point. Where it is impossible to trace all lines, because it would carry a work far beyond the limits intended, the usefulness of a compact genealogy can readily be appreciated.

James Spencer, No. 4, oldest son of William and Elizabeth Spencer, was twice married and died in Upper Dublin. Owing to the fact that he inherited his father's half of the Whitton estate, he removed from Northampton (Bucks county) to Upper Dublin, and his descendants are now very numerous in Montgomery county. He married Sarah Walton in 1761 and she dying in 1786, in 1788 he married Elizabeth Marple, widow of John Marple, of Horsham, her maiden name having been Lukens. She survived him. Louis Spencer Whitcomb, a well-known Justice of the Peace of Upper Dublin, occupies a property which he owned and where he resided. His son Abner, whose wife was Mary Muckleson, the ancestor of Louis S. Whitcomb, was bequeathed this property by the will of his father. It passed from Abner to his daughter Catharine Spencer Whitcomb, thence to its present owner. All James' children were by his first wife.

Spencer Shoemaker (27) married Sarah Gentle and had several children. Margaret (28) married Peter Lightcap. Margaret (34) married John Brand, the family living near Line Lexington.

Elizabeth (30) Cooper and her family lived in Illinois. Angeline Shoemaker, her sister, lived in Solebury, Bucks county.

Peter Shoemaker (26) married and left a child Adrianna who married Joseph M. Vandever, of Marlborough, Chester county.

Thomas (6) Spencer m. Mary Hallowell, Twelfth-month 16, 1760, at Horsham meeting-house.

His oldest son was William (93). He married Margaret (118) Spencer, daughter of Samuel, his first cousin, and was disowned therefor by Horsham Monthly Meeting, Tenth-month 17, 1788. All his children, four daughters, died unmarried.

Mary (95) married Isaac Walton, of Warwick, Bucks county. They had one child, a daughter who died unmarried.

Thomas (92) married Esther Worthington. His twin sister, Elizabeth, died in 1802, aged thirty-five, unmarried.

Margaret (97) born Second-month 19, 1770, married William Worthington, of Wrightstown, a brother to Esther, Margaret's brother Thomas' wife. Their children were Thomas, Mary, William, Jesse, Esther and Spencer Worthington, all of whom married. After Margaret's death, William married Mary Saner and had six children by her.

Amos (94) Spencer married Ann Brown. Among their children was John G. (103) Spencer, of Oxford Valley. Born in 1803, he taught school for some years, and in 1833 commenced storekeeping at Springville. In 1834, he married Elizabeth, daughter of George Fetter, of Montgomery county. In 1840 he purchased the store at Oxford Valley and removed to it. His son, C. Watson Spencer, succeeded him in business in 1873.

John G. Spencer survived to the great age of ninety-four years, dying in 1897. His wife died seventeen years earlier. He left four children—Amy Ann, wife of William R. Vandegrift, of Newportville; Amos L., for years a well-known teacher, though now retired; C. Watson, the merchant, and G. Franklin, a farmer near Breadysville. He was postmaster at Oxford Valley from the time of the establishment of the office in 1849 until a few years ago, when he resigned and Watson was appointed.

Chapter VII, page 134.

The following is the will of Mary Roberts, widow of Edward Roberts:

Whereas I, Mary Roberts of Richland in the County of Bucks, Widow, being weak in Body but of Sound Mind & Memory, do make and Commit to writing this my last Will & Testament in manner & form as follows,—

First, I give unto my Son Abel Roberts the sum of Four pounds Ten shillings. Item, I give unto my Son David Roberts the sum of Four pounds Ten shillings. Item, I give unto my Son Nathan Roberts the like sum of Four pounds Ten shillings. Item, I give unto my Daughter Margaret Roberts the like sum of Four pounds Ten shillings. Item, I give unto my Son Everard Roberts the sum of Eight pounds. Item, I give unto my daughter Mary the sum of Nine pounds & a Feather Bed with all its Appurtenances, and also my Dressing Table. Item, I give unto my daughter Jane the sum of Nine pounds, and a Feather Bed and all its Appurtenances thereunto belonging, & also my largest Looking Glass. Item, I give unto the three Eldest Daughters of Daughter Martha deceased, One Feather Bed with all its Appurtenances, & Six silver spoons, to be by a Just valuation equally divided between them.

Item, I Will that all the remainder of my Household Goods & Effects be by a Just Valuation Equally divided between my said two Daughters, Mary & Jane abovenamed.

Item, I give the sum of Ten pounds to be Equally divided between my Daughter Martha's other children, named Edward, John, William, Martha, & Sarah, share and share alike.——— and as my son Nathan abovenamed, has had the use of sundry of my Goods which were given me by my deceased Husband, whereby some of them are worn out, & others rendered of less value, it is therefore my Will that my Son Nathan shall make good the deficiency which shall appear in the value of the Goods which he hath had the Use of, so that Justice be done to my other Children & Grand Children respectively as above mentioned

Lastly I do Ordain & Appoint my Son in law Thomas Foulke & my Friend Samuel Foulke to be Executors of this my last Will & Testament. In witness whereof I have hereunto set my hand and seal this Eleventh Day of the First Month in the Year of our Lord 1781.

her

MARY X ROBERTS   [Seal]

mark

Sealed, Signed & Declared by the said Testatrix to be her last Will & Testament in the presence of us.

Everard Foulke Israel Foulke.   Proved Aug. 14th, 1784.

It must not be supposed that the custom, among very old people, of signing with a mark, was due to a lack of education. It was probably because of physical debility, often, perhaps. of a stroke of paralysis. Mary Roberts' age excuses the mark, as does that of Thomas Roberts and others. The author has in his possession fac-similes of the signatures of many of the older Richland Friends, and they all indicate fair educational advantages, such as members of the Society, for more than two centuries, have been accustomed to provide for their children.

Martha Roberts m. Benjamin Foulke, page 137. See also page 156, No. 6.

Martha F. Custard, daughter of George and Hannah Custard, and granddaughter of Benjamin and Martha (Roberts) Foulke, m. Samuel Kinsey. Their children: (1) Charles, m. Emma ———, they having two children, Lanneau and Charles; (2) George, m. first, Lizzie Roeder, they having two children, Martha and Cora, d. young; (3) John, d. unmarried; (4) Irene,

m. Dr. W. H. Meredith. Joseph, the brother of Martha (Custard) Kinsey (see page 156) d. unmarried.

Jane, second daughter of Benjamin and Martha (Roberts) Foulke, m. 4th-mo. 22, 1829, Thomas Strawn. Their children: (1) Martha, d. unmarried; (2) Rachel, d. unmarried; (3) Charles, m. Mary Warwick, they having three children, Harry, Frederick (d. unmarried), Jane F.

Chapter XI, page 164.

Extract from William Buckman's will, dated 7th-mo. 4, 1716, proved 10th-mo. 26, 1716.

"Item—I give unto my daughter Mary Strawhen Fifty Shillings current money, to be payed twelve months after my decease and to her five children, Ruth, Sarah, William, Henry and John, fifty shillings apiece to be paid to them respectively when they arrive at twenty one years of age."

William Buckman, with daughters, Mary and Sarah, arrived in this country in the year 1684.

Mary m., 1706, Henry Cooper, of Newtown, blacksmith. He died in 1710, leaving a widow, Mary, and five children, William, Henry, John, Sarah and Ruth as above.

Ruth m. Dennis Pursel and removed to Bethlehem township, Hunterdon Co., N. J.

Sarah m. Joseph Strickland at Buckingham in 1727, and after his death in 1737, m. (second husband) Jonathan Abbott.

Mary Cooper, widow, married Launcelot Strawhen, of Middletown, and had by him one son, Jacob, 1716.

Launcelot Strawhen died in Middleton township. Letters of administration were granted to his widow Mary, June 10, 1720.

The will of Mary Strawhen, dated June 7, 1738 (at Bethlehem, county of Hunterdon, N. J.), proved September 10, 1740, mentions daughters Ruth and Sarah, and William, Henry and John Cooper, to whom she devised 40 shillings each. The residue of her estate she bequeathed to her son, Jacob Strawhen, whom she named as executor.

Jacob Strawn, or Strawhen, obtained title to 255 acres of land in Haycock township, May 5, 1752, by deed from Joseph Tomlinson, of Makefield.

Jacob Strawn was a prominent man in his neighborhood. At the organization of the Committee of Safety, December 15, 1774, he was named as the member of that committee for Haycock, but with Abraham Stout and Thomas Foulke, of Richland, and John Chapman, of Wrightstown, he on July 21st, 1775, declined serving, on the ground that being Friends, "their consciences prevented them from taking part in some of the proceedings in which the Committee were required to participate."

Two of his sons were drafted into the army during the Revolutionary War, but substitutes were procured for them by their father.

Isaiah Strawn, page 166.

Perry A. Armstrong, his great-grandson, says of him:

Isaiah Strawn never had a lawsuit or made an active enemy. He took no interest in local politics and never sought or held an office except one—collector of taxes. Too generous to oppress the poor, he marked their taxes paid upon the tax roll but had to sell a whole pen full of his fat hogs to make up the shortage. This discouraged all further office holding. His lips were never stained with tobacco nor did they utter profane or really vulgar language. Liquors he kept, as was the custom in those days, as a means of showing hospitality to visitors, but he never tasted it himself. He never went in debt. "Pay as you go" was his favorite maxim and rule of his life. What he bought he paid for and what he could not pay for he did not buy even though he might need it ever so much. No man ever held the note of this Isaiah Strawn.

Joel Strawn, page 167.

Perry A. Armstrong, his grandson, says of him:

When volunteers were called to defend Lower Sandusky in the War of 1812, he was the first to respond and was elected Captain of the regiment and marched to the front in time to render material aid to the gallant Cragin. For the opportunities he had, few men excelled him in general, useful information. In no sense, however, was he a great man, but in every sense a good one. Like his parents he was a devout Methodist.

Capt. John Strawn, page 169.

Captain Strawn appears to have been an exceedingly eccentric character. Perry Armstrong says:

After his first marriage he moved from Pennsylvania to Perry county, Ohio, where he purchased and improved a farm which he sold in 1829 and then moved overland in a huge wagon made to order with a six horse team, each horse having a heavy string of bells attached to his harness. These bells made such a din that they could be heard for miles. He moved to a farm near where Logan now stands, in Marshall county, Ill. Here he purchased in a body twenty-four sections of fine government land at $1.25 per acre. He held all the land, but as the children married he gave each a farm. His buildings seem of the extravagant kind—fences must be in a straight line; buildings, barns, corncribs and hog pens must also range in line. His carriage drawn by four elephantine horses, must have a calliope, or, as he termed it, a music box attachment. This calliope was put in motion as he approached a village, or town, or farmhouse, as a kind of warning that Capt. John Strawn was near at hand. He died, leaving to his young widow a fine fortune. She married again, this time a young and thrifty man.

Jacob Strawn, page 169.

P. A. Armstrong says:

Jacob Strawn (the father) was a decided character. His fidelity to his engagements was proverbial and from the first from this fact he commanded the confidence of everybody who knew him and his reputation was as wide as the Union. He was never known to break his word, hence he could command any amount of money at any time and his word alone was required as security. Yet with his splendid financial standing he occasionally became hypochondriac. Fortunately, however, such spells were of but short duration, and infrequent.

Always busy, he never had time to think about politics and religion, and though a moral man we think he never belonged to any church. Close in his deal, yet he was naturally a very benevolent man. We were with him in the winter of 1845 when he asked a poor widow for a bowl of bread and milk. On being informed that she had but one cow to supply milk for herself and six children, he quietly placed three ten-dollar bills under the empty bowl and left the house ere the widow had perceived her good fortune in giving a bowl of milk to Jacob Strawn, the cattle king of Illinois.

Page 178.

Elizabeth Roberts, daughter of Thomas Roberts, Jr., born 1759.

Page 180.

Ethel Gertrude, daughter of Edward and Ella McCarty, is living; a sister, however, d. in infancy. Lewis Ellwood Roberts was born 12th-mo. 26, 1835.

John Penrose, page 206.

Clementine, daughter of Thomas Penrose (line 15), was born 10th-mo. 30, 1810, d. 2d-mo. 17, 1890. See page 59.

The seventh child of John and Ann Penrose was John, and not John J., as stated. See page 211. John J. was the son of Joseph and Margaret Penrose, as appears by the latter reference.

DEATHS AND BURIALS.

The following is a list of deaths and interments kept for many years by Abigail R. Heacock, of Quakertown, and continued after her death by her son, J. Levi Heacock. They consist largely of persons related to Richland families though at the time of their death often at a great distance. Other names are those of prominent Friends or of distinguished persons outside of the Society:

Spring, 1832.	Sarah Lancaster, Philadelphia.
2, 2, 1833.	Samuel Penrose, Horsham.
10th-mo., 1833.	Jacob Albertson, Plymouth.
4, 21, 1835.	Ann Roberts, Chester county.
6, 24, 1836.	John Roberts, Chester county.
6, 5, 1837.	Henry Trumbower, Milford.
2, 25, 1838.	Martha Hallowell, Abington.
9th-mo., 1838.	John Thomson, Abington.
1, 1, 1839.	Phebe Foulke, Philadelphia.
4, 3, 1839.	Clementine Roberts, Philadelphia.
4, 4, 1839.	Margaret Iden, Indiana.
4, 10, 1839.	Edith Weidner, Milford.
2, 8, 1840.	Jacob Siegel, New Jersey.

3d-mo.,	1840.	Hannah Iden, Buckingham.
10, 18,	1840.	John Flagler, Stroudsburg.
3, 4,	1841.	Lewis Lewis, Ohio.
4, 10,	1841.	Wm. Roberts, Chester county.
8th-mo.,	1841.	Rachel Griffith.
12th-mo.,	1841.	Jacob Ritter, Plymouth.
12th-mo.,	1841.	Rebecca Roberts, Chester county.
12th-mo.,	1841.	Samuel Ashton, Little Britain.
8, 18,	1844.	Samuel M. Foulke, Indiana.
10, 13,	1844.	Rowland Foulke, Philadelphia.
3, 27,	1845.	Christiana Heacock, Indiana.
7, 13,	1846.	John Thomson, Gwynedd.
8, 22,	1846.	Ann Ball, Indiana.
10th-mo.,	1847.	Priscilla Maginnis, Pottsville.
12, 1,	1847.	Miriam Heacock, Ohio.
3, 13,	1849.	George Lukens, Gwynedd.
1, 31,	1850.	Wm. Stokes, Doylestown.
6, 23,	1851.	Abigail W. Heacock, Germantown (bur.).
7, 10,	1851.	Mary Walton, Gwynedd.
1, 2,	1855.	Sarah Reed buried.
2, 20,	1857.	Martha Ingram, Ohio.
3, 8,	1857.	Martha Cleaver, Gwynedd.
4, 19,	1857.	Jonathan Carr buried.
5, 26,	1857.	John Cotton, Gwynedd.
6, 21,	1857.	Peter Lester, Philadelphia
9, 25,	1857.	Salathiel Cleaver (bur.), Gwynedd.
10, 4,	1857.	Mary Cleaver, Gwynedd.
10, 25,	1857.	Isaac Parry (bur.), Horsham.
12, 3,	1857.	Joseph Paul (bur.), Horsham.
5, 7,	1858.	Sarah Scotton (bur.).
2, 10,	1860.	Elizabeth Carey buried.
3, 15,	1860.	Martha Conard.
7, 14,	1861.	Jonah Heacock.
8, 14,	1861.	Lydia Leedom.
9, 7,	1861.	Antrim Foulke.
1, 9,	1863.	Mary Saylor buried.
2, 17,	1863.	Joseph Foulke buried.
3, 18,	1863.	Edward Artman buried.
3, 24,	1863.	Mary Lester, Philadelphia.
3, 26,	1863.	Joseph Williams, Plymouth.
9, 22,	1863.	Ezekiel Cleaver, Gwynedd.
11, 21,	1863.	Dr. Wm. Walton, Stroudsburg.
11, 23,	1863.	Wm. Penrose, Horsham.
12, 9,	1863.	Andora Sailor, Limerick Square.
1, 16,	1864.	John Bennett, Rockhill, bur.

1, 19, 1864.	Anna Maria Jenkins, Gwynedd, bur.
1, 20, 1864.	Daniel Sacks, Philadelphia, bur.
1, 21, 1864.	Letitia Walmsley, Philadelphia.
1, 28, 1864.	John Kinsey, Chester county, bur.
2, 3, 1864.	Ann Getman, Rockhill, bur.
2, 28, 1864.	Seth Roberts, Trappe, bur.
5, 6, 1864.	Hugh Foulke, Gwynedd, buried.
6, 8, 1864.	Henrietta Childs buried.
6, 9, 1864.	Jane Michener buried.
6, 16, 1864.	Ann Rebecca Carr, Plumstead, buried.
10, 10, 1864.	Edward Foulke, Philadelphia.
10, 12, 1864.	Morris Paul, Horsham.
11, 1, 1864.	Letitia Roberts, Montgomery county.
11, 27, 1864.	Ellwood P. Roberts, Gwynedd.
1, 7, 1865.	George O. Maugle, Quakertown.
1, 17, 1865.	Moses Wilson, Indiana.
2, 17, 1865.	John Hallowell, Abington.
4, 6, 1865.	Moses Philips, Stroudsburg, buried.
4, 7, 1865.	Edward Meredith, Gwynedd, bur.
4, 9, 1865.	Edward Kenderdine, Gwynedd, bur.
4, 14, 1865.	Abraham Lincoln assassinated.
5, 10, 1865.	John Kichline, Charlestown, bur.
6, 18, 1865.	Ellwood Heacock, Plumstead, bur.
8, 28, 1865.	Lydia Roberts, Norristown.
8, 29, 1865.	Emma Fleming's child bur.
12, 22, 1865.	John Nusky.
1, 5, 1866.	Barton Green, Philadelphia, bur.
4, 4, 1866.	Eleazer Shaw, Plumstead.
7, 12, 1866.	Dr. Charles F. Lott, Bethlehem, bur.
2, 8, 1867.	Charles F. Jenkins, Gwynedd.
2, 27, 1867.	Sarah Thomson, Gwynedd, bur.
7, 19, 1867.	Isaac Ellis, Gwynedd.
10, 12, 1867.	Joseph Walton, Horsham.
1, 2, 1868.	Hannah Cavender, Philadelphia.
2, 17, 1868.	Henry Ochs buried.
2, 26, 1868.	Joseph Roberts buried.
2, 28, 1868.	Abigail Wildman, Langhorne.
3, 15, 1868.	Martha Foulke, Gwynedd, bur.
3, 22, 1868.	Samuel Shellenberger bur.
4th-mo., 1868.	Abel Lester buried.
5th-mo., 1868.	Sarah Conrad buried.
8th-mo., 1868.	Mary J. Ambler buried.
8th-mo., 1868.	Lewis Forman buried.
9, 5, 1868.	John Heacock, Indiana, buried.
1, 5, 1869.	Ann Ochs, Bunker Hill.
1, 9, 1869.	Jane Iden, Richmond, Ind.

1, 30, 1869. Charles Leedom, Newtown, Pa.
2, 21, 1869. Mary Parry, Horsham.
5, 27, 1869. James Rutter, Philadelphia.
9, 18, 1869. Nathan Hicks, Horsham.
9, 23, 1869. Wm. Vanhouten, Richland.
3, 1, 1870. Maggie McCarty, Weatherly, Pa.
3, 10, 1870. Hannah Meredith, Gwynedd.
4, 15, 1870. John Roberts, Quakertown.
6, 11, 1870. Lewis R. Jacoby, Philadelphia.
10th-mo., 1870. John Hunt, N. J., buried.
10, 8, 1870. Wm. Mills, Philadelphia, buried.
11, 9, 1870. Alice Green, Philadelphia, buried.
11, 11, 1870. Andrew Ambler buried at Gwynedd.
1, 22, 1871. Hannah Smith, Charlestown, buried.
2, 16, 1871. Esther Lukens buried at Gwynedd.
2, 22, 1871. Cadwallader Roberts buried at Gwynedd.
2, 26, 1871. Jacob Felman, Tohickon.
3, 3, 1871. Phebe Conrad, Plymouth.
3, 31, 1871. Lydia Kemmerer, Quakertown.
5, 8, 1871. Meribah Green, Philadelphia, buried.
7, 13, 1871. Silas Shoemaker, Upper Dublin, buried.
8, 13, 1871. Cynthia Green, Gwynedd, buried.
9, 17, 1871. Daniel Comly, Horsham, buried.
9, 29, 1871. Mary Styer, Plymouth, buried.
10, 31, 1871. Elizabeth Wonsetler, Charlestown, buried.
12, 23, 1871. Rebecca Walton, Horsham, buried.
1, 1, 1872. Knowles Lancaster, Philadelphia, buried.
1, 2, 1872. Margaret Ellis, Gwynedd, buried.
1, 25, 1872. Lyman McCarty, Weatherly, buried.
1, 27, 1872. Matthias Moore, Philadelphia, buried.
1, 28, 1872. Jane Hallowell, Plymouth, buried.
1, 30, 1872. Elizabeth Newport, Philadelphia, buried.
2, 7, 1872. Louisa Matthews, Philadelphia, buried.
3, 28, 1872. Lucas Gillingham, Chicago.
4, 2, 1872. Ashton Roberts, Philadelphia.
5, 22, 1872. Tacy Shoemaker buried.
5, 30, 1872. Priscilla Walton buried.
6, 5, 1872. Sydenham Walton, Stroudsburg, buried.
6, 17, 1872. Annie Crew, Philadelphia.
10, 12, 1872. Catharine Dodson, Weatherly, buried.
10, 17, 1872. Millie Carr, Plumstead, buried.
12th-mo., 1872. Jane Dennis, buried, Salem, Ohio.
12, 12, 1872. George E. Lippincott, Philadelphia, buried.
2, 1, 1873. Charles Reeder, Wrightstown, buried.
3, 1, 1873. Jesse T. Heacock, Middletown, buried.

4,	25,	1873.	Henry Ridgway, Crosswicks, N. J., buried.
4,	19,	1873.	Martha Gilman's child buried, Doylestown.
7,	2,	1873.	Benjamin Tomlinson, Byberry.
8,	5,	1873.	Elizabeth Foulke, Gwynedd, buried.
8,	6,	1873.	Martha Mather, Abington, buried.
1,	15,	1874.	John Lester, California.
2,	21,	1874.	Samuel Haring, Valley Creek, buried.
4,	26,	1874.	Esther Heacock, Abington.
5,	1,	1874.	Rebecca Shaw Conrad, Plymouth, buried.
8,	3,	1874.	John Good, Wilmington, buried.
9,	19,	1874.	Charles Heacock's child buried.
10,	6,	1874.	George Heist, Charlestown, buried
10,	15,	1874.	William Dorsey, Philadelphia, buried.
12,	3,	1874.	Joseph Bancroft buried.
1,	1,	1875.	Alice Foulke, Illinois.
1,	7,	1875.	Robert Winder, Philadelphia.
2,	5,	1875.	Rachel Siegel, New Jersey.
4,	17,	1875.	Enos Strawn, Salem, Ohio.
4,	21,	1875.	Thomas Artman, Philadelphia, buried.
5,	8,	1875.	Enos Housekeeper, Charlestown, buried.
6,	13,	1875.	Wm. Levis, Philadelphia.
8,	3,	1875.	Mary Rich, Doylestown, buried.
8,	6,	1875.	Mary Philips, Philadelphia, buried.
1,	19,	1876.	Elizabeth Bleiler buried.
1,	26,	1876.	Ann Price, Doylestown, buried.
2,	26,	1876.	Albion I. Grove buried.
3,	31,	1876.	Elizabeth Warner, Horsham, buried.
4,	5,	1876.	Isaac Warner, husband of E. W., buried.
10,	24,	1876.	Sarah Heacock.
3,	15,	1879.	Nathan Heacock, Indiana.
7,	3,	1883.	Henry Kemmerer buried.
12,	3,	1883.	James Hibberd, Baltimore, buried.
12,	16,	1883.	Susan Roberts (wife of Frank) buried.
4,	25,	1884.	Amanda Hinkle, New Britain, buried.
4,	19,	1885.	Samuel J. Levick, Philadelphia, bur. at Merion.
5,	1,	1885.	Lewis B. Thompson, Doylestown, buried.
7th-mo.,		1885.	Benjamin Grant, formerly of Quakertown, died in Hawaii, of consumption.
8,	1,	1885.	Ann Foulke, Iowa; 93 years.
4,	10,	1886.	Henrietta Hill, Philadelphia, buried.
4,	27,	1886.	Wm. Bunstein buried.
7,	23,	1886.	Hattie Grow, Boyertown, buried.
8,	7,	1886.	Evaline Heacock, Philadelphia.
11,	19,	1887.	James C. Iden, Buckingham, buried.
11,	19,	1887.	Monroe Roberts buried.

12,	9,	1887.	Cettie Swank's mother bur. at Weatherly, Pa.
2,	8,	1888.	Charles Fellman, Richlandtown, buried.
2,	9,	1888.	Mary Wilson, Lewisville, Indiana.
2,	15,	1888.	Davis Walton, Stroudsburg.
2,	18,	1888.	Daniel Foulke, Gwynedd.
2,	20,	1888.	Harriet Applebach, Applebachsville, buried.
2,	20,	1888.	Lewis H. Fluck, Quakertown.
9,	4,	1888.	Emma Graver, Trumbauersville, buried.
9,	6,	1888.	Tacy Johnson, Salem, Ohio, buried.
10,	28,	1888.	Joseph Steinhauer, Quakertown.
10,	29,	1888.	Dominicus Mirken, Richlandtown.
11,	26,	1888.	Jacob Swartzgrove, Chestnut Hill, buried.
12,	29,	1888.	Lydia Mather, Gwynedd, buried.
1,	3,	1889.	George Mason, Indiana, buried.
6,	9,	1889.	Three of J. L. Smith's children, also his wife, buried. They were victims of the Johnstown flood, 5, 31, 1889.
7,	17,	1889.	Fanny Foulke, Stroudsburg, buried.
8,	14,	1889.	Henry Clymer, Quakertown.
8,	15,	1889.	Charles Taylor, Lansdale, buried.
1,	12,	1890.	John Jamison, Philadelphia.
1,	19,	1890.	Annie Heacock, Philadelphia.
1,	30,	1890.	Worman Stoneback, Quakertown, buried.
8,	6,	1890.	Samuel F. Scheetz, buried.
8,	11,	1890.	E. T. Ochs.
8,	29,	1890.	Martha Scypes buried.
8,	30,	1890.	Harriet Apgar, N. J., buried.
2,	25,	1891.	James V. Smith, Yardley, buried.
4	9,	1891.	Margaret Meredith, Gwynedd, buried.
4,	15,	1891.	Mary Bullock.
9,	17,	1891.	Caroline Ambler, Ambler, buried.
1,	26,	1892.	Maria Smith buried.
5,	30,	1892.	John Heacock, Melrose, Pa.
7,	15,	1892.	Richard Watson, Doylestown.
9,	16,	1892.	Eliza Heacock, Indiana.
12,	8,	1892.	Henry H. Smith buried.
9,	26,	1893.	Mary Jamison.

OTHER DEATHS.

Lydia Penrose 3, 6, 1874; 77 years.
Ann Penrose 7, 14, 1872; 71 years.
John Penrose 9, 12, 1881 ; 77 years.
Phebe Phillips 5, 19, 1885 ; 57 years ; Stroudsburg.
Christiana Phillips 8, 26, 1884; 90 years; Stroudsburg.
Mary C. Phillips 11, —, 1888; 72 years. (Daughter of Christiana.)
Sidney Strawn 8, 2, 1883.
James Shaw 2, 8, 1873; 48 years.

GENERAL INDEX.

www.ingramcontent.com/pod-product-compliance
Lightning Source LLC
Chambersburg PA
CBHW030238030426
42336CB00009B/154